Police Sergeant Exam

A Step-by-Step System to
Prepare for Your Promotion Exam

2nd Edition

LEARNINGEXPRESS®

NEW YORK

Library of Congress Cataloging-in-Publication Data:
Police sergeant exam : a step-by-step system to prepare for your promotion exam.—2nd ed.
    p. cm.
   ISBN 10: 1-57685-572-4
   ISBN 13: 978-1-57685-572-0
     1. Police—Examinations—Study guides. 2. Police—Vocational guidance. I. LearningExpress
(Organization)
HV7921.P5728 2006
363.2076—dc22

                          2006048654

Printed in the United States of America

9 8 7 6 5 4 3 2 1

Second Edition

ISBN 10: 1-57685-572-4
ISBN 13: 978-1-57685-572-0

Regarding the Information in This Book
We attempt to verify the information presented in our books prior to publication. It is always a good idea, however, to double-check such important information as minimum requirements, application and testing procedures, and deadlines with your local law enforcement agency, as such information can change from time to time.

For more information or to place an order, contact LearningExpress at:
   55 Broadway
   8th Floor
   New York, NY 10006

Or visit us at:
   www.learnatest.com

Contents

Contributors

Eileen F. Brennan, M.A., is a senior editor for a chain of weekly newspapers on Long Island, New York, and editor of the *Manhasset Press*. She reports regularly on the Nassau County Police Sixth Precinct.

Virginia M. Brennan, Ph.D., is an editor, test-development specialist, and teacher living in Nashville, Tennessee.

Deputy Chief of Police Charles Brooks works in the Haverford Township Police Department in Haverford, Pennsylvania. He has over 23 years of experience on the force.

Jan Gallagher, Ph.D., is an editor, test-development specialist, and teacher living in Jersey City, New Jersey.

Police Officer Mary Hesalroad has over 12 years of experience on the police force in Austin, Texas, and is experienced in test preparation and manuscript review.

Chief of Police Gary Hoover works in the Haverford Township Police Department in Haverford, Pennsylvania. He has over 30 years of experience on the force and has sat on the oral boards for numerous departments.

Police Officer Lawrence Morici is the Communications Officer of the Nassau County, New York, Sixth Precinct. He has 15 years of experience on the force.

Captain George Morrish is Commander of the Nassau County, New York, Sixth Precinct. He has served on the police force for over 32 years.

Christopher W. Ortiz, Ph.D., is a police sergeant in Glen Cove, New York. In addition to his work as a police officer, Dr. Ortiz has conducted multiple research projects for the Police Foundation, the Vera Institute of Justice, and Police Assessment Resource Center. Dr. Ortiz also holds adjunct teaching positions at John Jay College of Criminal Justice and Utica College.

Chief Michael A. Petrillo (retired) has over 25 years of experience on the police force in the state of New Jersey. He presently teaches at the Essex County Police Academy and the Princeton Educational Research Center (the DelBangno School for Police). He is the author of the multiple-choice questions in this book.

Jo Southard is an attorney and freelance writer living in Portland, Maine.

John Thompson, M.A., teaches writing at Widener University in Chester, Pennsylvania, and Neumann College in Philadelphia, Pennsylvania. In his spare time, he plots mystery novels and toils on construction projects.

How to ▶
Use This Book

Sergeant's stripes—they color the dreams of many police officers on the line. It's the goal of all the contributors of this book to make those dreams a reality for you. The contributors combine experience and expertise on police forces throughout the country with sharp writing and editorial skills. By working through this book, you will increase your understanding of and become well acquainted with the material covered on the police sergeant test.

This preface sketches out how our book is organized and how you can best take advantage of it. The focus is on test preparation. We want you to know the answers and be confident that you know them. The knowledge and self-confidence you will gain from preparing ahead will help propel you to the top of the sergeant eligibility list.

The book you have in your hands is unusual in that it consists primarily of practice exam questions and lengthy answer explanations. By giving you over 500 practice multiple-choice questions and detailed explanations of the correct answers, we aim to provide you with a firm foundation for taking the sergeant test. We think the best way to do well on a test is to prepare for it by taking practice tests that simulate both the content and the format of the actual test. This book gives you the opportunity to do just that.

In addition to lots of practice material and answer explanations, this book also includes a chapter on what it means to become a sergeant. Chapter 1, "So You Want to Be Promoted to Sergeant," gives you the big picture, explaining what steps you must go through to become sergeant, a bird's-eye view of the sergeant test, and what you can expect once you've scored well on the test.

Chapter 2, "The LearningExpress Test Preparation System," will give you invaluable advice on how to organize your time before and during the written exam. If you've had trouble with written exams in the past (anxiety, bad study habits, running out of time), you definitely don't want to skip this chapter—it even gives you great tips on how to choose the right multiple-choice answer when you're unsure. Even if written exams aren't that hard for you, be sure to take advantage of the sample study plans in this chapter. The best insurance for acing your exam is good preparation, and these study schedules will help you organize your time.

It's a fact of life in the United States that many laws differ from one jurisdiction to another. For example, there are "dry counties" in states such as North Carolina and Kentucky, where it is against the law to sell alcohol any time of the day, any day of the year, whereas in neighboring counties and states, it can be perfectly legal to buy and sell alcohol anytime, even at night or on a holiday. So how can a national book help you to prepare for a test that covers not only federal laws but local laws and ordinances as well? It can do so by teaching you how to find out about your area's laws. Chapter 3, "How to Bone Up on Local Laws and Procedures," tells you how to prepare for local material, giving tips about where to find the information you need and—just as important—how to remember it.

Chapter 4, "Police Sergeant Practice Exam 1," gives you your first shot at the core of the exam, the multiple-choice written test. The idea is that you take this 100-item test and figure out how well prepared you already are. How much do you know? What are your strengths and what are your weaknesses? Are there particular areas you need to focus on when you study? By taking this first practice test, you should be able to answer these questions. Furthermore, like all the remaining questions in the book (and there are over 400 more), these questions are paired with instructional answer explanations. So, when you miss one (and you will, because this stuff isn't easy), you can immediately read up on the material by reading the paragraph-long answer explanation.

In addition to studying the answer explanations for the practice exam, at this point you should start to study some of the law-enforcement material recommended at the end of Chapter 2. By using the study techniques recommended in Chapters 2 and 3 and

then identifying your strong and weak points by means of the first practice exam, in Chapter 4, you will be able to focus your study energy where it will do the most good.

We continue to use the same strategy of test preparation in the large Police Sergeant Minicourse in Chapter 5. This minicourse consists of over 300 test questions and answer explanations, organized according to the area they cover. There are questions on supervision, management, criminal procedure, constitutional law, criminal investigation, patrol practices, and community relations. In other words, there is a section of the minicourse for all the major topics typically covered on police sergeant exams.

Knowing your strengths and weaknesses from the practice exam will help you decide which sections of the minicourse to zero in on. In order to use your study time most efficiently, you should also find out which skills the department you're applying to will be testing. Then you can concentrate on the sections of the minicourse that cover material you are likely to face.

Having taken the pretest in Chapter 4 and then engaged in focused study and more practice testing by using the minicourse in Chapter 5, you'll be ready to take another practice test of the same length and description as a typical sergeant exam. That is what is offered to you in Chapter 6, "Police Sergeant Exam 2." Once again, our focus is on teaching, so we have included answer explanations for those questions you are unsure of.

Many departments now offer Assessment Center exercises as part of the evaluation of potential sergeants. What is an Assessment Center and what can you expect if your department uses one? Those questions and many more are answered in Chapter 7, "Preparing for Assessment Center Exercises."

The oral component of the sergeant test is a mystery to a lot of test takers, so we consulted with police supervisors who have served on orals boards in numerous jurisdictions to get their perspectives on the oral exam. Chapter 8 presents our findings—we cover everything from what to wear to how to phrase your answers. Additionally, we provide tips on how to get ready to think on your feet before a board consisting of both superior officers and civilian consultants.

Finally, some police jurisdiction may include a writing component on the sergeant exam. To cover that possibility, we have included Chapter 9, "Preparing for Your Writing Test." Those readers who will have to demonstrate their writing skills will find this chapter helpful in preparing. Remember, however, that most departments do not include essay writing as part of the test; find out if yours does as you begin to prepare for the sergeant test.

This book is here to help. It covers all the basics of what police departments across the country are looking for in a candidate for sergeant, and it gives you examples of what typical police sergeant exams are like. You've given yourself a big advantage by choosing to use this book. You should go on to use it and to use the law-enforcement material recommended for study at the end of Chapter 2. Your success in becoming a police sergeant depends largely on your desire to become one and the amount of work you're willing to put in, first by doing a great job as a police officer and then by getting ready to take the sergeant test.

Good luck!

CHAPTER

1 ▶ So You Want to Be Promoted to Sergeant

Thinking about the sergeant exam is a sign that you are ready to move forward in your career. This book is here to help. Over the course of the next eight chapters, our team of police professionals and writers will take you through the paces that will get you ready to take the next step up the ladder of law enforcement.

As you contemplate the possibility of becoming sergeant, and the steps you'll have to take to get there, it is good to focus periodically on the fact that you already know a lot. If you are thinking of becoming a sergeant, you've probably been on the job for a while. You know a lot about procedures, about people, and about the law. Now you have to start studying this material in a formal and precise way. You also have to start learning about being a supervisor and managing personnel. This is new territory for a lot of officers interested in moving up in rank. Reading this book, talking to friends on the squad, and watching your own sergeant will all help you make this transition effectively.

This book was written for a national audience. We have included all the material that sergeants and potential sergeants throughout the country should be in command of. There is a piece of the puzzle we can't supply, and that is what is unique to your department, jurisdiction, and state. The first step in moving on to become sergeant is keeping your ears open in your department and learning as much as you can in your present position. Only the best officers and detectives move up to the rank of sergeant. Work hard in your present job, learning everything you can that way and paying special attention to local ordinances and procedures that can only be picked up on the job.

One category of information you need to get on your own is the description of the sergeant test your department offers. In many cases, the exam is known as a *Chief's Test*; in that case, the chief of the department picks the exam's format. Most departments (including those with Chief's Tests) use multiple-choice tests as the core of the sergeant exam. The multiple-choice tests are demanding. Time is often kept short and the content is kept heavy—you have to know it cold. It's a tall order, but that's the kind of knowledge you will have after working through this book and studying the resources listed at the end of Chapter 2.

Be sure you find out what kinds of conditions usually prevail during sergeant exams in your department. By *conditions* we mean a few different things: How much time do you get for how many questions? Will other people be in the room? Will it be quiet, or will you have to grapple with noise and interruptions? What is the policy regarding going back to questions you skipped? How about wrong answers—do you get penalized? All these things matter and they're all local issues; make sure you ask around ahead of time so you know what to expect. (Chapter 2 of this book presents a system for test taking and test preparation that should be helpful no matter what the conditions are where you take the sergeant exam.)

The multiple-choice test at the core of most sergeant exams covers these areas:

- Supervision
- Management
- Criminal procedure
- Constitutional law
- Patrol practices
- Community relations

The bulk of this book—two complete practice exams and a 350-question minicourse (Chapters 4–

6)—is dedicated to getting you ready to take such a multiple-choice exam. The questions are tough and require a lot of study. We have provided extensive answer explanations to help you internalize all this information. Assuming you have the time, you should certainly also study by getting hold of some of the classics of police work recommended at the end of Chapter 2.

Many sergeant exams test your cool and your staying power as much as your brains and your knowledge. Be ready to face lengthy questions in which the real point is buried under a mass of detail. Watch out for information overload and misleading questions. Read carefully, taking notes and underlining where you need to, before answering the question. Don't be tricked into answering the wrong question.

Two other increasingly common and important components of sergeant exams are Assessment Centers and oral boards. Assessment Centers, covered in Chapter 7 of this book, give you the chance to perform as if you were on the job as a sergeant. During Assessment Center exercises, you might be faced with video simulations in which you have to issue orders for dealing with a difficult case, a packet of reports and photographs that you must process, or a role-playing task. During the oral board, you will face a panel of people—possibly from the police force and possibly *not*—who will ask you a lot of questions, both to hear your answers and to see how you perform in a pressure situation. Chapter 8 of this book covers the oral boards.

Civil service examiners are required to create questions that are job related. All the questions must relate to the job for which the test taker hopes to apply. A test must show the relationship between the process used to promote officers and the officers' job performance. While the ideal civil service examination tests your ability to understand these basic principles and concepts, you'd better get ready to see a few questions that you won't be able to answer unless you know the material intimately. Most exams include a few extremely difficult questions that will separate those who studied a little from those who prepared thoroughly for the promotional exam.

The overall strategy of learning the material's basic principles and concepts will certainly earn you a passing grade, but when your goal is to score high enough to get promoted, you have to know the material so well that your friends will swear you must have memorized it. As one newly promoted sergeant in Texas put it, "You better **know your stuff** before you sit down to take this test, because the person next to you surely does." Many departments are able to promote only two or three people per year to supervisory positions. As a result, competition for these top spots on the promotional list is fierce.

Valuable qualities needed for success on the sergeant exam are motivation, perseverance, test-taking skills, and reading comprehension. By working with this book, you should be able to improve upon your test-taking skills and reading comprehension. Motivation and perseverance must be developed on your own.

CHAPTER

2 ▶ The LearningExpress Test Preparation System

Taking the police sergeant exam can be tough. It demands a lot of preparation if you want to achieve a top score. Your rank on the eligibility list is often determined in large measure by this score. The LearningExpress Test Preparation System, developed exclusively for LearningExpress by leading test experts, gives you the discipline and attitude you need to be a winner.

First, the bad news: Taking the police sergeant exam is no picnic, and neither is getting ready for it. Your future career in law enforcement depends on your getting a high score on the various parts of the test, but there are all sorts of pitfalls that can keep you from doing your best on this all-important exam. Here are some of the obstacles that can stand in the way of your success:

- Being unfamiliar with the format of the exam
- Being paralyzed by test anxiety
- Leaving your preparation to the last minute
- Not preparing at all!
- Not knowing vital test-taking skills: how to pace yourself through the exam, how to use the process of elimination, and when to guess
- Not being in tip-top mental and physical shape
- Being distracted and uncomfortable on test day because you skipped breakfast or are too hot or cold

What's the common denominator in all these test-taking pitfalls? One word: *control*. Who's in control, you or the exam?

Now the good news: The LearningExpress Test Preparation System puts you in control. In just nine easy-to-follow steps, you will learn everything you need to know to make sure that you are in charge of your preparation and your performance on the exam. Other test takers may let the test get the better of them; other test takers may be unprepared or out of shape, but not you. You will have taken all the steps you need to take to get a high score on the police sergeant exam.

Here's how the LearningExpress Test Preparation System works: Nine easy steps lead you through everything you need to know and do to get ready to master your exam. Read each step and complete the accompanying activities. It's important that you do the activities along with the reading, or you won't be getting the full benefit of the system. Each step tells you approximately how much time that step will take you to complete.

We estimate that working through the entire system will take you approximately three hours, though it's perfectly OK if you work faster or slower than the time estimates assume. If you can take a whole afternoon or evening, you can work through the whole LearningExpress Test Preparation System in one sitting. Otherwise, you can break it up and do just one or two steps a day for the next several days. It's up to you—remember, *you're* in control.

Step 1. Get Information	30 minutes
Step 2. Conquer Test Anxiety	20 minutes
Step 3. Make a Plan	50 minutes
Step 4. Learn to Manage Your Time	10 minutes
Step 5. Learn to Use the Process of Elimination	20 minutes
Step 6. Know When to Guess	20 minutes
Step 7. Reach Your Peak Performance Zone	10 minutes
Step 8. Get Your Act Together	10 minutes
Step 9. Do It!	10 minutes
Total	**3 hours**

► Step 1: Get Information

Time to complete: 30 minutes
Activities: Read Chapter 1, "So You Want to Be
Promoted to Sergeant"

Knowledge is power. The first step in the Learning-Express Test Preparation System is finding out everything you can about your police sergeant exam. Contact your department, request a position announcement or exam bulletin, and ask when the next exam is scheduled. The exam bulletin usually gives a brief outline of what skills will be tested on the written exam. Once the exam is officially scheduled, the announcement and exam bulletin will be posted in a prominent place in the department, but it won't hurt to get a good head start by requesting one early.

What You Should Find Out

The more details you can find out about the exam, either from the bulletin or from speaking with others in your department, the more efficiently you'll be able to study. Here's a list of some things you might want to find out about your exam:

- What skills are tested
- How many sections are on the exam
- How many questions each section has
- Whether the questions are ordered from easy to hard or whether the sequence is random
- How much time is allotted for each section
- Whether there are breaks between sections
- What the passing score is and how many questions you must answer correctly in order to get that score
- How high a score you probably need to be chosen from the eligibility list
- How the test is scored: Is there a penalty for wrong answers?

- Whether you're permitted to go back to a prior section or move on to the next section if you finish early
- Whether you can write in the test booklet or will be given scratch paper
- What you should bring with you on exam day

What's on Most Police Sergeant Exams

The skills that the police sergeant exam tests vary from city to city. That's why it's important to find out from your own department what areas are covered. Below are the subjects that are tested most often on the written exam:

- Supervision and Management
- Constitutional Law
- Criminal Procedure
- Human Relations
- Patrol Practices
- Criminal Investigation
- Forensic Science
- Community Relations

► Step 2: Conquer Test Anxiety

Time to complete: 20 minutes
Activity: Take the Test Stress Test

Having complete information about the exam is the first step in getting control of the exam. Next, you have to overcome one of the biggest obstacles to test success: test anxiety. Test anxiety can not only impair your performance on the exam itself, but it can even keep you from preparing! In Step 2, you'll learn stress management techniques that will help you succeed on your exam. Learn these strategies now, and practice them as you work through the exams in this book, so they'll be second nature to you by exam day.

Combating Test Anxiety

The first thing you need to know is that a little test anxiety is a good thing. Everyone gets nervous before a big exam—and if that nervousness motivates you to prepare thoroughly, so much the better. It's said that Sir Laurence Olivier, one of the foremost British actors of the twentieth century, was ill before every performance. His stage fright didn't impair his performance; in fact, it probably gave him a little extra edge—just the kind of edge you need to do well, whether on a stage or in an examination room.

On the next page is the Test Stress Test. Stop here and answer the questions on that page to find out whether your level of test anxiety is something you should worry about.

Stress Management before the Test

If you feel your level of anxiety rising in the weeks before the test, here is what you need to do to bring the level down again:

- **Get prepared.** There's nothing like knowing what to expect and being prepared for it to put you in control of test anxiety. That's why you're reading this book. Use it faithfully, and remind yourself that you're better prepared than most of the people taking the test.
- **Practice self-confidence.** A positive attitude is a great way to combat test anxiety. This is no time to be humble or shy. Stand in front of the mirror and say to your reflection, "I'm prepared. I'm full of self-confidence. I'm going to ace this test. I know I can do it." Say it into a tape recorder and play it back once a day. If you hear it often enough, you'll believe it.
- **Fight negative messages.** Every time someone starts telling you how hard the exam is or how it's almost impossible to get a high score, start telling them your self-confidence messages. If the someone with the negative messages is you, telling yourself *you don't do well on exams, you just can't do this*, don't listen. Turn on your tape recorder and listen to your self-confidence messages.
- **Visualize.** Imagine yourself reporting for duty on your first day as a sergeant. Think of yourself wearing your uniform with pride and supervising your squad. Visualizing success can help make it happen—and it reminds you of why you're doing all this work in preparing for the exam.
- **Exercise.** Physical activity helps calm your body down and focus your mind. Besides, being in good physical shape can actually help you do well on the exam. Go for a run, lift weights, go swimming—and do it regularly.

Stress Management on Test Day

There are several ways you can bring down your level of anxiety on test day. They'll work best if you practice them in the weeks before the test, so you know which ones work best for you.

- **Deep breathing.** Take a deep breath while you count to five. Hold it for a count of one, then let it out on a count of five. Repeat several times.
- **Move your body.** Try rolling your head in a circle. Rotate your shoulders. Shake your hands from the wrist. Many people find these movements very relaxing.
- **Visualize again.** Think of the place where you are most relaxed: lying on the beach in the sun, walking through the park, or whatever works for you. Now close your eyes and imagine you're actually there. If you practice in advance, you'll find that you need only a few seconds of this exercise to experience a significant increase in your sense of well-being.

You need to worry about test anxiety only if it is extreme enough to impair your performance. The following questionnaire will provide a diagnosis of your level of test anxiety. In the blank before each statement, write the number that most accurately describes your experience.

0 = Never 1 = Once or twice 2 = Sometimes 3 = Often

___ I have gotten so nervous before an exam that I simply put down the books and didn't study for it.

___ I have experienced disabling physical symptoms such as vomiting and severe headaches because I was nervous about an exam.

___ I have simply not showed up for an exam because I was scared to take it.

___ I have experienced dizziness and disorientation while taking an exam.

___ I have had trouble filling in the little circles because my hands were shaking too hard.

___ I have failed an exam because I was too nervous to complete it.

___ **Total: Add up the numbers in the blanks above.**

Your Test Stress Score

Here are the steps you should take, depending on your score. If you scored:

- **Below 3**, your level of test anxiety is nothing to worry about; it is probably just enough to give you that little extra edge.

- **Between 3 and 6**, your test anxiety may be enough to impair your performance, and you should practice the stress management techniques listed in this section to try to bring your test anxiety down to manageable levels.

- **Above 6**, your level of test anxiety is a serious concern. In addition to practicing the stress management techniques listed in this section, you may want to seek additional, personal help. Call your local high school or community college and ask for the academic counselor. Tell the counselor that you have a level of test anxiety that sometimes keeps you from being able to take an exam. The counselor may be willing to help you or may suggest someone else you should talk to.

When anxiety threatens to overwhelm you right there during the exam, there are still things you can do to manage the stress level:

- **Repeat your self-confidence messages.** You should have them memorized by now. Say them quietly to yourself, and believe them!
- **Visualize one more time.** This time, visualize yourself moving smoothly and quickly through the test, answering every question correctly and finishing just before time is up. Like most visualization techniques, this one works best if you've practiced it ahead of time.
- **Find an easy question.** Skim over the test until you find an easy question, and answer it. Getting even one circle filled in gets you into the test-taking groove.
- **Take a mental break.** Everyone loses concentration once in a while during a long test. It's normal, so you shouldn't worry about it. Instead, accept what has happened. Say to yourself, "Hey, I lost it there for a minute. My brain is taking a break." Put down your pencil, close your eyes, and do some deep breathing for a few seconds. Then you're ready to go back to work.

Try these techniques ahead of time, and watch them work for you!

▶ Step 3: Make a Plan

Time to complete: 50 minutes
Activity: Construct a study plan
Maybe the most important thing you can do to get control of yourself and your exam is to make a study plan. Too many people fail to prepare simply because they fail to plan. Spending hours on the day before the exam poring over sample test questions not only increases anxiety, but it also is simply no substitute for careful preparation and practice over time.

Don't fall into the cram trap. Take control of your preparation time by mapping out a study schedule. There are four sample schedules on the following pages, based on the amount of time you have before the exam. If you're the kind of person who needs deadlines and assignments to motivate you for a project, here they are. If you're the kind of person who doesn't like to follow other people's plans, you can use the schedules suggested here to construct your own.

In constructing your plan, you should take into account how much work you need to do. If your score on the Police Sergeant Practice Exam 1 (Chapter 4) isn't what you hoped, consider taking some of the steps from Schedule A and fitting them into Schedule D, even if you do have only three weeks before the exam.

You can also customize your plan according to the information you gathered in Step 1. If the exam you have to take doesn't include a writing test, for instance, you can skip Chapter 9 and concentrate instead on the areas that are covered.

Even more important than making a plan is making a commitment. You can't increase your knowledge and good judgment overnight. You have to set aside some time every day for study and practice. Try for at least 20 minutes a day. Twenty minutes daily will do you much more good than two hours on Saturday.

If you have months before the exam, you're lucky. Don't put off your study until the week before the exam! Start now. Even ten minutes a day, with half an hour or more on weekends, can make a big difference in your score—and in your chances of becoming a sergeant!

Schedule A: The Leisure Plan

If no test has yet to be announced in your department, you may have a year or more in which to get ready. This schedule gives you six months to sharpen your skills. If an exam is announced in the middle of your preparation, you can use one of the later schedules to help you compress your study program. Study only the chapters that are relevant to the type of exam you'll be taking.

Time	Preparation
Exam minus 6 months	Read "How to Use This Book" and Chapter 1, "So You Want to be Promoted to Sergeant." Take Police Sergeant Practice Test 1 (Chapter 4). Note down your strengths and weaknesses, and study the answer explanations for the questions you answered incorrectly. Visit a library or bookstore to get the study material recommended at the end of this chapter covering material in your weak areas.
Exam minus 5 months	Read Chapter 3, "How to Bone Up on Local Laws and Procedures," and start gathering information about ordinances in your jurisdiction. Continue studying the material you got from the library or bookstore last month, focusing on the areas where you are weak, and making flash cards for points that are tough to remember. Begin working through the minicourse (Chapter 5) in this book, again taking notes and making flash cards to help in the areas where you are weak; you should get about one-third of the way through the minicourse this month.
Exam minus 4 months	Read Chapter 8, "Preparing for Your Oral Board," and get started forming a study group. Work with your study group on oral boards and local laws and procedures. Continue taking the minicourse (Chapter 5); you should be about two-thirds of the way through it by the end of this month. Continue using your flash cards and study materials.
Exam minus 3 months	Read Chapter 7, " Preparing for Assessment Center Exercises," and discuss it with your study group. Continue taking the minicourse (Chapter 5); you should finish it by the end of this month. Continue using your flash cards and study materials, and continue working with your study group.
Exam minus 2 months	Read Chapter 9, "Preparing for Your Writing Test," if your jurisdiction includes essay writing on the sergeant test, and practice your writing skills. Give your work to a friend for constructive criticism. Continue using your flash cards and study materials, and continue working with your study group.
Exam minus 1 month	Take Police Sergeant Practice Exam 2 (Chapter 6) in this book. Use your score to help you decide what to concentrate on this month. Go back to the relevant chapters and sections of the minicourse for review. Go back to the study materials recommended at the end of this chapter for further review. Continue working with your study group.
Exam minus 1 week	Review the practice exams. See how much you've learned in the last months. Concentrate on what you've done well, and resolve not to let any areas where you still feel uncertain bother you.
Exam minus 1 day	Relax. Do something unrelated to law enforcement. Eat a good meal and go to bed at your usual time.

Schedule B: The Just-Enough-Time Plan

If you have three to six months before the exam, that should be enough time to prepare for the multiple-choice test, especially if you score above 70 on the first practice exam (Chapter 4). This schedule assumes four months; stretch it out or compress it if you have more or less time, and study only the chapters that are relevant to the type of exam you'll be taking.

Time	Preparation
Exam minus 4 months	Read "How to Use this Book" and Chapter 1, "So You Want to Be Promoted to Sergeant." Take Police Sergeant Practice Exam 1 (Chapter 4), to determine where you need the most work, studying the answer explanations for the questions you answered incorrectly. Visit a library or bookstore to get the study material recommended at the end of this chapter covering material in your weak areas. Make flash cards for points that are tough to remember. Begin working through the minicourse (Chapter 5) in this book, again taking notes and making flash cards to help in the areas where you are weak; you should get about one-third of the way through the minicourse this month.
Exam minus 3 months	Read Chapter 3, "How to Bone Up on Local Laws and Procedures," and start gathering information about ordinances in your jurisdiction; make flash cards. Continue studying the material you got from the library or bookstore last month, focusing on the areas where you are weak. Continue taking the minicourse (Chapter 5); you should be about two-thirds of the way through it by the end of this month. Continue using your flash cards and study materials. Read Chapter 8, "Preparing for Your Oral Board."
Exam minus 2 months	Read Chapter 7, "Preparing for Assessment Center Exercises." Continue taking the minicourse (Chapter 5); you should finish it by the end of this month. Continue using your flash cards and study materials.
Exam minus 1 month	Take Police Sergeant Practice Exam 2 (Chapter 6) in this book. Use your score to help you decide what to concentrate on this month. Go back to the relevant chapters and sections of the minicourse for review. If your jurisdiction includes essay writing on the sergeant test, read Chapter 9, "Preparing for Your Writing Test."
Exam minus 1 week	Review the practice exams. See how much you've learned in the last months. Concentrate on what you've done well, and resolve not to let any areas where you still feel uncertain bother you.
Exam minus 1 day	Relax. Do something unrelated to law enforcement. Eat a good meal and go to bed at your usual time.

Schedule C: More Study in Less Time

If you have one to three months before the exam, you still have enough time for some concentrated study that will help you improve your score. This schedule is built around a two-month time frame. If you have only one month, spend an extra couple of hours a week to get all these steps in. If you have three months, take some of the steps from Schedule B and fit them in. Study only the chapters that are relevant to the type of exam you'll be taking.

Time	Preparation
Exam minus 8 weeks	Take Police Sergeant Practice Exam 1 (Chapter 4) to determine where you need the most work, studying the answer explanations for the questions you answered incorrectly. Visit a library or bookstore to get the study material recommended at the end of this chapter covering material in your weak areas. Make flash cards for points that are tough to remember. Begin working through the minicourse (Chapter 5) in this book, again taking notes and making flash cards to help in the areas where you are weak; you should get about halfway through the minicourse this month.
Exam minus 6 weeks	Read Chapter 3, "How to Bone Up on Local Laws and Procedures," and start gathering information about ordinances in your jurisdiction; make flash cards. Continue taking the minicourse (Chapter 5); you should be about halfway through it. Continue using your flash cards and study materials. Read Chapter 8, "Preparing for Your Oral Board."
Exam minus 4 weeks	Read Chapter 7, "Preparing for Assessment Center Exercises." Continue taking the minicourse (Chapter 5); you should be three-quarters of the way through it. Continue using your flash cards and study materials
Exam minus 2 weeks	Take Police Sergeant Practice Exam 2 (Chapter 6) in this book. Use your score to help you decide what to concentrate on this month. Finish the minicourse and go back to the relevant sections for review. If your jurisdiction includes essay writing on the sergeant test, read Chapter 9, "Preparing for Your Writing Test."
Exam minus 1 week	Review the practice exams. See how much you've learned in the last months. Concentrate on what you've done well, and resolve not to let any areas where you still feel uncertain bother you.
Exam minus 1 day	Relax. Do something unrelated to law enforcement. Eat a good meal and go to bed at your usual time.

If you have three weeks or less before the exam, you really have your work cut out for you. Carve half an hour out of your day, every day, for study. This schedule assumes you have the whole three weeks in which to prepare; if you have less time, you'll have to compress the schedule accordingly. Study only the chapters that are relevant to the type of exam you'll be taking.

Time	Preparation
Exam minus 3 weeks	Take Police Sergeant Practice Exam 1 (Chapter 4), studying the answer explanations for the questions you answered incorrectly. Visit a library or bookstore to get the study material recommended at the end of this chapter covering material in your weak areas. Make flash cards for points that are tough to remember. Begin working through the minicourse (Chapter 5) in this book, focusing on those areas the practice exam showed that you need to work on.
Exam minus 2 weeks	Read Chapter 3, "How to Bone Up on Local Laws and Procedures"; Chapter 7, "Preparing for Assessment Center Exercises"; and Chapter 8, "Preparing for Your Oral Board." Continue working through the minicourse (Chapter 5). Continue using your flash cards and study materials.
Exam minus 1 week	Take Police Sergeant Practice Exam 2 (Chapter 6) in this book. Use your score to help you decide what to concentrate on this week. Review the parts of the minicourse you had the most trouble with.
Exam minus 2 days	Review the practice exam. Make sure you understand the answer explanations.
Exam minus 1 day	Relax. Do something unrelated to law enforcement. Eat a good meal and go to bed at your usual time.

▶ Step 4: Learn to Manage Your Time

Time to complete: 10 minutes to read, many hours of practice!

Activities: Practice these strategies as you take the practice exams in this book

Steps 4, 5, and 6 of the LearningExpress Test Preparation System put you in charge of your exam by showing you test-taking strategies that work. Practice these strategies as you take the practice exams in this book, and then you'll be ready to use them on test day.

First, you'll take control of your time on the exam. The first step in achieving this control is to find out the format of the exam you're going to take. Some police sergeant exams have different sections that are each timed separately. If this is true of the exam you'll be taking, you'll want to practice using your time wisely on the practice exams and trying to avoid mistakes while working quickly. Other types of exams don't have separately timed sections. If this is the case, just practice pacing yourself on the practice exams so you don't spend too much time on difficult questions.

- **Listen carefully to directions.** By the time you get to the exam, you should know how the test works, but listen just in case something has changed.
- **Pace yourself.** Glance at your watch every few minutes, and compare the time to how far you've gotten in the section. When one-quarter of the time has elapsed, you should be a quarter of the way through the section, and so on. If you're falling behind, pick up the pace a bit.
- **Keep moving.** Don't spend too much time on any one question. If you don't know the answer, skip the question and move on. Circle the number of the question in your test booklet in case you have time to come back to it later.
- **Keep track of your place on the answer sheet.** If you skip a question, make sure you skip on the answer sheet too. Check yourself every 5–10 questions to make sure the question number and the answer sheet number are still the same.
- **Don't rush.** Though you should keep moving, rushing won't help. Try to keep calm. Work methodically and quickly.

▶ Step 5: Learn to Use the Process of Elimination

Time to complete: 20 minutes
Activity: Complete the worksheet "Using the Process of Elimination"

After time management, the next most important tool for taking control of your exam is using the process of elimination wisely. It's standard test-taking wisdom that you should always read all the answer choices before choosing your answer. This helps you find the right answer by eliminating wrong answer choices. And, sure enough, that standard wisdom applies to your exam, too.

For the sake of illustration, imagine you're facing a question that goes like this:

13. "Biology uses a *binomial* system of classification." In this sentence, the word *binomial* most nearly means
    a. understanding the law.
    b. having two names.
    c. scientifically sound.
    d. having a double meaning.

If you happen to know what *binomial* means, of course, you don't need to use the process of elimination, but let's assume that you don't. So you look at the answer choices. "Understanding the law" sure doesn't sound very likely for something having to do with biology. So you eliminate choice **a**—and now you have only three answer choices to deal with. Mark an **X** next to choice **a** so you never have to read it again.

On to the other answer choices. If you know that the prefix *bi-* means *two*, as in *bicycle*, you'll flag answer **b** as a possible answer. Make a check mark beside it, meaning "good answer, I might use this one."

Choice **c**, "scientifically sound," is a possibility. At least it's about science, not law. It could work here, though when you think about it, having a "scientifically sound" classification system in a scientific field is kind of redundant. You remember the *bi* thing in *binomial*, and probably continue to like answer **b** better. But you're not sure, so you put a question mark next to **c**, meaning "well, maybe."

Now, choice **d**, "having a double meaning." You're still keeping in mind that *bi-* means *two*, so this one looks possible at first. But then you look again at the sentence the word belongs in, and you think, "Why would biology want a system of classification that has two meanings? That wouldn't work very well!" If you're really taken with the idea that *bi* means *two*, you might put a question mark here. But if you're feeling a little more confident, you'll put an **X**. You've already got a better answer picked out.

Now your question looks like this:

13. "Biology uses a *binomial* system of classification." In this sentence, the word *binomial* most nearly means

  X **a.** understanding the law.

  ✔ **b.** having two names.

  ? **c.** scientifically sound.

  ? **d.** having a double meaning.

You've got just one check mark, for a good answer. If you're pressed for time, you should simply mark answer **b** on your answer sheet. If you've got the time to be extra careful, you could compare your check-mark answer to your question-mark answers to make sure that it's better. (It is: The *binomial* system in biology is the one that gives a two-part genus and species name like *homo sapiens.*)

It's good to have a system for marking good, bad, and maybe answers. We're recommending this one:

  X = bad

  ✔ = good

  ? = maybe

If you don't like these marks, devise your own system. Just make sure you do it long before test day—while you're working through the practice exams in this book—so you won't have to worry about it during the test.

Even when you think you're absolutely clueless about a question, you can often use the process of elimination to get rid of at least one answer choice. If so, you're better prepared to make an educated guess, as you'll see in Step 6. More often, the process of elimination allows you to get down to only two possibly right answers. Then you're in a strong position to guess. And sometimes, even though you don't know the right answer, you find it simply by getting rid of the wrong ones, as you did in the example above.

Try using your powers of elimination on the questions in the following worksheet, "Using the Process of Elimination." The answer explanations there show one possible way you might use the process to arrive at the right answer.

Using the Process of Elimination

Use the process of elimination to answer the following questions.

1. Ilsa is as old as Meghan will be in five years. The difference between Ed's age and Meghan's age is twice the difference between Ilsa's age and Meghan's age. Ed is 29. How old is Ilsa?

  a. 4

  b. 10

  c. 19

  d. 24

2. "All drivers of commercial vehicles must carry a valid commercial driver's license whenever operating a commercial vehicle." According to this sentence, which of the following people need NOT carry a commercial driver's license?

  a. a truck driver idling his engine while waiting to be directed to a loading dock

  b. a bus operator backing her bus out of the way of another bus in the bus lot

  c. a taxi driver driving his personal car to the grocery store

  d. a limousine driver taking the limousine to her home after dropping off her last passenger of the evening

3. Smoking tobacco has been linked to

    a. increased risk of stroke and heart attack.

    b. all forms of respiratory disease.

    c. increasing mortality rates over the past ten years.

    d. juvenile delinquency.

4. Which of the following words is spelled correctly?

    a. incorrigible

    b. outragous

    c. domestickated

    d. understandible

Answers

Here are the answers, as well as some suggestions as to how you might have used the process of elimination to find them.

1. d. You should have eliminated answer **a** off the bat. Ilsa can't be four years old if Meghan is going to be Ilsa's age in five years. The best way to eliminate the other answer choices is to try plugging them into the information given in the problem. For instance, for answer **b**, if Ilsa is 10, then Meghan must be 5. The difference in their ages is 5. The difference between Ed's age, 29, and Meghan's age, 5, is 24. Is 24 two times 5? No. Then answer **b** is wrong. You could eliminate answer **c** in the same way and be left with answer **d**.

2. c. Note the word *not* in the question, and go through the answers one by one. Is the truck driver in choice **a** "operating a commercial vehicle"? Yes, idling counts as "operating," so he needs to have a commercial driver's license. Likewise, the bus operator in answer **b** is operating a commercial vehicle; the question doesn't say the operator has to be on the street. The limo driver in **d** is operating a commercial vehicle, even if it doesn't have passenger in it. However, the cabbie in answer **c** is not operating a commercial vehicle, but his own private car.

3. a. You could eliminate answer **b** simply because of the presence of the word *all*. Such absolutes hardly ever appear in correct answer choices. Choice **c** looks attractive until you think a little about what you know— aren't *fewer* people smoking these days, rather than more? So how could smoking be responsible for a higher mortality rate? (If you didn't know that *mortality rate* means the rate at which people die, you might keep this choice as a possibility, but you'd still be able to eliminate two answers and have only two to choose from.) And choice **d** is unlikely and hard to support, so you could eliminate that one, too. And you're left with the correct choice, **a**.

4. a. How you used the process of elimination here depends on which words you recognized as being spelled incorrectly. If you knew that the correct spellings were *outrageous*, *domesticated*, and *understandable*, then you were home free. The odds are that you knew that at least one of those words was wrong.

The process of elimination is your tool for the next step, which is knowing when to guess.

► Step 6: Know When to Guess

Time to complete: 20 minutes
**Activity: Complete the worksheet "Your Guessing
Ability"**

Armed with the process of elimination, you're ready to take control of one of the big questions in test taking: Should I guess? The probable answer is yes. Unless the exam has a so-called guessing penalty, you have nothing to lose and everything to gain from guessing. The more complicated answer depends both on the exam and on you—your personality and your "guessing intuition."

Most police sergeant exams don't use a guessing penalty. The number of questions you answer correctly yields your score, and there's no penalty for wrong answers. So the first thing you must do is find out whether the test you are getting ready to take has a guessing penalty. That is, find out if points are taken off for answering incorrectly. If not, you don't have to worry—simply go ahead and guess. But if you find out that your exam does have a guessing penalty, you should read the section below to find out what that means for you.

How the Guessing Penalty Works

Here's how a guessing penalty works: Depending on the number of answer choices in a given exam, some proportion of the number of questions you got wrong is subtracted from the total number of questions you got right. For instance, if there were four answer choices per each question, typically the guessing penalty is one-third of your wrong answers.

Suppose you took a test of 100 questions. You answered 88 of them right and 12 of them wrong. If there's no guessing penalty, your score is simply 88. But if there's a one-third point guessing penalty, the scorers take your 12 wrong answers and divide by 3 to come up with 4. Then they *subtract* that 4 from your correct-answer score of 88 to leave you with a score of 84. Thus, you would have been better off if you had simply not answered those 12 questions that you weren't sure of. Then your total score would still be 88, because there wouldn't be anything to subtract.

Sticking with our example of an exam that has four answer choices per question, eliminating just one wrong answer makes your odds of choosing the correct answer one in three. That's the same as the one-out-of-three guessing penalty—even odds. If you eliminate two answer choices, your odds are one in two—better than the guessing penalty. In either case, you should go ahead and choose one of the remaining answer choices.

A guessing penalty really only works against *random* guessing—filling in the little circles to make a nice pattern on your answer sheet. If you can eliminate one or more answer choices, as outlined previously, you're better off taking a guess than leaving the answer blank, even on the sections that have a penalty.

What You Should Do about the Guessing Penalty

So, **if** your police sergeant test has a guessing penalty—and remember that most don't—you now know that marking your answer sheet at random doesn't pay. If you're running out of time on an exam that has a guessing penalty, you should not use your remaining seconds to mark a pretty pattern on your answer sheet. Take those few seconds to try to answer one more question correctly.

But as soon as you get out of the realm of random guessing, the guessing penalty no longer works against you. If you can use the process of elimination to get rid of even one wrong answer choice, the odds stop being against you and start working in your favor, even on tests with a guessing penalty.

Your Guessing Ability

The following are ten really hard questions. You're not supposed to know the answers. Rather, this is an assessment of your ability to guess when you don't have a clue. Read each question carefully, just as if you did expect to answer it. If you have any knowledge at all of the subject of the question, use that knowledge to help you eliminate wrong answer choices. Use this answer grid to fill in your answers to the questions.

1. (a) (b) (c) (d)   5. (a) (b) (c) (d)   9. (a) (b) (c) (d)
2. (a) (b) (c) (d)   6. (a) (b) (c) (d)   10. (a) (b) (c) (d)
3. (a) (b) (c) (d)   7. (a) (b) (c) (d)
4. (a) (b) (c) (d)   8. (a) (b) (c) (d)

1. September 7 is Independence Day in
   a. India.
   b. Costa Rica.
   c. Brazil.
   d. Australia.

2. Which of the following is the formula for determining the momentum of an object?
   a. $p = mv$
   b. $F = ma$
   c. $P = IV$
   d. $E = mc^2$

3. Because of the expansion of the universe, the stars and other celestial bodies are all moving away from each other. This phenomenon is known as
   a. Newton's first law.
   b. the big bang.
   c. gravitational collapse.
   d. Hubble flow.

4. American author Gertrude Stein was born in
   a. 1713.
   b. 1830.
   c. 1874.
   d. 1901.

5. Which of the following is NOT one of the Five Classics attributed to Confucius?
   a. *I Ching*
   b. *Book of Holiness*
   c. *Spring and Autumn Annals*
   d. *Book of History*

6. The religious and philosophical doctrine that holds that the universe is constantly in a struggle between good and evil is known as
   a. Pelagianism.
   b. Manichaeanism.
   c. neo-Hegelianism.
   d. Epicureanism.

7. The third Chief Justice of the Supreme Court was
   a. John Blair.
   b. William Cushing.
   c. James Wilson.
   d. John Jay.

8. Which of the following is the poisonous portion of a daffodil?
   a. the bulb
   b. the leaves
   c. the stem
   d. the flowers

9. The winner of the Masters golf tournament in 1953 was

  a. Sam Snead.

  b. Cary Middlecoff.

  c. Arnold Palmer.

  d. Ben Hogan.

10. The state with the highest per capita personal income in 1980 was

  a. Alaska.

  b. Connecticut.

  c. New York.

  d. Texas.

Answers

Check your answers against the correct answers below.

1. c.

2. a.

3. d.

4. c.

5. b.

6. b.

7. b.

8. a.

9. d.

10. a.

How Did You Do?

You may have simply gotten lucky and actually known the answers to one or two questions. In addition, your guessing was more successful if you were able to use the process of elimination on any of the questions. Maybe you didn't know who the third Chief Justice was (question 7), but you knew that John Jay was the first. In that case, you would have eliminated answer **d** and therefore improved your odds of guessing correctly from one in four to one in three.

According to probability, you should get $2\frac{1}{2}$ answers correct by guessing, so getting either two or three right would be average. If you got four or more right, you may be a really terrific guesser. If you got one or none right, you may not be a very strong guesser.

Keep in mind, though, that this is only a small sample. You should continue to keep track of your guessing ability as you work through the practice questions in this book. Circle the numbers of questions you guess on as you make your guess, or, if you don't have time while you take the practice exams, go back afterward and try to remember which questions you guessed at. Remember, on a test with four answer choices for each question, your chances of getting a right answer is one in four. So keep a separate "guessing" score for each exam. How many questions did you guess on? How many did you get right? If the number you got right is at least one-fourth of the number of questions you guessed on, you are at least an average guesser, maybe better—and you should go ahead and guess on the real exam. If the number you got right is significantly lower than one-fourth of the number you guessed on, you should not guess on exams where there is a guessing penalty unless you can eliminate a wrong answer. If there's no guessing penalty, you should always guess unless you are running out of time.

▶ Step 7: Reach Your Peak Performance Zone

Time to complete: 10 minutes to read; weeks to complete!

Activity: Complete the "Physical Preparation Checklist"

To get ready for a challenge like a big exam, you have to take control of your physical, as well as your mental, state. Exercise, proper diet, and rest will ensure that your body works with, rather than against, your mind on test day, as well as during your preparation.

Exercise

If you don't already have a regular exercise program going, the time during which you're preparing for an exam is actually an excellent time to start one. You'll have to be pretty fit to pass your physical ability test anyway. And if you're already keeping fit—or trying to get that way—don't let the pressure of preparing for an exam fool you into quitting now. Exercise helps reduce stress by pumping wonderful good-feeling hormones called endorphins into your system. It also increases the oxygen supply throughout your body, including your brain, so you'll be at peak performance on test day.

A half hour of vigorous activity—enough to raise a sweat—every day should be your aim. If you're really pressed for time, every other day is OK. Choose an activity you like and get out there and do it. Jogging with a friend always makes the time go faster, as does running with a radio.

But don't overdo it. You don't want to exhaust yourself. Moderation is the key.

Diet

First of all, cut out the junk. Go easy on caffeine, and try to eliminate alcohol and nicotine from your system at least two weeks before the exam.

What your body needs for peak performance is simply a balanced diet. Eat plenty of fruits and vegetables, along with protein and complex carbohydrates. Foods that are high in lecithin (an amino acid), such as fish and beans, are especially good "brain foods."

The night before the exam, you might "carboload" the way athletes do before a contest. Eat a big plate of spaghetti, rice and beans, or whatever your favorite carbohydrate is.

Rest

You probably know how much sleep you need every night to be at your best, even if you don't always get it. Make sure you do get that much sleep, though, for at least a week before the exam. Moderation is important here, too: Extra sleep will just make you groggy.

If you're not a morning person and your exam will be given in the morning, you should reset your internal clock so that your body doesn't think you're taking an exam at 3 A.M. You have to start this process well before the exam. Get up half an hour earlier each morning, and then go to bed half an hour earlier that night. Don't try it the other way around; you'll just toss and turn if you go to bed early without having gotten up early. The next morning, get up another half an hour earlier, and so on. How long you will have to do this depends on how late you're used to getting up.

Physical Preparation Checklist

During the week before the test, write down what physical exercise you engaged in and for how long and what you ate for each meal. Remember, you're trying for at least a half an hour of exercise every other day (preferably every day) and a balanced diet that's light on junk food.

Exam minus 7 days

Exercise: _____ for _____ minutes

Breakfast: _____

Lunch: _____

Dinner: _____

Snacks: _____

Exam minus 6 days

Exercise: _____ for _____ minutes

Breakfast: _____

Lunch: _____

Dinner: _____

Snacks: _____

Exam minus 5 days

Exercise: _____ for _____ minutes

Breakfast: _____

Lunch: _____

Dinner: _____

Snacks: _____

Exam minus 4 days

Exercise: _____ for _____ minutes

Breakfast: _____

Lunch: _____

Dinner: _____

Snacks: _____

Exam minus 3 days

Exercise: _____ for _____ minutes

Breakfast: _____

Lunch: _____

Dinner: _____

Snacks: _____

Exam minus 2 days

Exercise: _____ for _____ minutes

Breakfast: _____

Lunch: _____

Dinner: _____

Snacks: _____

Exam minus 1 day

Exercise: _____ for _____ minutes

Breakfast: _____

Lunch: _____

Dinner: _____

Snacks: _____

▶ Step 8: Get Your Act Together

Time to complete: 10 minutes to read; time to complete will vary
Activity: Complete the "Final Preparations" worksheet

You're in control of your mind and body; you're in charge of test anxiety, your preparation, and your test-taking strategies. Now it's time to take charge of external factors, such as the testing site and the materials you need to take the exam.

Find out Where the Test is and Make a Trial Run

The exam bulletin the recruiting office sent you will tell you when and where your exam is being held. Do you know how to get to the testing site? Do you know how long it will take you to get there? If not, make a trial run, preferably on the same day of the week at the same time of day. Make note, on the "Final Preparations" worksheet, of the amount of time it will take you to get to the exam site. Plan on arriving 10–15 minutes early so you can get the lay of the land, use the bathroom, and calm down. Then figure out how early you will have to get up that morning, and make sure you get up that early every day for a week before the exam.

Gather Your Materials

The night before the exam, lay out the clothes you will wear and the materials you have to bring with you to the exam. Plan on dressing in layers; you won't have any control over the temperature of the examination room. Have a sweater or jacket you can take off if it's warm. Use the checklist on the "Final Preparations" worksheet to help you pull together what you'll need.

Don't Skip Breakfast

Even if you don't usually eat breakfast, do so on exam morning. A cup of coffee doesn't count. Don't eat doughnuts or other sweet foods, either. A sugar high will leave you with a sugar low in the middle of the exam. A mix of protein and carbohydrates is best: Cereal with milk, or eggs with toast, will do your body a world of good.

▶ Step 9: Do It!

Time to complete: 10 minutes, plus test-taking time
Activity: Ace the Police Sergeant Exam!

Fast forward to exam day. You're ready. You made a study plan and followed through. You practiced your test-taking strategies while working through this book. You're in control of your physical, mental, and emotional state. You know when and where to show up and what to bring with you. In other words, you're probably better prepared than most of the other people taking the exam with you.

Just one more thing: When you're done with the exam, you will have earned a reward. Plan a celebration. Call up your friends and plan a party, have a nice dinner for two, or pick out a movie to see—whatever your heart desires. Give yourself something to look forward to.

And then do it. Go into the exam full of confidence and armed with test-taking strategies you've practiced till they're second nature. You're in control of yourself, your environment, and your performance on the exam. You're ready to succeed. So do it. Go in there and ace the exam. And look forward to your future career as a police sergeant!

Final Preparations

Getting to the Exam Site

Location of exam: _____

Date: _____

Time of exam: _____

Do I know how to get to the exam site?   Yes ___   No ___

(If no, make a trial run.)

Time it will take to get to exam site: _____

Things to Lay out the Night Before

Clothes I will wear   ___

Sweater/jacket   ___

Watch   ___

Photo ID   ___

Admission card   ___

4 No. 2 pencils   ___

_____   _____

_____   _____

▶ References

Adams, Thomas F. *Police Field Operations.* 6th ed. Upper Saddle River, N.J.: Prentice Hall, 2003.

Carlson, Daniel P. *When Cultures Clash: Strategies for Strengthened Police–Comunity Relations.* 2nd ed. Upper Saddle River, N.J.: Prentice Hall, 2004.

Coffey, Alan, Edward Eldefonso, and Walter Hartinger. *Human Relations: Law Enforcement in a Changing Community.* 3rd ed. Engelwood Cliffs, N.J.: Prentice Hall, 1981.

Franklin, Carl J. *Constitutional Law for the Criminal Justice Professional.* Boca Raton, F.L.: CRC Press., 1999.

Geller, William A., ed. *Local Government Police Management Study Guide.* 4th ed. Washington, D.C.: The International City Management Association (ICMS), 2003.

Holder, Angela Roddey, and John Thomas Roddey. *The Meaning of the Constitution.* 3rd ed. Hauppauge, N.Y.: Barron's Educational Series, Inc., 1997.

Hunter Ronald D., Thomas Barker, and Pamela D Mayhall. *Police-Community Relations and the Administration of Justice.* 6th ed. Upper Saddle River, N.J.: Prentice Hall, 2003.

Iannone, Nathan F., and M.D. Iannone. *Supervision of Police Personnel.* 6th ed. Upper Saddle River, N.J.: Prentice Hall, 2001.

Kamisar, Yale, Wayne R. LaFave, Jerold H. Israel, and Nancy J. King. *Basic Criminal Procedure: Cases, Comments & Questions.* 10th ed. Egan, M.N.: West Publishing, 2002.

Moenssens, Andre A., James E. Starrs, and Carol E. Henderson. *Scientific Evidence in Criminal Cases.* 4th ed. Eagan, M.N.: West Publishing, 1995.

O'Hara, Charles E., and Gregory L. O'Hara. *Fundamentals of Criminal Investigation.* 7th ed. Springfield, Ill.: C.C. Thomas Publishing Co., 2003.

Radelet, Louis A., and David L. Carter. *The Police and the Community.* 7th ed. Upper Saddle River, N.J.: Prentice Hall, 2001.

Schoroeder, Donald J., Frank Lombardo, and Jerry Strollo. *Management and Supervision of Law Enforcement Personnel.* Dayton, O.H.: Gould Publications, 1997.

CHAPTER

3 ▶

How to Freshen Up on Local Laws and Procedures

Many police sergeant exams include at least some questions on state and municipal laws and the procedures of the local department. With so many laws on the books and so many different procedures, how can you ever know it all? Well, you can't.

o exam realistically expects you to know everything. The trick becomes deciding what to spend your valuable time learning. First, and most obvious, is to study the exam guideline you are given for the police sergeant exam, if any. What does the guideline tell you? Is there a reading list? Does the order of the reading list tell you anything? If the reading list is not arranged alphabetically, then assume the most important sources are listed first. Give them top priority. The most effective use of study time is to prioritize. Why spend as much time memorizing facts that do not have as much probability of being asked as studying ones where the probability is high? Study is in some ways like police work. An investigation is most effective when the possibilities, suspects, and scenarios are identified. The same is true of effective study.

▶ Devise a Study Plan

First things first: Yes, you must schedule time to study. Don't think you will just make the time to study. Odds are you probably won't haphazardly make enough time to cover the pertinent material, unless study is given priority and scheduled right along with the other "must do" items in your day planner. Learning won't happen unless you allot specific study periods. How much time is there between today's date and the date of the test? In your day planner—if you are not using one, then this might be a good time to start—can you find at least one free hour a day for study? You may schedule more as the time gets closer to the test, but try for one hour a day to start with. One-hour blocks of time are ideal. Much less than that, and you may be just warming up and working hard when it's time to stop. Just as in a physical workout, in effective study there tends to be a warming up, a stretching of the gray matter, before the heavy lifting of facts takes place.

There are many advantages to regular study hours: Study will become a habit. You won't have to waste valuable energy trying to get yourself to study. You won't end up a few days before the police sergeant exam trying to "cram" all the important codes and procedures into a frantic brain. You will have acquired your knowledge in manageable bits and pieces, which is the proven path of study. One hint: Don't schedule your study hours during times that will be hard to stick to. Don't plan to study when you know your favorite television program is showing. Don't plan to study Monday evenings after 9:00 P.M. if you're a football fanatic. You won't study. But if you schedule study time from 8:00 P.M. until kickoff, the game can be a just reward for your efforts. Research has shown that people work better if they get immediate rewards for their efforts. Schedule realistic study periods and reward yourself for a job well done, but allow yourself to be flexible too. If life, as it is apt to do, throws you a curve and you can't study when scheduled, don't eliminate the study hour altogether. If your study schedule requires an adjustment, adjust. Trade the time for one task for another, but study. Then, once you have a workable schedule, it's time to plan how to use those hour-long slots of study time most effectively to cover the material you need to know for the police sergeant exam.

▶ What to Study

How do you decide what to spend your time on? What will you need to know for the exam? The place to start is with the exam notice. Study it carefully. It may tell you more than you think. Another resource is others who have taken police sergeant exams in the past. Talk to your sergeant, lieutenant, and chief, if possible. Glean as much information and advice as you can, since their experiences can be useful to you. Your exam will be different from the ones they took in the past, yet there will be similarities. The personal issues, how to study, what to study, how to prepare emotionally, and so on will be similar. Talking to someone who has experienced what you are about to encounter has a reassuring effect. After all, how much smarter than you are your sergeant, lieutenant, or chief? They passed. You can, too. They can also give you an idea of how many and what type of local codes might be asked about in the exam. For many departments giving standardized tests, there will not be a local component, though questions on local code could very well arise in the orals. Just as in police work in general, people are the first and most obvious source of pertinent information. Always use what information is available.

One area overlooked surprisingly often by prospective applicants for supervisory positions is the specific duties of the position to which they aspire. You will absolutely need to know the sergeant's duties and responsibilities in your department. If not addressed directly in the written exam, this information will be a crucial part of the oral exam. Do not neglect it. This information is readily available, both through the written job description for the job and from the personnel in the department. Be prepared to know in detail what the job entails. Know it as you know your own current position.

When you have finished your assessment of what you need to know, sit down and make a list of the information you need to master. Match this list of needed information to the materials supplying the information. Use the titles of the sections in the materials to locate the crucial, most often asked information. You don't need to know everything, but you need to know **which** information is crucial and **where** to find it, so you can include it in your study.

▶ Setting Goals

Having identified the material to be studied, you will need to go back to your day planner or calendar and develop your study plan further. This means setting goals for the individual study hours you have scheduled. For example, you may allot one hour to the goal of learning the specific duties and responsibilities of a sergeant in your department. The most efficient use of the study time will come when you have specific study goals. You won't need to stare at a high pile of thick books and wonder where to start. When learning is broken down into smaller tasks, information becomes easier to absorb.

▶ Maximizing Concentration

Setting specific study goals is not the only way to maximize your concentration. Something as simple as choosing a good environment is also important. The room you study in should be well lit and quiet. You should have a comfortable chair, but not one that makes you too relaxed. You should have all the materials you need: pens, pencils, highlighters, paper, and so on. It helps to tell family and friends of your specific study times so they can leave you alone during study hours. Assure them that you will return calls when you are finished studying. Taking the time at the beginning to ensure that your study environment is good will

increase the likelihood that once you achieve a decent level of concentration, you will not be sidetracked. If there is no room in your home that is conducive to a good study environment, consider using a quiet spot at the local library or even finding a secluded room at your police station. Try to use the same spot as often as possible. We are creatures of habit. If we get used to studying at a certain location at a certain time of day, we will automatically go into study mode when we go to that place.

▶ Alone or with a Group?

Some people find that studying with others helps them to concentrate. This can be a most effective strategy. You undoubtedly are not the only officer in your department who is taking the sergeant exam. A word of caution is called for here: Pick your partner or partners well. You don't want someone who is more of a distraction than an aid, and you don't want to spend your study time "shooting the breeze." Remember that the hour you designate as a study period is for study. That said, if you do find a good partner or partners, the benefits are many. You will have other "educated guesses" as to what material is important and what is not. You can test each other on the material. If you choose the right partner or partners, you can delegate segments of the material to each other to study. Each partner can do some of the sifting work to glean the important information from the material that needs to be considered. Then each partner can teach the others what he or she has learned. This strategy can save significant time and make your sessions together effectively do double duty. After all, part of your responsibilities as sergeant will be to delegate tasks and make the most effective use of everyone's time. Why not start now?

▶ Other Tricks

With the daunting task of preparing for questions relating to state and municipal law and the procedures of the local department, you should consider all available learning tactics. Have an open mind and find the tactics that work for you. You may want to use three-by-five-inch cards to make study aids, posing a question on one side and the answer on the other. Then whenever a spare moment arises, you can pull out your cards and test yourself. After you answer a question successfully enough times so that you are sure you know the answer, put it in a separate pile. Eventually, you will be carrying around only the things you still need to learn and not wasting time on what you already know. Don't throw the mastered cards away just yet, though. You will want to retest yourself again after some time. Overlearn the material. Go over it several times after you think you already have it down cold. This way, you won't be sitting at the exam sure you know a fact yet unable to recall what you so surely know. Just writing the material down, whether on cards or in a notebook, has a beneficial effect. It has been found that the act of writing something down, engaging the part of your brain that controls the motor skills along with thought, enhances memory.

Don't forget the other senses. Many of us are more auditory. A small recorder may come in handy. You can record items that your research has shown to be important. You can record sample questions and test yourself on material until you know it cold. Using a recorder, you can study at times that might otherwise not occur to you. You can listen to your tape while driving, cooking, gardening, or jogging. Use your imagination. This is a study tool that should not be overlooked. Make tapes of the material that you are having the most trouble remembering and the material that requires rote memorization. This way, you will be able to study at times when reading would be impossible. Consider using the tapes, or any of the other study tools, before going to bed. For some people, reviewing material before sleep adds to comprehension. You might try this and test yourself in the morning. Remember to keep an open mind. Results are what count.

There is no way to memorize a 700-page municipal code. But if you have done your research and have an idea what is most important and most likely to be asked, you can begin to make the task manageable. There are ways to organize material so that it can be more easily remembered. Our minds like to group ideas. If you can manage to group things you need to learn in a way that makes sense to you, you have a better shot at recall. You may not remember the item you want at first, but if you know what group it belongs to, the remembering of the other items can often enable recall of the item you want. You can make up a catchphrase. For example, to remember the license plate number **DBV-528**, you might make up the phrase *Dandy Black Vehicle 5 minutes 2 the diner where you 8 breakfast.* You get the idea. Be creative. Similarly, a catchword may help to jog memory. Say you need to know the psychological defense mechanisms *denial, repression, projection, and identification.* You could use the catchword **DRIP** to jog your memory.

Whatever the techniques you employ to memorize material, try to space out your memory work over many sessions. Don't rely on massive memory work. If you space it out, you won't overload and you'll be surprised how much material you can master.

Police Sergeant Practice Exam 1

With this chapter, your police sergeant exam preparation begins in earnest. Take the following practice exam as a means of assessing the state of your knowledge: Are you in command of all the facts, procedures, laws, and theories that might show up on your sergeant exam? By taking this practice exam, you will be able to see where you are in good shape and where you need to spend some study time.

Think ahead before you begin this exam. Decide whether you are going to limit yourself to the same amount of time that you will get when taking the actual sergeant exam. In one New Jersey department, the time allowed worked out to just over a minute per question. That isn't much time. To give yourself a similarly high-pressure test, allot 1 hour and 45 minutes for the practice exam. You might instead, however, choose to get your feet wet by taking this first practice test at your own pace.

Whichever approach you take to timing, be sure to answer all the questions before looking at the answers, and **study** the answer explanations once you've scored yourself. The information provided in the answer explanations is straight to the point, and these bite-size lessons are a good way to ingest material you'll need to have on exam day.

The questions on this exam are organized according to the following content chart:

QUESTION RANGE	TOPICS COVERED
Questions 1–16	Constitutional Law and Criminal Procedure
Questions 17–60	Supervision and Management
Questions 61–75	Criminal Investigation and Forensic Science
Questions 76–85	Community Relations
Questions 86–100	Patrol Practices

After you finish the practice exam and score yourself, be sure to check your results against this chart. That way, you can determine for yourself what content areas give you the most trouble. Use what you learn to decide what to spend your time studying.

Police Sergeant Practice Exam 1

1.	ⓐ	ⓑ	ⓒ	ⓓ
2.	ⓐ	ⓑ	ⓒ	ⓓ
3.	ⓐ	ⓑ	ⓒ	ⓓ
4.	ⓐ	ⓑ	ⓒ	ⓓ
5.	ⓐ	ⓑ	ⓒ	ⓓ
6.	ⓐ	ⓑ	ⓒ	ⓓ
7.	ⓐ	ⓑ	ⓒ	ⓓ
8.	ⓐ	ⓑ	ⓒ	ⓓ
9.	ⓐ	ⓑ	ⓒ	ⓓ
10.	ⓐ	ⓑ	ⓒ	ⓓ
11.	ⓐ	ⓑ	ⓒ	ⓓ
12.	ⓐ	ⓑ	ⓒ	ⓓ
13.	ⓐ	ⓑ	ⓒ	ⓓ
14.	ⓐ	ⓑ	ⓒ	ⓓ
15.	ⓐ	ⓑ	ⓒ	ⓓ
16.	ⓐ	ⓑ	ⓒ	ⓓ
17.	ⓐ	ⓑ	ⓒ	ⓓ
18.	ⓐ	ⓑ	ⓒ	ⓓ
19.	ⓐ	ⓑ	ⓒ	ⓓ
20.	ⓐ	ⓑ	ⓒ	ⓓ
21.	ⓐ	ⓑ	ⓒ	ⓓ
22.	ⓐ	ⓑ	ⓒ	ⓓ
23.	ⓐ	ⓑ	ⓒ	ⓓ
24.	ⓐ	ⓑ	ⓒ	ⓓ
25.	ⓐ	ⓑ	ⓒ	ⓓ
26.	ⓐ	ⓑ	ⓒ	ⓓ
27.	ⓐ	ⓑ	ⓒ	ⓓ
28.	ⓐ	ⓑ	ⓒ	ⓓ
29.	ⓐ	ⓑ	ⓒ	ⓓ
30.	ⓐ	ⓑ	ⓒ	ⓓ
31.	ⓐ	ⓑ	ⓒ	ⓓ
32.	ⓐ	ⓑ	ⓒ	ⓓ
33.	ⓐ	ⓑ	ⓒ	ⓓ
34.	ⓐ	ⓑ	ⓒ	ⓓ
35.	ⓐ	ⓑ	ⓒ	ⓓ

36.	ⓐ	ⓑ	ⓒ	ⓓ
37.	ⓐ	ⓑ	ⓒ	ⓓ
38.	ⓐ	ⓑ	ⓒ	ⓓ
39.	ⓐ	ⓑ	ⓒ	ⓓ
40.	ⓐ	ⓑ	ⓒ	ⓓ
41.	ⓐ	ⓑ	ⓒ	ⓓ
42.	ⓐ	ⓑ	ⓒ	ⓓ
43.	ⓐ	ⓑ	ⓒ	ⓓ
44.	ⓐ	ⓑ	ⓒ	ⓓ
45.	ⓐ	ⓑ	ⓒ	ⓓ
46.	ⓐ	ⓑ	ⓒ	ⓓ
47.	ⓐ	ⓑ	ⓒ	ⓓ
48.	ⓐ	ⓑ	ⓒ	ⓓ
49.	ⓐ	ⓑ	ⓒ	ⓓ
50.	ⓐ	ⓑ	ⓒ	ⓓ
51.	ⓐ	ⓑ	ⓒ	ⓓ
52.	ⓐ	ⓑ	ⓒ	ⓓ
53.	ⓐ	ⓑ	ⓒ	ⓓ
54.	ⓐ	ⓑ	ⓒ	ⓓ
55.	ⓐ	ⓑ	ⓒ	ⓓ
56.	ⓐ	ⓑ	ⓒ	ⓓ
57.	ⓐ	ⓑ	ⓒ	ⓓ
58.	ⓐ	ⓑ	ⓒ	ⓓ
59.	ⓐ	ⓑ	ⓒ	ⓓ
60.	ⓐ	ⓑ	ⓒ	ⓓ
61.	ⓐ	ⓑ	ⓒ	ⓓ
62.	ⓐ	ⓑ	ⓒ	ⓓ
63.	ⓐ	ⓑ	ⓒ	ⓓ
64.	ⓐ	ⓑ	ⓒ	ⓓ
65.	ⓐ	ⓑ	ⓒ	ⓓ
66.	ⓐ	ⓑ	ⓒ	ⓓ
67.	ⓐ	ⓑ	ⓒ	ⓓ
68.	ⓐ	ⓑ	ⓒ	ⓓ
69.	ⓐ	ⓑ	ⓒ	ⓓ
70.	ⓐ	ⓑ	ⓒ	ⓓ

71.	ⓐ	ⓑ	ⓒ	ⓓ
72.	ⓐ	ⓑ	ⓒ	ⓓ
73.	ⓐ	ⓑ	ⓒ	ⓓ
74.	ⓐ	ⓑ	ⓒ	ⓓ
75.	ⓐ	ⓑ	ⓒ	ⓓ
76.	ⓐ	ⓑ	ⓒ	ⓓ
77.	ⓐ	ⓑ	ⓒ	ⓓ
78.	ⓐ	ⓑ	ⓒ	ⓓ
79.	ⓐ	ⓑ	ⓒ	ⓓ
80.	ⓐ	ⓑ	ⓒ	ⓓ
81.	ⓐ	ⓑ	ⓒ	ⓓ
82.	ⓐ	ⓑ	ⓒ	ⓓ
83.	ⓐ	ⓑ	ⓒ	ⓓ
84.	ⓐ	ⓑ	ⓒ	ⓓ
85.	ⓐ	ⓑ	ⓒ	ⓓ
86.	ⓐ	ⓑ	ⓒ	ⓓ
87.	ⓐ	ⓑ	ⓒ	ⓓ
88.	ⓐ	ⓑ	ⓒ	ⓓ
89.	ⓐ	ⓑ	ⓒ	ⓓ
90.	ⓐ	ⓑ	ⓒ	ⓓ
91.	ⓐ	ⓑ	ⓒ	ⓓ
92.	ⓐ	ⓑ	ⓒ	ⓓ
93.	ⓐ	ⓑ	ⓒ	ⓓ
94.	ⓐ	ⓑ	ⓒ	ⓓ
95.	ⓐ	ⓑ	ⓒ	ⓓ
96.	ⓐ	ⓑ	ⓒ	ⓓ
97.	ⓐ	ⓑ	ⓒ	ⓓ
98.	ⓐ	ⓑ	ⓒ	ⓓ
99.	ⓐ	ⓑ	ⓒ	ⓓ
100.	ⓐ	ⓑ	ⓒ	ⓓ

▶ Police Sergeant Practice Exam 1

1. As a newly appointed sergeant, you observe one of your officers approach a person who she reasonably suspects to be selling packets of cocaine. The officer begins to question the person and then conducts a pat-down search of the person's jacket, attempting to locate where the drugs are secreted. As a supervisor, you should tell the officer that this type of search is
   a. justifiable because possession/sale of drugs is a serious crime.
   b. not justifiable because the person was not under arrest.
   c. justifiable because the officer had probable cause to search.
   d. not justifiable because the officer had only reasonable suspicion.

2. You, as the sergeant, observe one of your officers stop a vehicle and arrest the lone driver of the vehicle. The officer then places the arrestee, handcuffed, in the rear seat of the patrol car and asks you if he can now search the car that the arrestee was driving. Which of the following is the best answer you can give to your officer under these circumstances?
   a. A full search of the vehicle can be made.
   b. A full search of the vehicle can be made for weapons only.
   c. A search of the passenger compartment and the trunk can be made for weapons and evidence.
   d. The passenger compartment and any containers found there, whether opened or closed, can be searched.

3. When evidence is obtained by the police in violation of a person's constitutional rights, that evidence may be inadmissible in any subsequent criminal trial against that person for which the evidence was a key component. This is known as
   a. the left out rule.
   b. constitutional exclusion rule.
   c. the exclusionary rule.
   d. the illegal search and seizure rule.

4. What is needed for a police officer to make a lawful search of a person's premises in the absence of exigent circumstances? Choose the best answer.
   a. probable cause
   b. reasonable suspicion that criminal activity is afoot
   c. reasonable belief that the person inside the premises in question has committed a felony
   d. a search warrant

5. According to the Supreme Court, what standard of proof must be forwarded by a police officer conducting a common law right of inquiry?
   a. a founded suspicion of criminality
   b. probable cause
   c. reasonable suspicion
   d. blanket suspicion

6. Which of the following constitutional amendments contains the due process clause?
   a. Fifth Amendment only
   b. Fourth Amendment only
   c. Fifth and Fourteenth Amendments
   d. Tenth Amendment only

7. What is true with regard to the First Amendment to the Constitution?

   a. The rights contained in the First Amendment are absolute rights.

   b. The rights contained in the First Amendment are not absolute rights but conditional rights.

   c. The First Amendment establishes the right of the government to take private property for public use.

   d. The First Amendment establishes the right to hold, express, teach, or advocate any opinion, and to join with others to express it, except if such opinion is grossly repugnant to the vast majority of the citizenry.

8. If probable cause exists to search a motor vehicle, then

   a. the entire vehicle can be searched.

   b. only the passenger compartment and any containers found there can be searched.

   c. if the motor vehicle is parked, a search warrant must be obtained.

   d. if the vehicle can be readily moved, the entire vehicle can be searched.

9. According to the Supreme Court, the Fouth Amendment to the Constitution protects

   a. places.

   b. people.

   c. the home.

   d. people and places.

10. Probable cause is

   a. a rigid concept.

   b. a fluid concept.

   c. to be adjudicated by utilizing the science or philosophy of law.

   d. a bright line rule.

11. Two police officers boarded a bus during a stopover from another city. They wore badges and insignia, and one of them was holding a zipper pouch containing a pistol. Although they lacked express reasons for suspicion, the officers picked out the defendant and asked to inspect his ticket and identification, which he gave to them. These items were immediately returned to the defendant as unremarkable. However, the two police officers then explained that they were narcotics agents on the lookout for illegal drugs and asked the defendant's consent to search his luggage. They specifically advised the defendant that he had the right to refuse consent. The search uncovered a quantity of cocaine in one of the defendant's suitcases. The defendant was arrested and charged with trafficking in cocaine. The Supreme Court held that

   a. the evidence must be suppressed because seizure of a person without probable cause is illegal.

   b. the evidence must be suppressed because seizure without articulable reasonable suspicion in a situation where the defendant feels he or she is not free to leave is illegal.

   c. the actions of the two officers were lawful and no reasonable suspicion was required because the defendant gave his consent to the search.

   d. the actions of the two officers were justified based on a recognized exception to the warrant requirement.

12. Which of the following is a recognized exception of the Fourth Amendment search warrant requirement?

   a. movable vehicle

   b. abandoned property

   c. *Terry* type search for drugs

   d. plain view

13. A field interview by a police officer does not involve detention in the constitutional sense so long as the officer does not deny the individual the right to move. What else is true of this scenario?
   a. The person approached may not be detained even momentarily unless the officer has reasonable objective grounds for detaining the person.
   b. If the police officer is not armed with reasonable suspicion of criminal activity, the person approached need not answer any question put to him or her; indeed, he or she may decline to listen to the questions at all and leave.
   c. When the officer has reasonable suspicion that a particular person committed a crime, he or she may lawfully stop that person and detain him or her long enough to dispel or build on the suspicion, but the suspect does not have to answer any questions put to him or her by the police.
   d. All of the above statements are true.

14. According to a recent Supreme Court decision, which of the following is NOT considered a necessary condition characteristic of plain view seizures?
   a. The officer must be lawfully in the viewing area.
   b. The officer must have probable cause to believe the evidence is somehow associated with criminal activity.
   c. The discovery of the evidence must be inadvertent.
   d. All of the above are necessary prongs of the plain view doctrine.

15. Which of the following is an exception to the exclusionary rule?
   a. good faith
   b. public safety
   c. inevitable discovery
   d. all of the above

16. In modern police management, it is generally accepted that the punishment and admonishing of an officer should not be carried out in front of the public or fellow officers. When would it be appropriate for a supervisor to violate this practice?
   a. when the officer is disrespectful to the supervisor
   b. when the officer is recalcitrant
   c. when the officer's violation was minor
   d. when the officer conducted an overt act of misconduct

17. An order will most often be better accepted and carried out if it is given as a
   a. request.
   b. command.
   c. recommendation.
   d. suggestion.

18. Which orders should not ordinarily be used with the inexperienced or undependable worker?
   I. direct commands
   II. implied orders
   III. orders in the form of suggestions
   IV. orders in the form of requests
   V. calls for volunteers
   a. I and II
   b. II and III
   c. IV only
   d. V only

19. In emergency situations when immediate action is called for, the most appropriate type of order is a(n)
   a. request for volunteers.
   b. direct command.
   c. request.
   d. implied order.

20. Uncertainty in the language a supervisor uses is problematic primarily because it is often interpreted as
   a. indecision.
   b. apathy.
   c. sarcasm.
   d. weakness.

21. You are a newly appointed sergeant and you are put in charge of a group of people who are your friends, some of whom joined the police department with you. Under the circumstances, what is the best course for you to take?
   a. Maintain your friendships, but don't allow them to influence your actions.
   b. Slowly weaken your friendships until your relationship is the same with each of your subordinates.
   c. Explain in a tactful manner why you can no longer maintain the same relationships.
   d. Request that your friends be transferred to another squad.

22. One sergeant says to another, "You know, I don't receive complaints from my personnel." Any sergeant who makes this statement should realize that
   a. everything is going along well in his or her squad.
   b. he or she is probably seen as unapproachable.
   c. his or her subordinates are well trained.
   d. his or her subordinates lack communication skills.

23. According to experts in the field of supervision and management, female police officers
   a. are less affected by physical conditions than are men.
   b. invariably look upon their jobs as permanent positions.
   c. react to supervision about the same way men do.
   d. are far more emotional than male police officers.

24. As a supervisor, you should know that the evaluation of your subordinates' performance is best conducted
   a. yearly.
   b. monthly.
   c. weekly.
   d. continuously.

25. One of the most important skills of a supervisor, and one that is basic to understanding the subordinate's point of view, is the ability to
   a. train and educate subordinates.
   b. plan and research duties.
   c. cultivate clear and concise communication.
   d. supervise and follow up with subordinates.

26. The period between the end of the police academy training and the end of the probationary period is considered to be part of the
  a. training process.
  b. selection process.
  c. hiring process.
  d. recruitment process.

27. Which of the following will most likely happen when the training function in a police department is poorly performed or not performed at all?
  a. low morale
  b. waste
  c. preventable errors
  d. all of the above

28. During shift training, the sergeant is imparting information on a recent rash of burglaries in the area that the shift patrols. After completing the training session, how should the sergeant best assess whether the message got through and ensure that subordinates will continue to pay attention during future shift trainings?
  a. utilize a short paper and pencil test of multiple-choice questions
  b. have one or two of the trainees repeat what was taught
  c. question subordinates individually about the topics covered
  d. give a short synopsis in the form of a repeat of important police topics

29. The number of people that a supervisor can effectively manage is known as
  a. span of control.
  b. effective quotient.
  c. efficiency ratio.
  d. span of management.

30. With regard to the process of delegation, which of the following statements is least accurate?
  a. Delegation is closely related to span of control: If the supervisor is responsible for more than he or she can be expected to accomplish alone, he or she must delegate the detail work to subordinates.
  b. The supervisor can successfully avoid responsibility if he or she delegates tasks to others.
  c. When a task is delegated, enough authority to complete it must also be delegated.
  d. The supervisor must exercise care that he or she does not delegate tasks beyond the capacity of his or her subordinates.

31. Assume that you as a sergeant have an important job to assign that will require three people to work on it at the same time. The three people you select to do this job are all of equal rank and seniority. You are assigned an important task from your chief, and time constraints will not enable you to supervise the job as you originally planned. What would be the best way for you to delegate authority?
  a. Give one officer responsibility for seeing that the job is done and the power to give orders to the other two.
  b. Give each officer responsibility for completing the job and the power to give orders to the other two on the job.
  c. Give no one full responsibility for seeing that the job is completed or the power to give orders. Encourage all three to work together.
  d. Give one officer responsibility for seeing that the job is done but not the authority to give orders to the other two.

32. As a sergeant, you find that one person on your squad is continually getting into trouble despite your repeated efforts to train and assist him or her. This subordinate shows little regard for his or her duties or appearance, and his or her relationships with fellow officers are poor. After all attempts at positive training failed, you began a progressive discipline process of punitive measures, but nothing seems to have worked. Under the circumstances, what is the best course of action?
- **a.** Continue to train him or her until he or she comes around.
- **b.** Assign him or her to a job that demands little responsibility.
- **c.** Transfer the officer to a more demanding unit.
- **d.** Recommend that he or she be dismissed from the force.

33. When considering punishments for violations of policy and procedure, it is most important for a supervisory officer to ensure that his or her punishments are
- **a.** consistent.
- **b.** proportionate.
- **c.** equal.
- **d.** fair.

34. Every supervisor should understand the teaching process. Probably the best way to determine whether or not learning has taken place is to
- **a.** administer a test.
- **b.** observe the learning process.
- **c.** research the material presented.
- **d.** know the student's background.

35. Which of the following factors is least significant in determining the number of subordinates one supervisor can effectively control?
- **a.** quality of the subordinates supervised
- **b.** working conditions
- **c.** organizational structure
- **d.** personality of the supervisor

36. Which of the following most clearly gives direction to the various divisions within a police department?
- **a.** the investigation unit
- **b.** the patrol division
- **c.** the research and planning unit
- **d.** the juvenile division

37. Why have a large number of police departments in our country not developed a suitable formal training program?
- **a.** the high cost of training
- **b.** insufficient personnel
- **c.** failure to grasp the importance of training
- **d.** lack of educational material

38. What is the fundamental reason a sergeant's position is of key importance in the police organization?
- **a.** Ultimate responsibility for his or her subordinates' performance rests with the sergeant.
- **b.** Subordinates look to their sergeant for advice and direction.
- **c.** Follow-up procedures are usually the sergeant's responsibility.
- **d.** The sergeant must see that the objectives of the department are achieved.

39. Every good supervisor should know that the creation of good public relations within a community is the responsibility of
a. the police sergeant.
b. specifically assigned staff personnel.
c. the police chief.
d. every member of the police department.

40. Fill in the blank: When two people are communicating, it is better if neither party does all the talking, since two-way conversations _____ one-way conversations.
a. are faster than
b. are more effective than
c. don't require as much feedback as
d. are simpler than

41. One of the most common mistakes made by supervisors in the delegation of tasks to subordinates is
a. overcommunicating the message.
b. delegating too many routine tasks to subordinates.
c. delegating too much authority to subordinates.
d. not giving instructions on how to proceed with the task.

42. Which of the following supervisory functions is the least expendable?
a. coordination of human effort
b. procedural planning
c. organizing
d. reporting upward

43. How can an administrator make maximum use of the personnel available to him or her?
a. assign the personnel in equal numbers to shifts
b. assign the personnel to areas of equal geographical size
c. assign the personnel to equal beats
d. assign the personnel according to the times when they are needed

44. Although a supervisor's orders to his or her employees can be general or detailed, oral or written, it is most important that they be
a. simple.
b. courteous.
c. clear.
d. explained.

45. Which of the following is a sign of a good unit leader?
a. the leader's popularity in his or her unit
b. high productivity of the organization as a whole
c. high morale within the organization as a whole
d. a high level of discipline in the leader's unit

46. A formal structure of authority for coordinating work units is most accurately referred to as a(n)
a. procedural plan.
b. staff assignment plan.
c. organization.
d. schedule.

47. When a supervisor works out a broad outline of things to do, this is referred to as
a. directing.
b. planning.
c. coordinating.
d. reporting.

48. Orders should be memorialized in writing when
   a. they are simple orders.
   b. they are direct orders.
   c. they are given to a small specialized unit.
   d. strict accountability is required.

49. The type of organization that is found in all but the very smallest police agencies today is the
   a. line organization.
   b. line and staff organization.
   c. functional organization.
   d. military organization.

50. A plan that would provide police personnel with guidance and direction as to what to do in their normal routine performance is a(n)
   a. operational plan.
   b. procedural plan.
   c. auxiliary plan.
   d. none of the above

51. What does the following sentence describe?
   It denotes the process of directing and controlling people and things so that organizational objectives can be accomplished.
   a. assessment
   b. management
   c. intervention
   d. recruitment

52. Which of the following statements about morale is least accurate?
   a. If the supervisor's morale is high, the morale of his or her subordinates will also be high.
   b. Morale cannot be legislated or induced by logic.
   c. The supervisor can influence morale.
   d. Morale is more than a sense of duty.

53. Which one of the following most accurately completes the statement about personnel evaluations? Personnel rating systems are
   a. usually standardized.
   b. procedurally oriented.
   c. inherently subjective.
   d. objective instruments if used properly.

54. What is considered the most common error in personnel rating systems?
   a. personal bias
   b. being too lenient
   c. overweighting the most recent period of time
   d. giving good marks in every category because of a good performance in one or two areas ("the halo effect")

55. Sergeant Weiss comes to you and tells you that he is so busy that he cannot find time to complete his assigned duties. He is rather frustrated and wonders how you and the other sergeants can do it. Based on this information, what could you assume about Sergeant Weiss?
   a. Sergeant Weiss is unpopular with his workers.
   b. Sergeant Weiss needs additional training in his duties.
   c. Sergeant Weiss is probably not delegating.
   d. Sergeant Weiss needs to learn the principle of completed staff work.

56. At what point is it usually appropriate for a supervisor to intervene when he or she discovers his or her subordinate has a work-related problem that calls for intervention?
   a. without unnecessary delay
   b. after a short cooling-off period
   c. after a significant waiting period
   d. the timing depends on the experience of the worker

57. Which of the following is the single most important skill of a supervisor?
　　a. being able to communicate clearly with others
　　b. keeping his or her subordinates happy
　　c. teaching his or her subordinates well
　　d. disseminating information in a timely manner

58. When a supervisor conducts an interview, the most frequently recommended procedure is to
　　a. listen more than talk.
　　b. attempt to balance his or her talking with listening.
　　c. talk more than listen.
　　d. let the interviewee do all the talking.

59. The concept of unity of command dictates that subordinates should report
　　a. directly to the chief.
　　b. to one supervisor.
　　c. to staff personnel.
　　d. to any supervisor of appropriate rank.

60. Studies of police officers have revealed some distinct dissatisfaction about organizational rules and regulations and how supervisors apply them. What did the researchers find was mentioned most often as the cause of subordinate dissatisfaction?
　　a. the regulation of subordinates' conduct off-duty
　　b. violation of subordinates' personal rights
　　c. supervisors' inconsistency in enforcing rules and regulations
　　d. recent court decisions

61. The police assigned to investigate a case where there are no suspects would have three basic aims: to identify the guilty party, to locate him or her, and to
　　a. prosecute him or her to the fullest extent of the law.
　　b. establish the motives for his or her criminality.
　　c. provide evidence of his or her guilt or innocence.
　　d. none of the above

62. What is the ultimate goal of a police investigator?
　　a. to apprehend suspects
　　b. to present sufficient evidence to a court of law to justify a conviction
　　c. to prosecute the alleged defendant and to obtain a conviction
　　d. to ensure that the defendant receives a fair and just trial

63. It is often said that the "three *Is*" of the police investigator are information, interrogation, and instrumentation. It is further agreed that the most important of the three is information, simply because it answers the central question of any police investigation. What is that central question?
　　a. Who did it?
　　b. Why did it happen?
　　c. Where did it happen?
　　d. Who is the victim?

64. When police apprehend someone suspected of a crime, what is normally true of the suspect?
  a. The suspect will have an irresistible urge to talk.
  b. The suspect will place the blame elsewhere.
  c. The suspect will be inclined to fault his or her environment.
  d. The suspect will wish to be left alone and will remain silent.

65. With regard to a valid confession of guilt, which one of the following statements is most accurate?
  a. It is considered corroborative evidence.
  b. It is a form of *corpus delicti*.
  c. It is seldom sufficient by itself in proving guilt.
  d. It is valid only when written out.

66. Officer Moua is an average performing officer. On the day before she is scheduled to undergo a performance review, Officer Moua apprehends three armed gunmen as they are exiting a bank that they had just robbed. When completing Officer Moua's review, Sergeant Hall recalls the previous day's heroics and gives Officer Moua exceptional ratings in every category based upon her performance during the bank robbery. Sergeant Hall committed the rating error known as
  a. overweighting.
  b. halo effect.
  c. leniency.
  d. related traits.

67. When an investigator proceeds from the general to the particular, applying a general theory to the particular instance represented by the criminal occurrence, he or she is engaged in
  a. nonconstructive reasoning.
  b. inductive reasoning.
  c. deductive reasoning.
  d. chance reasoning.

68. In criminal investigations, the investigator's notebook is invaluable. Among other things, it should contain the raw material from which the final report of the investigation is ultimately fashioned. Which of the following statements about investigators' notebooks is least accurate?
  a. Notes should be gathered in chronological order corresponding to the investigative steps or receipt of the information.
  b. Ink is preferred to pencil for permanence.
  c. Loose-leaf notebooks are just as suitable as bound notebooks.
  d. Under examination by defense counsel, the investigator must be able to account for all entries in the notebook.

69. *Strip*, *spiral*, *zone*, and *wheel* are terms most accurately used for what purpose?
  a. qualification of firearms
  b. fingerprint classification
  c. defensive driving tactics
  d. crime scene search methods

70. Officer Martinez arrests a suspect who has in her possession a large quantity of marijuana. The marijuana is
  a. associative evidence.
  b. direct evidence.
  c. tracing evidence.
  d. *corpus delicti* evidence.

71. Perishable specimens or blood are ideally stored at a temperature between
  a. 20–30° F
  b. 40–50° F
  c. 75–100° F
  d. 0–10° C

72. When a police officer investigating a crime has finished the warm-up with the interviewee and is ready to get information, what is the best way to proceed?
   a. Begin the questioning by asking the interviewee simple questions and slowly progress to more difficult ones.
   b. Ask questions designed to give responses that cannot be answered by a yes or no.
   c. Ask questions about the subject's background and personal life and attempt to understand the person.
   d. Allow the interviewee to give a complete uninterrupted account of what he or she knows.

73. When a suspect gives a statement that is self-incriminatory but falls short of an acknowledgement of guilt, this is most accurately referred to as what?
   a. a confession
   b. an admission
   c. testimony
   d. a deposition

74. Is a confession sufficient enough to establish *corpus delicti*?
   a. Yes, a confession establishes guilt.
   b. No, you need additional corroborating evidence.
   c. Yes, a confession is reliable proof.
   d. No, you need proof of intent.

75. A secretor is someone who carries in his or her bloodstream a group-specific substance that makes it possible to determine the blood group from other body fluids. It has been estimated that what percent of the U.S. population are secretors?
   a. 15%
   b. 25%
   c. 60%
   d. 80%

76. According to experts in the field of community relations, the primary mission of a police force is
   a. promotion and maintenance of order in the community.
   b. arresting violators of the law.
   c. law enforcement.
   d. protection of property.

77. A teaching method in which the student assumes the attitude of the character and responds the way he or she thinks the character would is called
   a. conference leading.
   b. self-reflective analysis.
   c. projection.
   d. role-playing.

78. As a supervisor, your first duty at a crime scene is to
   a. ensure that you have ample numbers of officers.
   b. notify the patrol lieutenant.
   c. determine whether a warrant is needed.
   d. notify the crime scene unit.

79. The most common characteristic of a fingerprint is
   a. loop.
   b. swirl.
   c. arch.
   d. whorl.

80. An officer at a crime scene finds a shell from an expended round on the ground. In later marking the shell for evidentiary reasons, you should instruct the officer to mark the shell on the
   a. base.
   b. rim.
   c. side.
   d. primer.

81. In the long run, the goals of the organization and the goals of the individual worker
   a. differ substantially.
   b. grow further apart.
   c. remain unchanged.
   d. are the same.

82. What is at the top rung on Maslow's ladder of basic human needs?
   a. sustenance
   b. safety
   c. belonging
   d. self-actualization

83. Most police departments now invite citizens to ride in patrol vehicles with police officers as they perform their regular patrol duties. The only shortcoming of such programs is that
   a. those who ride along are sometimes injured.
   b. those who ride along sometimes develop more negative attitudes than positive ones.
   c. those who choose to ride along already have respect for the police.
   d. most persons do not wish to ride with the police.

84. Experts in police community relations agree that the police are considered to be the interpreters of the law on the street. They interpret the law through
   a. their expert knowledge.
   b. their discretion.
   c. their interpretation of case precedents.
   d. their impartial enforcement of the law.

85. Consider the following statement and then choose the best answer:
   According to experts in community relations, close supervision and strict discipline of police personnel amount to harassment and are therefore unwarranted.
   This statement is
   a. false, because close supervision and strict discipline of police personnel are absolutely vital.
   b. true, because the nature of police work does not lend itself to constant supervision.
   c. false, because close supervision and strict discipline may be considered harassment, but they are never unwarranted.
   d. true, because police who are properly trained require little to no supervision and discipline.

86. When an officer assigned alone to a patrol unit finds it necessary to stop a motorist who has committed a traffic violation, he or she should carefully evaluate the circumstances before committing to a particular course of action. He or she should follow the same general procedures as for a two-person unit traffic stop with any modification needed. Under these conditions, what should be the officer's main consideration?
   a. the officer's own safety
   b. the safety of the offender
   c. fairness and objectivity
   d. the action of positioning the police vehicle in relation to the offender's vehicle

87. When the level of enforcement is proportional to traffic accidents with respect to time, place, and type of violation causing the accidents, this type of enforcement is referred to as
   a. differential.
   b. selective.
   c. sporadic.
   d. primary.

88. A mass of data on the effectiveness of two-person patrol cars versus one-person patrol cars supports
   a. the effectiveness of a two-person patrol for ordinary operations.
   b. the effectiveness of a one-person patrol for ordinary operations.
   c. the effectiveness of a one-person patrol for unusual operations.
   d. that neither is superior to the other under any circumstances.

89. What is the most economical type of patrol?
   a. mounted patrol
   b. motorized patrol
   c. foot patrol
   d. bicycle patrol

90. How should the search for a suspect proceed in multistory buildings (whenever practicable)?
   a. from the top to the bottom in order to flush the suspects out into the street
   b. from the bottom to the top in order to corner the suspects on the roof
   c. with the team divided into two squads, one squad searching from the bottom upward and the other searching the neighborhood
   d. with the search team searching those floors with fire escapes first, then searching from the top downward in order to flush the suspects out into the street

91. A good rule of thumb that provides a reasonable safety margin for a driver following another car on dry pavement is to
   a. stay at least two seconds behind the car in front of you.
   b. stay at least one car length behind for every 5 miles per hour you are traveling.
   c. stay at least one car length behind for every 10 miles per hour you are traveling.
   d. stay at least two car lengths behind for every 10 miles per hour you are traveling.

92. The ability to understand and apply report-writing skills and other forms of written communication is absolutely essential for a competent supervisory officer. Which one of the following terms names the style of writing for a narrative account of an event that simplifies expression and provides the clearest description of what happened?
   a. basic style
   b. systems style
   c. newspaper style
   d. report style

93. The amount of evidence that, on its face, is sufficient to prove the *corpus delicti* until overcome by other evidence is most accurately referred to as
   a. sufficient proof.
   b. *prima facie* proof.
   c. insufficient proof.
   d. proof beyond a reasonable doubt.

94. An inventory search of the contents of an arrestee's vehicle is conducted in order to
   a. find additional evidence.
   b. look for contraband.
   c. look for proceeds of the crime.
   d. safeguard the arrestee's property.

95. When an officer testifying in a jury trial is asked a question by either counsel or the judge, he or she should
   a. face the jury while the question is being asked, then deliver the answer while facing the person who asked the question.
   b. start by delivering the answer facing the counsel that asked the question and then turn to the jury for the completion of the answer.
   c. face the person asking the question, then deliver the answer facing the jury.
   d. face the person who asked the question and continue to face that person while delivering the answer.

96. The main goal of a criminal investigation is to
   a. identify the perpetrator.
   b. successfully prosecute the crime.
   c. get a confession.
   d. find evidence.

97. If an injury caused by the criminal may cause the death of a victim, the best course of action for the officer to take is to
   a. make an effort to obtain a dying declaration without delay.
   b. concentrate his or her efforts on obtaining witnesses and preventing their departure.
   c. immediately secure the scene and prevent persons from entering.
   d. notify headquarters immediately and apprise them of the situation so they can assist and send experts to the scene.

98. The most important action for a police officer to take when arriving first at an accident scene where there are injuries is to
   a. protect the scene.
   b. aid the injured.
   c. notify headquarters of the circumstances.
   d. secure witnesses and prevent their departure from the scene.

99. After stopping a motor vehicle, an officer should make an immediate appraisal to determine which of the below?
   a. Is the vehicle in good condition or not?
   b. Does the motorist have a valid driver's license?
   c. Does the motorist have a positive attitude?
   d. Is the motorist possibly under the influence of alcohol or a drug?

100. If an officer is convinced that a suspect holding a hostage is really willing to kill and has no fear of the consequences, then it must be assumed that the suspect is exceedingly dangerous and that
   a. attempts to communicate with the suspect in a calm, patient manner could further aggravate this situation.
   b. the suspect should not be encouraged to talk.
   c. every attempt should be made to stall for time.
   d. the suspect should be killed as soon as possible, provided this action does not substantially endanger innocent persons.

► Answers

1. a. This type of situation is consistent with a *Terry* type limited search. The officer only had reasonable suspicion to believe that the person was selling drugs and therefore, did not have the much higher standard of probable cause. According to *Terry v. Ohio*, if an officer reasonably suspects that someone is involved in criminal activity, that officer may conduct a stop of that person for limited questioning. During that time, if the officer reasonably suspects that the person may be armed, that officer may conduct a limited pat-down search of the person's clothing to ensure safety. The search is not to be used to search for contraband, such as drugs.

2. d. Based on the United States case *New York v. Belton*, following a lawful arrest of a driver, that driver and the passenger compartment of the vehicle and any containers found there, whether opened or closed, may lawfully be searched as a search "incident to a lawful arrest." The court allowed the search to prevent the destruction of evidence, to stop a successful escape, and to prevent the use of weapons. Note that the arrest must be lawful and the search must be contemporaneous with (following closely in time) the arrest.

3. c. The exclusionary rule decrees that evidence obtained in violation of a person's constitutional rights is inadmissible at any subsequent proceedings against that person.

4. d. Probable cause, the notion behind answers **a**, **b**, and **c**, is not enough by itself to justify crossing the threshold of a person's premises. Without consent or probable cause **and** an exigency (something requiring immediate action), a search warrant is required (*New York v. Payton*).

5. a. A *common law right of inquiry* is defined as a limited stop by a police officer. During this stop, the officer may ask certain questions of the person stopped, such as "Where are you going?" The person stopped does not have to answer the officer's questions and may even walk away. According to the Supreme Court, the standard of proof required for a common law right of inquiry is "a founded suspicion that criminality is afoot." Reasonable suspicion is a higher standard of proof and allows for greater intrusion than that allowed in a common law right of inquiry; probable cause is still higher, allowing for the arrest of the subject.

6. c. The Fifth and the Fourteenth Amendments contain the due process clause. (The Fourteenth Amendment also contains the equal protection clause.) The Fifth applies to federal matters and the Fourteenth applies to states.

7. b. The rights contained in the First Amendment are not absolute rights but are conditioned by the doctrine of clear and present danger. A person cannot yell "Fire!" in the theater when there is no fire, for example, since doing so would endanger people without cause. Similarly, a person does not have an absolute right to worship: If worship practices are dangerous (for example, worship that involves drinking poison), they may be prohibited. These considerations rule out **a**. Choice **c** is not true; **d** is wrong because repugnancy is not what conditions the First Amendment.

8. d. Although **a** is on the right track, it is incomplete. If the government is armed with probable cause to search a motor vehicle, then the entire vehicle and all parts of it can be lawfully searched without a warrant if the vehicle can be readily moved. Even when the vehicle is on private property (a situation normally necessitating a search warrant), a warrantless search can be undertaken if the vehicle might be moved before a warrant can be obtained.

9. b. The Fourth Amendment protects people, not places. What a person knowingly exposes to the public, even in his own home or office, is not subject to Fourth Amendment protection, but what he seeks to preserve as private, even in an area accessible to the public, may be constitutionally protected (*Katz v. United States*).

10. b. Probable cause is not a rigid concept, but instead calls for a common sense analysis. It is adjudicated not by utilizing the science or philosophy of law or a bright-line rule, but by using practical, nontechnical reasoning.

11. c. In such a situation, the appropriate inquiry is whether a reasonable person would feel free to decline the officers' requests or otherwise terminate the encounter. The crucial test is whether, taking into account all of the circumstances surrounding the encounter, the police conduct would have communicated to a reasonable person that he was not at liberty to ignore the police presence and go about his business. *Florida v. Bostick*, 501 U.S. 429, 111 Sup. Ct. 2382 (1991).

12. c. During a *Terry* type stop, a police may not search the suspect for drugs. The officer may conduct a limited search of outer garments for weapons. The courts have ruled that there is no expectation of privacy in abandoned property, such as trash and items left in the plain view of the public. Also, there is an exception for movable vehicles because evidence can be lost or destroyed due to ease of transport.

13. d. While choice **c** is true, under the circumstances set forth the suspect would not be able to leave until the investigation was concluded (as long as it was concluded within a reasonable amount of time).

14. c. In 1990, the Supreme Court reexamined the plain view doctrine and eliminated the inadvertence requirement. *Horton v. California*, 496 U.S. 128 (1990). This may or may not be the case in a particular state.

15. d. The exclusionary rule was created by the court to deter official misconduct and to maintain judicial integrity.

16. d. Although it is generally accepted that officers should be punished in private and praised in public, overt acts of misconduct must be dealt with immediately. The supervisor should deal with serious acts of misconduct immediately, regardless of the presence of other officers or the public.

17. a. The supervisor should recognize that the manner in which an order is given is more often resented than the order itself. If it is framed as a request, a task will most often be accepted and carried out without resentment.

18. b. Implied orders or orders made in the form of suggestions may be used effectively with reliable, experienced employees but are not ordinarily used with the inexperienced or undependable worker.

19. b. Direct commands work best during emergency situations when subordinates must be quickly dispatched to perform necessary duties in a short period of time.

20. a. The supervisor should avoid uncertain or vacillating language because it will often be interpreted by his or her subordinates as indecision. The supervisor should play back in his or her mind any order before administering it.

21. a. Try to make all your subordinates your friends and have and maintain an open-door policy. Making it easy for people to approach you is key to good supervision.

22. b. A sergeant cannot afford to take a lack of complaints as a good sign. The more approachable he or she is to his or her troops, the more he or she will learn about the goings on in his or her squad; hearing complaints directly from the line personnel is one sign that the sergeant is approachable.

23. c. Many of the stereotyped beliefs that some supervisors have retained are not founded on fact. Legal requirements and factual research both agree that men and women are equal with respect to supervision in police work.

24. d. The evaluation of subordinates' performance occurs on a continuous basis. Supervisors should strive to observe all aspects of an officer's performance so that they can better assess that officer's strengths and weaknesses, training needs, and manner of conducting work. This will greatly aid the supervisor when formalized performance review mechanisms are conducted at a later date.

25. c. Although skill in communication is among the most important for a supervisor, experts in police work agree that it is the skill most often neglected.

26. b. The probationary period is a part of the selection process. If a probationary police officer cannot properly perform the tasks required of him or her, then that officer needs to be fired. Although this period is also a period of great learning for officers, it cannot be considered training, because training occurs on a continual basis in policing. This period is obviously not hiring or recruitment, because both usually happen before acceptance into a police academy.

27. d. Inadequate training results in inefficiency, waste, and low morale, all of which are tremendously costly to the organization.

28. c. By asking questions of individuals, the trainer can randomly pick through the group to ascertain whether they've gotten the message. A paper-and-pencil test will take too long, and questioning only one or two members is not enough to make sure that the message got through to the entire group. Repeating would not be productive because it would take too much time. Remember that this is roll-call training, which lasts only about 15 minutes.

29. a. The *span of control* is defined as the number of subordinates that a supervisor can effectively manage. All the other answer choices are nonexistent terms.

30. b. The supervisor cannot avoid responsibility for tasks when he or she delegates. The final responsibility always rests with the supervisor.

31. a. In choice **a**, the delegation process is complete. When you properly delegate, you must give the authority to complete the task along with the responsibility. Choice **a** also preserves the principle of unity of command: All subordinates should know to whom they are directly accountable.

32. d. Positive training must always be administered until it fails, but if the employee cannot be trained, start the process toward his or her removal.

33. d. Punishments should always be fair. Equal and consistent punishment is not always indicated. For example, if you have two officers that commit the same violation but one has a long history of committing violations, you would not give equal punishment to both officers. Likewise, you would not give each officer proportionate punishment.

34. a. Most authors on the subject of supervision principles agree that there are five steps in the instructional process, and that testing is one of them: (1) introduction, (2) presentation of the subject matter, (3) application (the student applies what he or she has learned), (4) testing (assessment of what the student has learned), and (5) follow-up.

35. c. The quality of those supervised affects control in that if the workers are effective and reliable, they need less control. Working conditions play a part, since it is not easy to control employees who are uncomfortable or in unsafe conditions. Finally, if the employees don't like or respect the supervisor, they are less apt to perform satisfactorily for him or her, and whether they like him or her is a function of the supervisor's personality. The organizational structure, in contrast, does not relate in any direct way to effective control of subordinates.

36. c. The research and planning unit is officially responsible for inspecting and planning departmental tasks. While suggestions may pass informally among other units, they are not mandated to give direction in the same way that research and planning is.

37. a. Most department heads understand the importance of a formal functioning training unit, realizing that they will be safer from lawsuits and better able to protect their own well-being if they have highly trained personnel. The cost of training is high, however. While **b** is often true, insufficient personnel is the result of insufficient funds, making **a** the more inclusive and therefore better answer.

38. d. This is a tough question because choices **b** and **c** have some merit. The most inclusive choice is **d**, however, and since the question asks for the fundamental reason sergeants are important, you should choose it. (Choice **a** is simply false, since ultimate responsibility rests with the chief.)

39. d. Remember that public relations is a one-way street, with the police giving information to the public but not vice versa. Community relations, in contrast, is a two-way street: The police give information to the public but also receive information back from the public. It is the responsibility of every member of the police force to become a public relations and community relations officer.

40. b. Two-way communication allows for feedback, which tends to cut down on misunderstanding.

41. d. Most experts would agree that when delegating a task, there should be at least some instructions on how to proceed. Remember that training is the key to the delegation process.

42. a. None of the other functions is feasible without coordination of human effort; even in the absence of planning, organizing, and reporting, however, it is possible to accomplish some tasks simply by coordinating the work of the available staff.

43. d. Workers must be assigned to the places where they are needed at the times they are needed. They should not be assigned in equal numbers to shifts, to days of the week, or to beats of equal geographical size, since to do so would make an equalization of the work load among officers and the establishment of area responsibility impossible.

44. c. An order can be simple or complex, and it can be delivered in a highly courteous or a somewhat abrupt manner, but it must be clear in order to ensure that the job gets done. While an order should be explained, this is true only when time permits.

45. d. If a unit is highly disciplined, that is a sign that the unit has a good and effective leader. While high productivity and high morale in the leader's unit would be a sign of the leader's success, the answers offered in choices **b** and **c** refer to high productivity of the organization as a whole, which is less relevant. Popularity is not a sign of good (or bad) leadership, ruling out **a**.

46. c. The overall structure for planning work is known as an organization; staff assignments and scheduling are important parts of that process, but don't encompass everything, ruling out **b** and **d**. A procedural plan is a plan that tells how to do something, not who does what, ruling out **a**. Be aware of examiners' practice of distracting you from the best answer with a partially correct one, and you will do well on your examinations.

47. b. If you read the question carefully, you realize that it refers to "working out things to be done and the way in which to do them"; choice **b** fits this definition. Directing, choice **a**, is nothing more than order giving. Coordinating takes planning but it does not involve the broad outline of things that require doing; reporting takes place after the fact, not ahead of time.

48. d. Orders should generally be memorialized in writing when they are to have longstanding applicability, when they deal with the operations of a large and varied number of units, and when strict accountability for the subject of the order is required.

49. b. Military organization and line organization are two names for the same simple type of organization in which lines of communication are direct and authority is absolute; because of its simplicity, this form of organization is usually adopted by the very smallest police forces. The line and staff organization is a combination of line organization and functional organization (grouping of staff by the kind of job they do), and it characterizes most larger police forces. The functional type of organization is rarely used alone in police departments.

50. a. The best choice is **a**, operational plan, because an operational plan is simply one that lays out what to do in normal situations. Procedural plans tell how to do something (rather than what to do), and they are equally useful for everyday and unusual tasks. Auxiliary plans are those that implement operations such as the recruitment of personnel, public and community relations activities, and the like, and these are not routine tasks for most members of the police force.

51. b. Only choice **b**, management, fits the definition.

52. a. The only false statement is made in choice **a**.

53. c. Personnel rating systems are usually not standardized and are never objective. Since they involve a personal audit of one person by another, some subjectivity always creeps in.

54. b. The error of leniency is by far the most common of all errors in the rating of personnel. It occurs when the rater gives an inordinately large number of individuals very high marks.

55. c. Weiss's symptoms are typical of failure to delegate tasks in order to free himself up for more important duties that only he should handle.

56. a. When an employee has a work-related problem in which the supervisor should become involved, the supervisor should do so without delay. Training to work out the problem is of paramount importance; the supervisor should also make a follow-up inspection to see that the employee has improved.

57. a. Choices **b**, **c**, and **d**, while having some merit, all presuppose the ability to communicate. The most inclusive and therefore best choice is **a**.

58. a. Ideally, mutual trust and confidence should be fostered between interviewer and interviewee, and in order to accomplish this, the interviewer must listen more than talk. He or she cannot avoid talking altogether, however, since at certain strategic points, the interviewer will have to direct the talk by asking open-ended questions.

59. b. Unity of command dictates that subordinates should report to one supervisor. That supervisor becomes accountable for the operations of those subordinates under his or her command.

60. c. During this study, all of the answer choices except **d** were mentioned by police officers surveyed, but choice **c** was mentioned most frequently.

61. c. It is the job of any investigating officer to gather facts to determine what actually happened, and that entails proving the innocence or guilt of a suspect. Choice **a** is the job of a prosecutor, not the police. Establishing the motive, while often helpful, is not necessary in most investigations. Remember that the job of the police is either to find probable cause for an offense to be charged or to gather evidence to clear a suspect.

62. b. Though he or she can and will make arrests, it is not the goal of the police investigator to apprehend suspects, but to gather evidence. Choice **c** is the responsibility of the prosecutor's office, and choice **d** is the responsibility of all of the officers of the court (the prosecuting staff, the defense counsel, and the judge and jury).

63. a. Answers to the questions in **b**, **c**, and **d** are important to ascertain, but the most important of all is **a**. If you can show who committed the crime, the prosecutor can get a conviction, but not otherwise.

64. a. A suspect's need to talk underlies the success of most police interrogation.

65. c. The confession is, of course, an excellent means of identifying the criminal, but from the point of view of proving guilt at the trial, it must be supported by corroborative evidence. Early in a criminal trial, the prosecution must prove the *corpus delicti* (literally, *body of the crime*), which is the fact that a crime was committed. The *corpus delicti* must be separately established in order to support a conviction.

66. a. The rating error known as overweighting occurs when a recent good or bad event forms the basis for a rater's positive or negative rating. In essence, the entire review is based on one single event.

67. c. Both inductive and deductive reasoning are important during investigations; deductive reasoning is reasoning from general principles to particular conclusions. Inductive reasoning, in contrast, is beginning with particular facts and inferring general rules.

68. c. The truth of the matter in a bound notebook creates a more favorable impression in the courtroom than does the loose-leaf type because its form does not suggest the possible removal or rearrangement of pages.

69. d. In the *strip* method, the area is blocked out in the form of a rectangle. The searches proceed slowly at the same pace along paths parallel to one side of the rectangle. When a piece of evidence is found, the finder announces his or her discovery and all halt until the evidence is processed. In the *zone* method, one searcher is assigned to each subdivision of a quadrant. In the *wheel* method, the area is approximately circular. The searchers gather at the center and proceed outward along the radii, or spokes. In the *spiral* method, the searching team starts from the center of the crime scene and works its way outward in a spiral motion.

70. d. *Corpus delicti* evidence consists of objects or substances that are an essential part of the body of the crime. For example, the stolen object is part of the *corpus delicti* of a larceny. The narcotic found in the suspect's possession is part of the *corpus delicti* of a narcotics violation.

71. b. High temperatures, such as 95° F, greatly accelerate the decomposition of blood and other perishable specimens. Similarly, freezing temperatures may affect the evidentiary value of perishable specimens. Ideally, the preserving temperature for blood or other perishable specimens is between 40° and 50° F.

72. d. Following the warm-up, the interviewee must be allowed to give his or her account without interruption. After the full account of the incident in question is given, it is suitable to ask questions that are to the point. There are times when the investigating officer will have to phrase questions for a direct yes or no response, but he or she should do so without interrupting the interviewee and only when it is safe to assume the interviewee has given a full account.

73. b. An admission is an acknowledgement of a fact or circumstance from which guilt may be inferred. It implicates but does not directly incriminate. On the other hand, a confession is a direct acknowledgment of the truth of the guilty fact as charged or of some essential part of the commission of the criminal act itself.

74. b. *Corpus delicti* is a term used to refer to the principle of law that you must prove that a crime actually occurred before a person can be found guilty of the crime. A confession by itself does not establish that a crime occurred. You need additional corroborating evidence, such as the proceeds from a burglary, a body in a murder case, or the statement of a victim, to prove that a crime actually occurred.

75. c. Some of the fluids of a secretor that are of value are saliva, semen, tears, urine, perspiration, and nasal secretions.

76. a. This mission statement made by community relations experts is close to the mission statement for most police administrators, committing them to the protection of life and property. Only a small percentage of the police officer's time is spent on law enforcement. Most is spent on maintaining order and performing services to the citizenry.

77. d. In this sort of training, widely used in Assessment Centers, the student plays various roles in order to better understand how conflicts develop and how best to deal with them.

78. c. If a crime happens on a public street, then a warrant is not needed to begin searching for and collecting evidence connected to that crime. If a crime occurs in a private residence, you will need to get a search warrant to begin searching through the crime scene, unless it is the scene of a homicide and the victim is the only person that resides in the residence.

79. a. *Loops* are the most common characteristic of fingerprints.

80. c. Expended shells should be marked on the side in order to preserve the firing pin markings for later comparison to a suspected weapon.

Expended rounds should be marked on the base to preserve rifling markings for comparison.

81. d. The long-term goals of the workers in an organization and the goals of the organization are basically the same. Security, success, and growth are common goals of both the workers and the organization.

82. d. Maslow's hierarchy of needs in ascending order is sustenance, safety, belonging, self-esteem, and self-actualization. To realize one's full potential is to reach self-actualization. Maslow contends that people cannot reach this point unless and until the lower needs are satisfied.

83. c. Studies have demonstrated that the ride-along experience can help to change negative attitudes of youth toward the police and vice versa. However, to be most effective, such programs would need to reach out to those who would not seek them out.

84. b. Police, through their discretionary judgments, are street interpreters of law. In a practical sense, police selectively determine which laws are to be enforced and how. Police discretionary decisions are most frequently street decisions, directly affecting individual citizens and neighborhoods. Mutual respect and support between the police and the community they serve are often defined by how fairly, objectively, and impartially police discretionary judgment calls are made.

85. a. Police work must always be of high quality; public respect must be not only earned but also maintained. Close supervision and strict discipline of police personnel are absolutely vital in pursuing these goals.

86. a. Contrary to popular belief, a police officer's primary concern in dangerous or potentially dangerous situations is not for the safety of others before him- or herself. The officer must be safe first, then he or she can attend to his or her duties. It is foolhardy for a police officer to place him- or herself in needless danger. He or she can not very well assist others if he or she is injured or killed. Choices **b**, **c**, and **d** are important, but they must take a back seat to **a**.

87. b. When the enforcement effort is proportional to traffic accidents with respect to time, place, and type of violation causing the accidents, this is referred to as selective enforcement. Experts describe *selective enforcement* as concentrating the police enforcement efforts on the times and places where accidents result in serious bodily injury or death.

88. b. Unquestionably, there are situations in which two-person units are justified because of the unusual nature of the population served, the area, the time, and the hazards present, but a mass of data has supported the effectiveness of a one-person patrol for ordinary operations. If officers are properly trained to avoid needless risks while alone by calling for assistance when needed, trained in patrol techniques, and given effective communications and safety equipment, the major weakness of a one-person operation, which is lack of safety, can be overcome.

89. b. Motorized patrol is the most economical type of patrol, since it provides the greatest mobility and flexibility of operation. Wider coverage is possible and considerably more incidents can be handled with fewer personnel than with any other type of patrol.

90. a. Before any building search begins, there should be officers on the bottom floors surrounding the building; they are referred to as *cover officers*. If the suspect is forced to the top of the premises, he or she might become more dangerous or escape over adjoining rooftops. If he or she is forced downward, the cover officers can capture him or her with relative safety. As each portion of the building is searched, it should be secured or kept under observation while the searching officers move to the next room or portion of the building.

91. a. The old rule is choice **c**, but the better is the two-second rule. This rule is applied by picking an object, such as a traffic sign or some marking in the roadway, that the vehicle in front of you passes. At the instant the vehicle passes the object, count two seconds: "one thousand one, one thousand two." Your vehicle must not reach the object you have chosen before the two seconds elapse.

92. c. The newspaper style of writing is associated with using short, clear sentence structure and declaring the essence of what the writer intends to establish by setting up the main idea of the paragraph within the first sentence or two. This style of narrative report also gives information in a logical and systematic way.

93. b. *Prima facie* evidence of a crime is that amount of evidence, which, on its face, is sufficient to prove that a crime occurred.

94. d. An *inventory search* is a search conducted in order to safeguard an arrestee's property and to protect officers from dangerous conditions. Courts have held that inventory searches conducted in order to find evidence or contraband are unconstitutional searches. Further, inventory searches are to be conducted in accordance with a written departmental protocol.

95. c. This is not only proper protocol, but respects the fact that it is extremely important for the jury to hear your response.

96. a. An investigation should be directed at identifying the perpetrator of the crime. Although one might think that the goal would be the successful prosecution, that is not the main goal of the investigation.

97. a. Despite slight differences in state laws, the meaning of the dying declaration is in general an exception to the hearsay rules of evidence. There are conditions that must be met for a statement to be considered a dying declaration: The person making the declaration has to believe he or she is going to die and has to have given up all hope of recovery; the person must die; the testimony is usually narrowly confined to information relating to the death.

98. a. Protecting the scene will prevent other motor vehicles from striking you, other persons involved in the accident, and any witnesses that are present. The accident happened for a reason and could reoccur if the scene is not protected properly. Protection of the scene can be as simple as parking your police vehicle in a strategic position before leaving it. Then the injured can be aided. Then notify headquarters, and then secure witnesses.

99. d. It must be understood that, in all of the United States, the law prohibits the police from stopping a motorist unless there is at least a substantial police need to do so.

100. c. The police should present a calm demeanor and the suspect should be encouraged to talk.

Police Sergeant Minicourse

You are now well advanced on your journey toward the police sergeant exam. By this point, the introduction "How to Use This Book" and Chapters 1 and 2 have helped you get a good sense of what to expect—and your own conversations with other personnel in your department have solidified this sense. You should have a plan of study tailored to both your style and the time available to you before the actual test is administered. In Chapter 3, you learned about how to cover material specific to your local jurisdiction.

The first practice exam, in Chapter 4, gave you the information you need to tailor your study to the content that is most challenging for you. The categories used there for organizing questions are also used here. Take a minute to go back over your notes on the practice exam to see where you need the most work. Compare them with the following chart.

MINICOURSE SECTION	CONTENT AREA	NUMBER OF QUESTIONS
1	Supervision and Management	150
2	Criminal Procedure and Constitutional Law	100
3	Criminal Investigation	50
4	Patrol Practices	35
5	Community Relations	15

The minicourse provided in this chapter is very comprehensive. There are over 300 questions, and every one of them comes with an explanation of the correct answer. If you have lots of time, we encourage you to take the whole course by answering every question and studying the answer explanations. If your time is limited, though, concentrate on those sections of the minicourse where you need the most work.

ANSWER SHEET

Section 1: Supervision and Management

1.	ⓐ	ⓑ	ⓒ	ⓓ	51.	ⓐ	ⓑ	ⓒ	ⓓ	101.	ⓐ	ⓑ	ⓒ	ⓓ
2.	ⓐ	ⓑ	ⓒ	ⓓ	52.	ⓐ	ⓑ	ⓒ	ⓓ	102.	ⓐ	ⓑ	ⓒ	ⓓ
3.	ⓐ	ⓑ	ⓒ	ⓓ	53.	ⓐ	ⓑ	ⓒ	ⓓ	103.	ⓐ	ⓑ	ⓒ	ⓓ
4.	ⓐ	ⓑ	ⓒ	ⓓ	54.	ⓐ	ⓑ	ⓒ	ⓓ	104.	ⓐ	ⓑ	ⓒ	ⓓ
5.	ⓐ	ⓑ	ⓒ	ⓓ	55.	ⓐ	ⓑ	ⓒ	ⓓ	105.	ⓐ	ⓑ	ⓒ	ⓓ
6.	ⓐ	ⓑ	ⓒ	ⓓ	56.	ⓐ	ⓑ	ⓒ	ⓓ	106.	ⓐ	ⓑ	ⓒ	ⓓ
7.	ⓐ	ⓑ	ⓒ	ⓓ	57.	ⓐ	ⓑ	ⓒ	ⓓ	107.	ⓐ	ⓑ	ⓒ	ⓓ
8.	ⓐ	ⓑ	ⓒ	ⓓ	58.	ⓐ	ⓑ	ⓒ	ⓓ	108.	ⓐ	ⓑ	ⓒ	ⓓ
9.	ⓐ	ⓑ	ⓒ	ⓓ	59.	ⓐ	ⓑ	ⓒ	ⓓ	109.	ⓐ	ⓑ	ⓒ	ⓓ
10.	ⓐ	ⓑ	ⓒ	ⓓ	60.	ⓐ	ⓑ	ⓒ	ⓓ	110.	ⓐ	ⓑ	ⓒ	ⓓ
11.	ⓐ	ⓑ	ⓒ	ⓓ	61.	ⓐ	ⓑ	ⓒ	ⓓ	111.	ⓐ	ⓑ	ⓒ	ⓓ
12.	ⓐ	ⓑ	ⓒ	ⓓ	62.	ⓐ	ⓑ	ⓒ	ⓓ	112.	ⓐ	ⓑ	ⓒ	ⓓ
13.	ⓐ	ⓑ	ⓒ	ⓓ	63.	ⓐ	ⓑ	ⓒ	ⓓ	113.	ⓐ	ⓑ	ⓒ	ⓓ
14.	ⓐ	ⓑ	ⓒ	ⓓ	64.	ⓐ	ⓑ	ⓒ	ⓓ	114.	ⓐ	ⓑ	ⓒ	ⓓ
15.	ⓐ	ⓑ	ⓒ	ⓓ	65.	ⓐ	ⓑ	ⓒ	ⓓ	115.	ⓐ	ⓑ	ⓒ	ⓓ
16.	ⓐ	ⓑ	ⓒ	ⓓ	66.	ⓐ	ⓑ	ⓒ	ⓓ	116.	ⓐ	ⓑ	ⓒ	ⓓ
17.	ⓐ	ⓑ	ⓒ	ⓓ	67.	ⓐ	ⓑ	ⓒ	ⓓ	117.	ⓐ	ⓑ	ⓒ	ⓓ
18.	ⓐ	ⓑ	ⓒ	ⓓ	68.	ⓐ	ⓑ	ⓒ	ⓓ	118.	ⓐ	ⓑ	ⓒ	ⓓ
19.	ⓐ	ⓑ	ⓒ	ⓓ	69.	ⓐ	ⓑ	ⓒ	ⓓ	119.	ⓐ	ⓑ	ⓒ	ⓓ
20.	ⓐ	ⓑ	ⓒ	ⓓ	70.	ⓐ	ⓑ	ⓒ	ⓓ	120.	ⓐ	ⓑ	ⓒ	ⓓ
21.	ⓐ	ⓑ	ⓒ	ⓓ	71.	ⓐ	ⓑ	ⓒ	ⓓ	121.	ⓐ	ⓑ	ⓒ	ⓓ
22.	ⓐ	ⓑ	ⓒ	ⓓ	72.	ⓐ	ⓑ	ⓒ	ⓓ	122.	ⓐ	ⓑ	ⓒ	ⓓ
23.	ⓐ	ⓑ	ⓒ	ⓓ	73.	ⓐ	ⓑ	ⓒ	ⓓ	123.	ⓐ	ⓑ	ⓒ	ⓓ
24.	ⓐ	ⓑ	ⓒ	ⓓ	74.	ⓐ	ⓑ	ⓒ	ⓓ	124.	ⓐ	ⓑ	ⓒ	ⓓ
25.	ⓐ	ⓑ	ⓒ	ⓓ	75.	ⓐ	ⓑ	ⓒ	ⓓ	125.	ⓐ	ⓑ	ⓒ	ⓓ
26.	ⓐ	ⓑ	ⓒ	ⓓ	76.	ⓐ	ⓑ	ⓒ	ⓓ	126.	ⓐ	ⓑ	ⓒ	ⓓ
27.	ⓐ	ⓑ	ⓒ	ⓓ	77.	ⓐ	ⓑ	ⓒ	ⓓ	127.	ⓐ	ⓑ	ⓒ	ⓓ
28.	ⓐ	ⓑ	ⓒ	ⓓ	78.	ⓐ	ⓑ	ⓒ	ⓓ	128.	ⓐ	ⓑ	ⓒ	ⓓ
29.	ⓐ	ⓑ	ⓒ	ⓓ	79.	ⓐ	ⓑ	ⓒ	ⓓ	129.	ⓐ	ⓑ	ⓒ	ⓓ
30.	ⓐ	ⓑ	ⓒ	ⓓ	80.	ⓐ	ⓑ	ⓒ	ⓓ	130.	ⓐ	ⓑ	ⓒ	ⓓ
31.	ⓐ	ⓑ	ⓒ	ⓓ	81.	ⓐ	ⓑ	ⓒ	ⓓ	131.	ⓐ	ⓑ	ⓒ	ⓓ
32.	ⓐ	ⓑ	ⓒ	ⓓ	82.	ⓐ	ⓑ	ⓒ	ⓓ	132.	ⓐ	ⓑ	ⓒ	ⓓ
33.	ⓐ	ⓑ	ⓒ	ⓓ	83.	ⓐ	ⓑ	ⓒ	ⓓ	133.	ⓐ	ⓑ	ⓒ	ⓓ
34.	ⓐ	ⓑ	ⓒ	ⓓ	84.	ⓐ	ⓑ	ⓒ	ⓓ	134.	ⓐ	ⓑ	ⓒ	ⓓ
35.	ⓐ	ⓑ	ⓒ	ⓓ	85.	ⓐ	ⓑ	ⓒ	ⓓ	135.	ⓐ	ⓑ	ⓒ	ⓓ
36.	ⓐ	ⓑ	ⓒ	ⓓ	86.	ⓐ	ⓑ	ⓒ	ⓓ	136.	ⓐ	ⓑ	ⓒ	ⓓ
37.	ⓐ	ⓑ	ⓒ	ⓓ	87.	ⓐ	ⓑ	ⓒ	ⓓ	137.	ⓐ	ⓑ	ⓒ	ⓓ
38.	ⓐ	ⓑ	ⓒ	ⓓ	88.	ⓐ	ⓑ	ⓒ	ⓓ	138.	ⓐ	ⓑ	ⓒ	ⓓ
39.	ⓐ	ⓑ	ⓒ	ⓓ	89.	ⓐ	ⓑ	ⓒ	ⓓ	139.	ⓐ	ⓑ	ⓒ	ⓓ
40.	ⓐ	ⓑ	ⓒ	ⓓ	90.	ⓐ	ⓑ	ⓒ	ⓓ	140.	ⓐ	ⓑ	ⓒ	ⓓ
41.	ⓐ	ⓑ	ⓒ	ⓓ	91.	ⓐ	ⓑ	ⓒ	ⓓ	141.	ⓐ	ⓑ	ⓒ	ⓓ
42.	ⓐ	ⓑ	ⓒ	ⓓ	92.	ⓐ	ⓑ	ⓒ	ⓓ	142.	ⓐ	ⓑ	ⓒ	ⓓ
43.	ⓐ	ⓑ	ⓒ	ⓓ	93.	ⓐ	ⓑ	ⓒ	ⓓ	143.	ⓐ	ⓑ	ⓒ	ⓓ
44.	ⓐ	ⓑ	ⓒ	ⓓ	94.	ⓐ	ⓑ	ⓒ	ⓓ	144.	ⓐ	ⓑ	ⓒ	ⓓ
45.	ⓐ	ⓑ	ⓒ	ⓓ	95.	ⓐ	ⓑ	ⓒ	ⓓ	145.	ⓐ	ⓑ	ⓒ	ⓓ
46.	ⓐ	ⓑ	ⓒ	ⓓ	96.	ⓐ	ⓑ	ⓒ	ⓓ	146.	ⓐ	ⓑ	ⓒ	ⓓ
47.	ⓐ	ⓑ	ⓒ	ⓓ	97.	ⓐ	ⓑ	ⓒ	ⓓ	147.	ⓐ	ⓑ	ⓒ	ⓓ
48.	ⓐ	ⓑ	ⓒ	ⓓ	98.	ⓐ	ⓑ	ⓒ	ⓓ	148.	ⓐ	ⓑ	ⓒ	ⓓ
49.	ⓐ	ⓑ	ⓒ	ⓓ	99.	ⓐ	ⓑ	ⓒ	ⓓ	149.	ⓐ	ⓑ	ⓒ	ⓓ
50.	ⓐ	ⓑ	ⓒ	ⓓ	100.	ⓐ	ⓑ	ⓒ	ⓓ	150.	ⓐ	ⓑ	ⓒ	ⓓ

Section 2: Criminal Procedure and Constitutional Law

1.	ⓐ	ⓑ	ⓒ	ⓓ	36.	ⓐ	ⓑ	ⓒ	ⓓ	71.	ⓐ	ⓑ	ⓒ	ⓓ
2.	ⓐ	ⓑ	ⓒ	ⓓ	37.	ⓐ	ⓑ	ⓒ	ⓓ	72.	ⓐ	ⓑ	ⓒ	ⓓ
3.	ⓐ	ⓑ	ⓒ	ⓓ	38.	ⓐ	ⓑ	ⓒ	ⓓ	73.	ⓐ	ⓑ	ⓒ	ⓓ
4.	ⓐ	ⓑ	ⓒ	ⓓ	39.	ⓐ	ⓑ	ⓒ	ⓓ	74.	ⓐ	ⓑ	ⓒ	ⓓ
5.	ⓐ	ⓑ	ⓒ	ⓓ	40.	ⓐ	ⓑ	ⓒ	ⓓ	75.	ⓐ	ⓑ	ⓒ	ⓓ
6.	ⓐ	ⓑ	ⓒ	ⓓ	41.	ⓐ	ⓑ	ⓒ	ⓓ	76.	ⓐ	ⓑ	ⓒ	ⓓ
7.	ⓐ	ⓑ	ⓒ	ⓓ	42.	ⓐ	ⓑ	ⓒ	ⓓ	77.	ⓐ	ⓑ	ⓒ	ⓓ
8.	ⓐ	ⓑ	ⓒ	ⓓ	43.	ⓐ	ⓑ	ⓒ	ⓓ	78.	ⓐ	ⓑ	ⓒ	ⓓ
9.	ⓐ	ⓑ	ⓒ	ⓓ	44.	ⓐ	ⓑ	ⓒ	ⓓ	79.	ⓐ	ⓑ	ⓒ	ⓓ
10.	ⓐ	ⓑ	ⓒ	ⓓ	45.	ⓐ	ⓑ	ⓒ	ⓓ	80.	ⓐ	ⓑ	ⓒ	ⓓ
11.	ⓐ	ⓑ	ⓒ	ⓓ	46.	ⓐ	ⓑ	ⓒ	ⓓ	81.	ⓐ	ⓑ	ⓒ	ⓓ
12.	ⓐ	ⓑ	ⓒ	ⓓ	47.	ⓐ	ⓑ	ⓒ	ⓓ	82.	ⓐ	ⓑ	ⓒ	ⓓ
13.	ⓐ	ⓑ	ⓒ	ⓓ	48.	ⓐ	ⓑ	ⓒ	ⓓ	83.	ⓐ	ⓑ	ⓒ	ⓓ
14.	ⓐ	ⓑ	ⓒ	ⓓ	49.	ⓐ	ⓑ	ⓒ	ⓓ	84.	ⓐ	ⓑ	ⓒ	ⓓ
15.	ⓐ	ⓑ	ⓒ	ⓓ	50.	ⓐ	ⓑ	ⓒ	ⓓ	85.	ⓐ	ⓑ	ⓒ	ⓓ
16.	ⓐ	ⓑ	ⓒ	ⓓ	51.	ⓐ	ⓑ	ⓒ	ⓓ	86.	ⓐ	ⓑ	ⓒ	ⓓ
17.	ⓐ	ⓑ	ⓒ	ⓓ	52.	ⓐ	ⓑ	ⓒ	ⓓ	87.	ⓐ	ⓑ	ⓒ	ⓓ
18.	ⓐ	ⓑ	ⓒ	ⓓ	53.	ⓐ	ⓑ	ⓒ	ⓓ	88.	ⓐ	ⓑ	ⓒ	ⓓ
19.	ⓐ	ⓑ	ⓒ	ⓓ	54.	ⓐ	ⓑ	ⓒ	ⓓ	89.	ⓐ	ⓑ	ⓒ	ⓓ
20.	ⓐ	ⓑ	ⓒ	ⓓ	55.	ⓐ	ⓑ	ⓒ	ⓓ	90.	ⓐ	ⓑ	ⓒ	ⓓ
21.	ⓐ	ⓑ	ⓒ	ⓓ	56.	ⓐ	ⓑ	ⓒ	ⓓ	91.	ⓐ	ⓑ	ⓒ	ⓓ
22.	ⓐ	ⓑ	ⓒ	ⓓ	57.	ⓐ	ⓑ	ⓒ	ⓓ	92.	ⓐ	ⓑ	ⓒ	ⓓ
23.	ⓐ	ⓑ	ⓒ	ⓓ	58.	ⓐ	ⓑ	ⓒ	ⓓ	93.	ⓐ	ⓑ	ⓒ	ⓓ
24.	ⓐ	ⓑ	ⓒ	ⓓ	59.	ⓐ	ⓑ	ⓒ	ⓓ	94.	ⓐ	ⓑ	ⓒ	ⓓ
25.	ⓐ	ⓑ	ⓒ	ⓓ	60.	ⓐ	ⓑ	ⓒ	ⓓ	95.	ⓐ	ⓑ	ⓒ	ⓓ
26.	ⓐ	ⓑ	ⓒ	ⓓ	61.	ⓐ	ⓑ	ⓒ	ⓓ	96.	ⓐ	ⓑ	ⓒ	ⓓ
27.	ⓐ	ⓑ	ⓒ	ⓓ	62.	ⓐ	ⓑ	ⓒ	ⓓ	97.	ⓐ	ⓑ	ⓒ	ⓓ
28.	ⓐ	ⓑ	ⓒ	ⓓ	63.	ⓐ	ⓑ	ⓒ	ⓓ	98.	ⓐ	ⓑ	ⓒ	ⓓ
29.	ⓐ	ⓑ	ⓒ	ⓓ	64.	ⓐ	ⓑ	ⓒ	ⓓ	99.	ⓐ	ⓑ	ⓒ	ⓓ
30.	ⓐ	ⓑ	ⓒ	ⓓ	65.	ⓐ	ⓑ	ⓒ	ⓓ	100.	ⓐ	ⓑ	ⓒ	ⓓ
31.	ⓐ	ⓑ	ⓒ	ⓓ	66.	ⓐ	ⓑ	ⓒ	ⓓ					
32.	ⓐ	ⓑ	ⓒ	ⓓ	67.	ⓐ	ⓑ	ⓒ	ⓓ					
33.	ⓐ	ⓑ	ⓒ	ⓓ	68.	ⓐ	ⓑ	ⓒ	ⓓ					
34.	ⓐ	ⓑ	ⓒ	ⓓ	69.	ⓐ	ⓑ	ⓒ	ⓓ					
35.	ⓐ	ⓑ	ⓒ	ⓓ	70.	ⓐ	ⓑ	ⓒ	ⓓ					

Section 3: Criminal Investigation

1.	ⓐ ⓑ ⓒ ⓓ		18.	ⓐ ⓑ ⓒ ⓓ		35.	ⓐ ⓑ ⓒ ⓓ
2.	ⓐ ⓑ ⓒ ⓓ		19.	ⓐ ⓑ ⓒ ⓓ		36.	ⓐ ⓑ ⓒ ⓓ
3.	ⓐ ⓑ ⓒ ⓓ		20.	ⓐ ⓑ ⓒ ⓓ		37.	ⓐ ⓑ ⓒ ⓓ
4.	ⓐ ⓑ ⓒ ⓓ		21.	ⓐ ⓑ ⓒ ⓓ		38.	ⓐ ⓑ ⓒ ⓓ
5.	ⓐ ⓑ ⓒ ⓓ		22.	ⓐ ⓑ ⓒ ⓓ		39.	ⓐ ⓑ ⓒ ⓓ
6.	ⓐ ⓑ ⓒ ⓓ		23.	ⓐ ⓑ ⓒ ⓓ		40.	ⓐ ⓑ ⓒ ⓓ
7.	ⓐ ⓑ ⓒ ⓓ		24.	ⓐ ⓑ ⓒ ⓓ		41.	ⓐ ⓑ ⓒ ⓓ
8.	ⓐ ⓑ ⓒ ⓓ		25.	ⓐ ⓑ ⓒ ⓓ		42.	ⓐ ⓑ ⓒ ⓓ
9.	ⓐ ⓑ ⓒ ⓓ		26.	ⓐ ⓑ ⓒ ⓓ		43.	ⓐ ⓑ ⓒ ⓓ
10.	ⓐ ⓑ ⓒ ⓓ		27.	ⓐ ⓑ ⓒ ⓓ		44.	ⓐ ⓑ ⓒ ⓓ
11.	ⓐ ⓑ ⓒ ⓓ		28.	ⓐ ⓑ ⓒ ⓓ		45.	ⓐ ⓑ ⓒ ⓓ
12.	ⓐ ⓑ ⓒ ⓓ		29.	ⓐ ⓑ ⓒ ⓓ		46.	ⓐ ⓑ ⓒ ⓓ
13.	ⓐ ⓑ ⓒ ⓓ		30.	ⓐ ⓑ ⓒ ⓓ		47.	ⓐ ⓑ ⓒ ⓓ
14.	ⓐ ⓑ ⓒ ⓓ		31.	ⓐ ⓑ ⓒ ⓓ		48.	ⓐ ⓑ ⓒ ⓓ
15.	ⓐ ⓑ ⓒ ⓓ		32.	ⓐ ⓑ ⓒ ⓓ		49.	ⓐ ⓑ ⓒ ⓓ
16.	ⓐ ⓑ ⓒ ⓓ		33.	ⓐ ⓑ ⓒ ⓓ		50.	ⓐ ⓑ ⓒ ⓓ
17.	ⓐ ⓑ ⓒ ⓓ		34.	ⓐ ⓑ ⓒ ⓓ			

Section 4: Patrol Practices

1.	ⓐ ⓑ ⓒ ⓓ		13.	ⓐ ⓑ ⓒ ⓓ		25.	ⓐ ⓑ ⓒ ⓓ
2.	ⓐ ⓑ ⓒ ⓓ		14.	ⓐ ⓑ ⓒ ⓓ		26.	ⓐ ⓑ ⓒ ⓓ
3.	ⓐ ⓑ ⓒ ⓓ		15.	ⓐ ⓑ ⓒ ⓓ		27.	ⓐ ⓑ ⓒ ⓓ
4.	ⓐ ⓑ ⓒ ⓓ		16.	ⓐ ⓑ ⓒ ⓓ		28.	ⓐ ⓑ ⓒ ⓓ
5.	ⓐ ⓑ ⓒ ⓓ		17.	ⓐ ⓑ ⓒ ⓓ		29.	ⓐ ⓑ ⓒ ⓓ
6.	ⓐ ⓑ ⓒ ⓓ		18.	ⓐ ⓑ ⓒ ⓓ		30.	ⓐ ⓑ ⓒ ⓓ
7.	ⓐ ⓑ ⓒ ⓓ		19.	ⓐ ⓑ ⓒ ⓓ		31.	ⓐ ⓑ ⓒ ⓓ
8.	ⓐ ⓑ ⓒ ⓓ		20.	ⓐ ⓑ ⓒ ⓓ		32.	ⓐ ⓑ ⓒ ⓓ
9.	ⓐ ⓑ ⓒ ⓓ		21.	ⓐ ⓑ ⓒ ⓓ		33.	ⓐ ⓑ ⓒ ⓓ
10.	ⓐ ⓑ ⓒ ⓓ		22.	ⓐ ⓑ ⓒ ⓓ		34.	ⓐ ⓑ ⓒ ⓓ
11.	ⓐ ⓑ ⓒ ⓓ		23.	ⓐ ⓑ ⓒ ⓓ		35.	ⓐ ⓑ ⓒ ⓓ
12.	ⓐ ⓑ ⓒ ⓓ		24.	ⓐ ⓑ ⓒ ⓓ			

Section 5: Community Relations

1.	ⓐ ⓑ ⓒ ⓓ		6.	ⓐ ⓑ ⓒ ⓓ		11.	ⓐ ⓑ ⓒ ⓓ
2.	ⓐ ⓑ ⓒ ⓓ		7.	ⓐ ⓑ ⓒ ⓓ		12.	ⓐ ⓑ ⓒ ⓓ
3.	ⓐ ⓑ ⓒ ⓓ		8.	ⓐ ⓑ ⓒ ⓓ		13.	ⓐ ⓑ ⓒ ⓓ
4.	ⓐ ⓑ ⓒ ⓓ		9.	ⓐ ⓑ ⓒ ⓓ		14.	ⓐ ⓑ ⓒ ⓓ
5.	ⓐ ⓑ ⓒ ⓓ		10.	ⓐ ⓑ ⓒ ⓓ		15.	ⓐ ⓑ ⓒ ⓓ

▶ Section 1: Supervision and Management

1. When workers obey a supervisor because of fear, their behavior is called
   a. resistance.
   b. yielding.
   c. commanding.
   d. obedience.

2. Which of the following is the most common weakness in an employee rating program?
   a. indifference of the supervisors doing the rating
   b. employee pressures thwarting the evaluation system
   c. failing to train the raters
   d. neglect on the part of management to inform ratees of their strengths and weaknesses

3. The type of leader who tells his or her subordinates what to do, allowing no discussion, is most accurately referred to as a(n)
   a. autocratic leader.
   b. democratic leader.
   c. free-rein leader.
   d. command presence leader.

4. What is the prime objective of the employment interview?
   a. to train the workers
   b. to improve the workers' performance
   c. to appraise an applicant's qualifications for employment
   d. all of the above

5. Sergeant McKinley is conducting performance reviews of the officers in his unit. Sergeant McKinley should be careful not to make the most common rating error. This is known as the error of
   a. halo effect.
   b. leniency.
   c. related traits.
   d. subjectivity.

6. Most experts consider the primary function of the supervising sergeant to be presiding over the process of
   a. unity of command.
   b. span of control.
   c. division of work.
   d. delegation.

7. During an employee-centered counseling session, the supervisor should
   a. give his or her advice or opinion.
   b. direct the subordinate in solving his or her problem.
   c. permit full reflection by the subordinate.
   d. all of the above

8. Sergeant Rasheed is conducting a training session on the use of deadly force and self-defense tactics. Sergeant Rasheed realizes that she must ask good questions in order to determine what the students learned. If the sergeant wants to stimulate discussion on a contribution requiring emphasis or elaboration, what types of questions should she use?
   a. reverse and relay questions
   b. rhetorical and converse questions
   c. inquisitive and follow-up questions
   d. factual and rhetorical questions

9. Public employees have always been liable for their own negligent or wrongful acts. Damages awarded because of pain and suffering are termed
   a. compensatory damages.
   b. exemplary damages.
   c. civil damages.
   d. tort damages.

10. Whenever counseling an employee with a drinking problem, the initial conversation should ordinarily be directed toward
    a. the worker's drinking problem.
    b. the worker's performance.
    c. the worker as an individual.
    d. the worker's attitude.

11. Which of the following would be the first step in the process of removing an employee from the organization for the good of the service?
    a. oral or written reprimand
    b. positive discipline
    c. counseling
    d. negative discipline

12. Which of the following statements is most accurate with regard to communication among members of the police force?
    a. Formal communications are always more accurate than informal conversations.
    b. Communication between people of the same rank allows for about the same amount of feedback as communication between supervisors and subordinates.
    c. Too much insistence that employees follow formal communication channels will tend to impede the passing of information upward, downward, and across organizational lines.
    d. All of the above statements are true.

13. Sergeant Xiang is conducting a training session on pursuit driving. After a ten-minute lecture, Sergeant Xiang asks a question to the entire class. This type of question is known as a(n)
    a. relay question.
    b. reverse question.
    c. rhetorical question.
    d. overhead question.

14. You, as the sergeant in charge, arrive at the scene of a shooting where one of your officers shot and killed a suspect. You realize that the coroner must hold an inquest to determine the cause of death. In order to be most consistent with sound supervisory practices, the best course for you to take regarding the inquest is to
    a. refer the matter to the local prosecutor's office.
    b. make a formal request for a transcript of the proceedings.
    c. attend the inquest.
    d. conduct a separate investigation as to the cause of death.

15. Lenient supervisors who tend to rate all their subordinates alike tend to be
a. overtly respected.
b. overtly disrespected.
c. covertly respected.
d. covertly disrespected.

16. Sergeant King is at the scene of a large public event at which there are multiple platoons assigned. Sergeant King observes an officer who is not under her direct supervision yelling and using profanity toward a member of the community. Sergeant King should
a. notify that officer's direct supervisor.
b. intervene immediately.
c. notify the platoon lieutenant.
d. ignore the situation.

17. The continuing task of making decisions and turning them into specific and general orders and instructions is best termed
a. direction.
b. planning.
c. organizing.
d. coordination.

18. One of the primary measures of the level of discipline within the police force is the
a. list of commendations earned by the department.
b. number of complaints generated by employees.
c. number of complaints generated by superior officers.
d. orderliness of the police force on a day-to-day basis.

19. Officer Garcia is going through a very difficult divorce. Sergeant Jackson has not observed any negative effect on the officer's performance. Sergeant Jackson decides to counsel Officer Garcia about the situation in order to head off any potential work-related problems. Sergeant Jackson's action were
a. wise; a problem such as this can have a devastating effect on an officer's performance.
b. unwise; other officers may see this as favoritism.
c. wise; divorce can often lead to larger problems like alcoholism.
d. unwise; Officer Garcia's performance at work has not been affected.

20. The key to the effective application of the exception principle is
a. authority.
b. delegation.
c. accountability.
d. investigation.

21. A supervisor can distinguish him- or herself most of all by the manner in which he or she deals with discipline problem situations. Therefore, it is important for him or her to understand that effective discipline of subordinates is preceded by
a. understanding.
b. training.
c. rules and regulations.
d. self-discipline.

22. Sergeant Hall is dealing with a subordinate who she knows is going through a difficult personal problem. At which point would it be most appropriate to approach the officer concerning this problem?
   a. immediately after she learns of the problem
   b. when other officers in the unit begin to notice
   c. when it negatively affects the officer's performance
   d. never; it is a personal problem

23. Work in a police department may be divided according to various criteria: (i) purpose, (ii) function, (iii) geographic area, and (iv) clientele. Which of the following would be an example of division of work by purpose?
   a. beats
   b. traffic control
   c. youth activities
   d. all of the above

24. Which of the following is a disadvantage of autocratic communications?
   a. arbitrariness
   b. speed
   c. directness
   d. all of the above

25. The following five-step teaching process has been widely accepted by experts in the field of training: (i) introduction, (ii) presentation, (iii) application, (iv) testing, and (v) evaluation and follow-up. When instructing a group of police officers, using instructional aids is particularly important during which steps?
   a. presentation and testing
   b. introduction and presentation
   c. presentation and application
   d. evaluation and follow-up

26. Under which of the following situations should the separation interview not be held?
   a. when someone voluntarily resigns
   b. when someone goes on regular retirement voluntarily
   c. when someone is fired because of a serious infraction
   d. the separation interview should always be held

27. Which one of the following most likely precedes effective learning?
   a. competition
   b. rewards
   c. attention
   d. cooperation

28. The various principles of organization—among them unity of command, span of control, and authority commensurate with responsibility—are very important for the police sergeant, although their apparent similarity is sometimes confusing. A more detailed study of them, however, reveals the subtle differences. The principle of unity of command most accurately refers to
   a. how many direct supervisors an employee has.
   b. how many employees a supervisor oversees.
   c. how much freedom an employee has in carrying out a task.
   d. both **a** and **b**

29. Communications theorists refer to the static that interferes with the transmission of messages as
   a. filtering.
   b. sentiments.
   c. noise.
   d. overloading.

30. From the following, select the false statement about free-rein communications.

  a. Free-rein communications provide for a maximum number of contacts.

  b. Leadership and guidance are often absent in the free-rein type of communication.

  c. Misunderstandings, misapprehensions, and mistakes often flourish in the free-rein communications process.

  d. Subordinates never realize the benefits of two-way communication.

31. Sergeant Flores overhears officers in his unit complaining about a new policy. Sergeant Flores knows that the officers are just venting and will accept the policy completely after a short adjustment period. When asked by his superior how the new policy change is proceeding, Sergeant Flores should tell his superior that

  a. the officers are complaining about the change.

  b. everything is going well.

  c. he is not sure.

  d. she should inquire herself.

32. A key to the success of any supervisor is the ability to delegate. Supervisors should know that it is important to delegate to subordinate officers any work assignment that they are capable of completing and to retain only those tasks that can be performed only by him or her. This concept is known as

  a. completed staff work.

  b. the exception principle.

  c. delegated authority.

  d. the retention principle.

33. Periodically conducting conferences, especially when the participants are of equal rank, is paramount for good problem solving. A big part of the success or failure of a conference is the leader's skillful use of questions. Which type of question (i) is asked of a specific participant for response, and (ii) helps get more reticent participants to speak up?

  a. rhetorical question

  b. indirect question

  c. direct question

  d. overhead question

34. In order to gain the respect and confidence of his or her subordinate officers, the first thing a supervisor must do is

  a. know each of his or her officers personally.

  b. know how to communicate.

  c. set an example through his or her own conduct.

  d. demand respect and confidence.

35. When the lesson material is being analyzed and the teaching plan is being prepared so that the presentation can be arranged in the most logical order, which of the following points of view should the police instructor have in mind?

  a. the learner's point of view

  b. the instructor's point of view

  c. the department's point of view

  d. the chief's point of view

36. Choose the most accurate comment regarding the following claim:

In a situation in which complex operations or numerous persons are affected, the best way to give orders is verbally, leaving time for a response.

a. The statement is true as written.

b. The statement is false as written.

c. No orders should be given in this situation.

d. The orders should be verbal, but there should not be an opportunity to respond.

37. Choose the best comment regarding the following claim:

In order to conserve time, effort, and money, supervisors should review procedural plans relating to standard operating procedures only when a need is evident.

a. The statement is true as written.

b. The statement is false as written.

c. Standard operating procedures never need review.

d. Only outside experts should review standard operating procedures.

38. Choose the best comment regarding the following claim:

Lines of authority and channels of communication usually become less distinct when an organization increases in complexity.

a. The statement is true as written.

b. The statement is false as written.

c. It is impossible to predict how increased complexity will affect lines of authority and communication.

d. Communication channels become less distinct but lines of authority become clearer as the organization becomes more complex.

39. In which of the following types of organization are the lines of authority laid out in a simple hierarchy?

a. straight-line

b. functional

c. line-and-staff

d. staff

40. Normally, a staff supervisor has

a. command over staff personnel.

b. line command over all subordinates in his or her unit.

c. command over line personnel.

d. authority over subordinates throughout the organization.

41. Lieutenant Gray continually bypasses Sergeant Cruz and gives orders directly to Sergeant Cruz's subordinates. In doing so, what principle of management does she violate?

a. chain of command

b. unity of command

c. span of control

d. authority commensurate with responsibility

42. Lieutenant Pearson ordered Sergeant Patel to write a memo directing all patrol personnel to make sure each shotgun carried in patrol cars was loaded with four rods of ammunition. When Sergeant Patel completed the task, Lieutenant Pearson read the memo and approved it. This describes what has been most accurately referred to as

a. span of authority.

b. personnel development.

c. completed staff work.

d. completed line work.

43. Two sergeants are discussing the process of discipline. Sergeant Simmons begins to discuss different forms of positive discipline. Sergeant Simmons should know that the best example of positive discipline is
a. training.
b. punishment.
c. reassignment.
d. delegation.

44. Which of the following is considered to be a prime cause of friction in any organization?
a. functional overlapping between units
b. the use of the exception principle by the hierarchy on a daily basis
c. as complete a delegation of duties as possible
d. lines of communications that are definite and straight

45. The one of the following types of leadership that holds the greatest promise for success in most normal operations is
a. free-rein.
b. autocratic.
c. democratic.
d. *laissez-faire.*

46. Which one of the following should be distributed, if at all possible, to those persons searching for a bomb in a building?
a. fresh batteries
b. mirrors
c. magnifying lenses
d. all of the above

47. When the morale of a sergeant is high, the morale of the officers in his or her unit is
a. low.
b. high.
c. at a good level.
d. possibly high or low.

48. In carrying out his or her role in disaster control operations, the supervisor's primary function is to
a. obtain and transmit field intelligence to headquarters.
b. deploy his or her unit as expeditiously as possible.
c. evacuate the area as quickly as possible.
d. treat the injured as quickly as possible.

49. Sergeant O'Brien was asked by her lieutenant to create a report about an accident-prone intersection. Sergeant O'Brien creates the report and is concerned that it contains too much information. Sergeant O'Brien should
a. submit the report unchanged.
b. shorten the report before submitting it.
c. seek advice from a fellow sergeant.
d. seek advice from a subordinate officer.

50. Officer Watts believes that in order to be an effective supervisor, a sergeant should possess advanced technical knowledge in all aspects of the work performed by his or her subordinates. Officer Watts's belief is
  a. correct; supervisors need to know all aspects of the work being performed.
  b. incorrect; supervisors do not need to know anything about the work being performed.
  c. correct; supervisors need to solve problems and need to have advanced knowledge.
  d. incorrect; supervisors need only have a working knowledge of the work being performed.

51. When training succeeds in changing the trainee's job performance, the objective achieved is a
  a. subsidiary objective.
  b. general objective.
  c. secondary objective.
  d. specific objective.

52. Raters often tend to rate higher than is justified those persons they know well and like and those who subscribe to the same opinions as the rater. Those who are not liked or who are not compatible with the rater's own particular likes or dislikes are likely to be rated lower than is justified. This error is most accurately referred to as
  a. the halo effect.
  b. personal bias.
  c. a contrast error.
  d. a leniency error.

53. Marking an inordinately large number of rating reports in the highest one or two categories on personnel evaluations results from
  a. a central-tendency error.
  b. the halo effect.
  c. association.
  d. leniency.

54. Captain Brassner delegates the task of performing a report to Lieutenant Newman. Lieutenant Newman delegates the task to Sergeant Mendez who, in turn, delegates it to Officer Iqbal. Who is responsible for the completion of the report?
  a. Captain Brassner
  b. Lieutenant Newman
  c. Sergeant Mendez
  d. Officer Iqbal

55. According to the experts in the field of supervision and management, what is the least preferred type of punishment to administer to an erring employee?
  a. loss of accumulated compensatory time
  b. one-day suspension
  c. loss of regular days off
  d. loss of annual leave

56. Sergeant Vaughn arrives at the scene of a fire in progress. One of her rookie officers asks what his primary duties in this situation are. Sergeant Vaughn should tell the rookie officer to
  a. assist the fire department.
  b. save lives and property.
  c. administer first aid.
  d. control vehicular and pedestrian traffic.

57. A supervisor hears that one of his or her troops has driven up unexpectedly to the scene of a house fire. The supervisor drives to the scene. One of the first actions a supervisor should take when he or she arrives at the scene is to
   a. attempt to locate any injured or trapped persons.
   b. begin to deploy his or her personnel immediately.
   c. ensure that the fire department has been notified.
   d. transmit the type and size of the fire, the type of property involved, wind direction, endangered structures, and emergency routes to the scene.

58. When a problem drinker claims that he or she can take or leave alcohol alone, he or she is engaging in
   a. rationalization.
   b. denial.
   c. projection.
   d. compensation.

59. Which of the following types of orders most facilitates systematic follow-up and provides a basis for establishing accountability for failures?
   a. written orders
   b. direct commands
   c. request-type orders
   d. implied or suggested orders

60. Understanding basic psychology is of paramount importance for the police supervisor. At times, a frustrated individual may regress, that is, revert to infantile or childish behavior, in the face of emotional stress. When this occurs, the greatest risk is of
   a. occasional immature reactions to orders.
   b. continuing absence of mature behavior.
   c. lessened ability to perform on the job.
   d. loss of problem-solving ability.

61. Which one of the following has the tendency to reduce the halo effect when rating employees?
   a. individual-trait rating
   b. validation-trait rating
   c. composite-trait rating
   d. related-trait rating

62. Which of the following establishes policy in a police organization?
   a. rules and regulations
   b. tactical plans
   c. general orders
   d. operational plans

63. A supervisor derives his or her official authority from
   a. his or her subordinates.
   b. his or her superior officer.
   c. management.
   d. his or her experience.

64. When disciplinary action is called for, it is most important that the discipline be
   a. positive.
   b. severe.
   c. prompt.
   d. negative.

65. Experienced managers agree that when positive methods fail in bringing an employee within accepted standards of conduct in the police department, negative discipline must be administered. Which of the following is considered a form of negative discipline?
  I. training
 II. suspension
III. counseling
 IV. oral reprimand
  a. II only
  b. III only
  c. IV only
  d. II and IV

66. A new policy has been developed regarding the response to hostage situations. Sergeant Benson has been instructed to instruct his officers about the change. Sergeant Benson should know that change is most readily accepted when
  a. the policy is written.
  b. acceptance of the policy is demanded.
  c. the reason for the change is explained.
  d. advance notice about the change is given.

67. In teaching, past training and experience and the ability to integrate these with new learning and experience are known as the student's
  a. motivational base.
  b. apperceptive base.
  c. cognitive base.
  d. perceptive base.

68. In the police organizational structure, polices and plans should be the most detailed and comprehensive at the
  a. administrative level.
  b. supervisory level.
  c. staff level.
  d. lowest level.

69. A supervisor can best reduce the frustration felt by workers through his or her
  a. demeanor.
  b. empathy.
  c. proper job placement.
  d. listening.

70. In a police department, what is the disadvantage to using a departmental (or line-type) organizational structure?
  a. Various specialists share responsibility and authority.
  b. Failure to recognize line and staff relationships causes friction.
  c. Supervisors are too often required to perform the duties of specialists.
  d. There is a lack of coordination because of functional overlap between units.

71. What is the name for the process of directing and controlling the resources of an organization (such as its personnel, materials, and equipment)?
  a. management
  b. supervision
  c. organization
  d. planning

72. Most police organizations, with the exception of extremely small organizations, are

a. line and staff organizations.

b. line organizations.

c. functional organizations.

d. staff organizations.

73. It is extremely important for the supervisor to understand the job of a good conference leader. The conference leader's primary role should be as

a. monitor.

b. mentor.

c. instructor.

d. demonstrator.

74. When a supervisor is integrating the different parts of the work process, he or she is most accurately

a. planning.

b. coordinating effort.

c. training.

d. inspecting or following up.

75. When a police organization makes procedural plans, for what level of organization should the plans be most precise?

a. the lower levels

b. the upper levels

c. the middle-level planning units

d. every level of the hierarchy

76. Human beings can react in multiple ways to failure. Some reactions are positive and some are negative. The most common reaction to failure is

a. fear.

b. anger.

c. indifference.

d. rationalization.

77. In a police organization, when does the need for coordination become greater?

a. when the organization decreases in size

b. when communication breaks down

c. when the organization increases in rank

d. when the organization increases in size

78. The majority of complaints against a police officer involve

a. criminal conduct.

b. corruption.

c. bribe receiving.

d. noncriminal conduct.

79. The greatest and most frequent cause of friction in a police organization is generally thought to be the failure of

a. line personnel to understand their limitations.

b. staff personnel to recognize their limited line authority.

c. line personnel to recognize and use their authority over staff personnel.

d. management to differentiate line and staff authority.

80. Which of the following statements about punishment is least accurate?

a. Law enforcement agencies must have uniform penalties for offenses.

b. It is imperative that punishment fit the individual as well as the offense.

c. Negative discipline comes after positive discipline has failed.

d. An individual's prior performance record must always be considered when meting out punishments.

81. When a subordinate is under the direct command of only one superior officer, this is referred to as
a. chain of command.
b. delegation of authority.
c. command presence.
d. unity of command.

82. Statistics bear out the claim that most complaints against police officers today involve
a. excessive physical abuse of prisoners.
b. theft from prisoners.
c. physical abuse of nonprisoners.
d. rude treatment of citizens.

83. A fair and impartial disciplinary system should probably NOT include which of the following?
a. performance feedback
b. job performance evaluations
c. an appeals procedure
d. automatic purging of negative information from officers' files

84. Sergeant Yates has discovered through his own observation that one of his officers, Officer Rios, has failed in performing some task. In order to be most consistent with sound supervisory and management principles, Sergeant Yates should first carefully analyze Officer Rios's personnel file to determine
a. what Officer Rios's work record was prior to joining the police department.
b. if Officer Rios is suitable to remain on the police force.
c. if Officer Rios has been previously warned about inadequate performance.
d. if Officer Rios lacked instruction in performing the particular incident.

85. A supervisor who has had the disciplinary cases he or she has administered against his or her subordinates overruled will most probably
a. be reluctant to initiate future disciplinary actions.
b. become excessively autocratic and strict.
c. continue to handle disciplinary problems in the same manner.
d. become free rein and ignore infractions completely.

86. For the most part, procedures to be followed in receiving and disposing of complaints against subordinates will be dictated by
a. the subordinate.
b. the first line supervisors.
c. organizational policy.
d. individual infractions.

87. Sergeant Higgins is about to conduct an interview with an employee regarding a recent performance evaluation. Sergeant Higgins should know that the main purpose of an employee performance interview is to
a. call attention to past performance problems.
b. engage the officer in self-appraisal.
c. show that the department is watching officers' performance.
d. get the officer's explanation for performance problems.

88. One widely accepted reason why supervisors are not always good at listening to what their subordinates are saying is that they are
a. preoccupied by the subordinate's problems.
b. more used to speaking and giving orders.
c. not interested in what the subordinate is saying.
d. afraid of what they may hear.

89. Sergeant Doyle is talking to a subordinate about an incident when she concludes that the resentment and anger the employee feels over the incident are totally without merit. Sergeant Doyle's best course of action is to
- **a.** point out how foolish the subordinate is being.
- **b.** allow the employee him- or herself to see how foolishly he or she is acting.
- **c.** allow the employee to speak freely and appear to agree with him or her.
- **d.** understand that the reason her subordinate is angry and resentful is real to him or her.

90. Widely recognized basic human drives include all of the following EXCEPT
- **a.** the desire for security.
- **b.** the need to maintain the status quo.
- **c.** the desire for recognition.
- **d.** the need for responsiveness from others.

91. It is believed that by studying the management process, you can increase your effectiveness as a manager. Effective managers and supervisors can be developed from among the rank and file. Such development requires two things, most nearly
- **a.** motivated personnel and adequate training.
- **b.** education and testing.
- **c.** intelligence and wide-ranging interests.
- **d.** performance and competition.

92. Sergeant Cobb is attempting to understand how communication within a police department operates. Regarding informal lines of communication, Sergeant Cobb should know that informal lines of communication
- **a.** are poisonous to a police department.
- **b.** consist of only rumor.
- **c.** can be useful for transmitting information.
- **d.** should not be allowed.

93. Sergeant Pope is asked to examine the current division of patrol services. Sergeant Pope should know that the most reliable indicator of the need for patrol time is
- **a.** linear miles.
- **b.** square miles.
- **c.** street miles.
- **d.** population.

94. You, as the sergeant in charge, just received a new order from management. You know the order is going to be very unpopular with your officers. Under the circumstances, what is the best thing for you to say?
- **a.** "Although I don't agree, that's the way our bosses want it, so that's how it has to be done."
- **b.** "I know you people don't like this order, but management gave it to me so I have to give it to you."
- **c.** "This is my new order, and I both defend and support it."
- **d.** "I know this order is unpopular with you; however, you must obey it until I can get a chance to get it changed by management."

95. The most valuable interpersonal skill needed by a supervisor is widely thought to be
- **a.** the ability to follow up effectively.
- **b.** the ability to communicate effectively.
- **c.** the ability to earn respect.
- **d.** the ability to make referrals to subordinates.

96. When a supervisor earns the respect and confidence of his or her subordinates, it is said that he or she gains
- **a.** official authority.
- **b.** actual authority.
- **c.** informed authority.
- **d.** peer authority.

97. The immediate supervisors of police departments must remain abreast of all conditions that could affect the department. The supervisor can best accomplish this task by
   a. using formal communications networks.
   b. using informal communications networks.
   c. using both formal and informal communications networks.
   d. using lateral communications networks.

98. When a person repeatedly makes the same response to a problem, despite the fact that such response has been ineffective in the past, he or she is said to have a(n)
   a. fixation.
   b. sublimation.
   c. inferiority complex.
   d. regressive behavior pattern.

99. Which kind of authority do all police managers who act in an advisory capacity to other managers possess?
   a. line
   b. staff
   c. line and staff
   d. functional

100. A police organization is composed of workers and managers. The managers form a hierarchy, which is usually composed of three levels: the top, the middle, and the operating level. The primary functions of top and middle managers are
   a. planning, directing, and controlling.
   b. delegating, controlling, and inspecting line personnel.
   c. budgeting, recording, and reporting.
   d. reporting, observing, and creating.

101. It is very important for sergeants to understand the distinction between lines of command and organizational structure. If a captain who is a community relations specialist directs the activities of one of his or her own subordinates at a street demonstration, this would most nearly be an example of
   a. a manager with functional authority exercising line authority.
   b. a manager with staff authority exercising line authority.
   c. a manager with staff authority exercising staff authority.
   d. a manager with functional authority exercising functional authority.

102. Delegation benefits the police agency for all of the following reasons EXCEPT
   a. it increases the technical skills of workers.
   b. it enhances worker initiative.
   c. it contributes to rote assignments.
   d. it creates a pool of employees who are able to fill in for supervisors.

103. At what stage in the evaluation interview should the rater talk to the ratee about the appeals process?
   a. at the beginning
   b. when he or she gives the ratee the copy of the report
   c. when future actions are discussed
   d. at the conclusion

104. When an employee complains that management is violating some provision of the union contract, this is most properly termed
  a. a grievance.
  b. a contract violation.
  c. an employee complaint.
  d. all of the above

105. When investigating allegations of minor infractions by employees, the supervisor must verify that an infraction indeed occurred and
  a. verify that the officer who allegedly committed the infraction has been notified of the investigation.
  b. discuss the matter with the alleged offending employee.
  c. verify that the officer who allegedly committed the infraction has received a copy of the formal complaint lodged against him.
  d. identify the officer who allegedly committed the infraction.

106. The manner in which personnel complaints should be handled depends more than anything else on
  a. the seriousness of the offense.
  b. the type of complainant.
  c. the timing of the complaint.
  d. the person receiving the complaint.

107. After all forms of positive discipline fail, what is the best way to deal with a problem employee?
  a. resort to more training
  b. fire the employee
  c. punishment
  d. request his or her resignation

108. With regard to counseling subordinates, which of the following statements is least accurate?
  a. Counseling should not be undertaken until a problem exists, or the supervising counselor will be perceived by his subordinates as a meddler.
  b. Effective counseling demands that the counseling supervisor know his or her subordinates in depth.
  c. Supervisors should meet informally on a regular basis with each of their immediate subordinates for the purpose of getting to know each subordinate as an individual.
  d. Formal meetings should be one-on-one, take place at least once a month, and last for at least 20 minutes.

109. One particular method of training is used mostly
  ▪ to inform employees of recent changes in the law
  ▪ to impart information concerning a rash of related criminal incidents occurring in a certain neighborhood
  ▪ to reinforce existing procedures
  This method of training is
  a. shift training.
  b. in-service training.
  c. field training.
  d. entry-level training.

110. It has been stated that learning requires change and that before any learning or change can occur the trainer must catch and hold the attention of the trainee. What is the best means of getting and maintaining the trainee's attention?
  a. pulling organizational rank
  b. displaying extensive knowledge
  c. appealing to the trainee's own best interests
  d. understanding the trainee

111. Sergeant Maeda is conducting a counseling session with an officer about a disciplinary problem. Sergeant Maeda should know that the best time for him to take notes about what was said is
  a. during the entire session.
  b. after the session ends.
  c. continually.
  d. every ten minutes.

112. One of the greatest burdens a supervisor faces in his or her efforts to maintain a high level of overall discipline is
  a. a lack of backing from the hierarchy.
  b. sudden policy changes.
  c. outdated rules and regulations.
  d. a lack of enforcement of rules and regulations.

113. The ultimate purpose of a discussion between a supervisor and employee is to
  a. test out new procedures.
  b. develop better relations.
  c. define the goals of the department.
  d. exchange information and improve attitudes.

114. Which of the following divisions of labor is not an example of division by purpose?
  a. traffic enforcement unit
  b. crime scene unit
  c. patrol beats
  d. detective division

115. When distributing available field personnel, the first consideration must be given to
  a. days of the week.
  b. shifts.
  c. beats.
  d. hours of the day.

116. Officers assigned to patrol activities should be distributed according to the
  a. area, including street miles.
  b. proportionate need for their services.
  c. current crime patterns.
  d. needs of the citizenry.

117. Weighing factors to determine the proportionate allocation of available patrol time is
  a. an exact science.
  b. a subjective process.
  c. not possible.
  d. an objective process.

118. Of the following factors, the one that has the least bearing on communicative interaction is
  a. attitude.
  b. emotion.
  c. mood.
  d. setting.

119. In general, communication is most difficult in which of the following circumstances?

    a. a police chief addressing a captain

    b. a lieutenant addressing a captain

    c. a sergeant addressing a patrol officer

    d. a captain addressing a sergeant

120. It has been said that people rarely pay equal attention to all the parts of a complex message. They usually tend to focus on the parts that are

    a. most useful to them.

    b. most important to them.

    c. most understandable to them.

    d. least understandable to them.

121. Assume that you are a sergeant working a street detail. While on your tour of duty, you receive numerous complaints from local merchants that the double parking in front of their stores prevents them from getting deliveries in a timely manner. Which of the following is the most appropriate action for you to take?

    a. Detail a sector car to respond and issue traffic summonses.

    b. Begin by discussing the issue with patrol officers who cover that area.

    c. Go to the area and observe firsthand whether there is any truth to the complaints.

    d. Do nothing for the time being until you can check records to corroborate the complaints.

122. The first step in devising a training program is discovering the training needs. To do this, the specific requirements of the job being considered should be examined to insure that they are in keeping with the agency goals. What else would help in identifying training needs?

    a. analyzing complaints from sources within or outside the agency

    b. inspecting the agency's personnel to see if they follow agency policy

    c. knowing the differences between the requirements of the specific job and the present employee competence level

    d. analyzing performance evaluations or informally assessing firsthand knowledge of supervisors

123. What is the process or activity by which the human and material resources of an organization are coordinated to achieve a specific goal?

    a. supervision

    b. control

    c. management

    d. pyramiding

124. When a group of people interact to achieve stated purposes, this is most nearly

    a. management.

    b. control.

    c. delegation.

    d. organization.

125. Coordination of effort is extremely important to a properly functioning police organization. Supervisors should be aware that the most important type of communication for ensuring coordination of effort is
a. upward communication.
b. downward communication.
c. lateral communication.
d. oral communication.

126. Who is it that most administration experts agree shoulders the greatest responsibility for maintaining discipline within the police organization?
a. the chief executive officer
b. upper management
c. the first line supervisor
d. the sergeant

127. One of your patrol officers, Officer Peters, wants very much to be a sergeant. In fact, she is studying for the examination. She asks you, "Hey, Sarge, what is the most valuable skill for a supervisor to develop?" If you want to tell her what most experts think, what should your response to Officer Peters be?
a. interpersonal skills
b. paperwork skills
c. technical skills
d. analytical skills

128. One of your subordinates comes to you and asks you, the sergeant, to help her out. She informs you that she understands that leadership is the most important role of a good sergeant and she understands that it is best accomplished by getting unsupervised subordinates to do a good job willingly. But she continues, saying, "What I don't know is how I get unsupervised subordinates to act this way." To be most accurate, you should tell your employee that the best way to accomplish this is by
a. studying your textbooks.
b. listening to subordinates' problems.
c. being skilled in human relations.
d. understanding that being a good leader is inborn.

129. Consider the situation where all members of a watch have been given a copy of a recent change in the law. A training session has been scheduled to discuss dangers brought about by the new law. What is the most common mistake made during training?
a. assuming that the trainees know more than they actually do
b. not preparing for the equipment needed
c. the trainer not possessing the needed knowledge of the subject matter
d. the improper allotment of time for the demonstration

130. In the matter of internal discipline, the burden of proof is on
a. the courts.
b. the immediate supervisor.
c. the person presiding over the hearing.
d. the agency.

131. One of the common causes of work-related employee complaints is physical plant and equipment problems. Under which one of the following circumstances must a supervisor be relentless in his or her efforts to bring about repair or replacement of any deficiency in the physical plant or operating equipment?
   a. any complaints concerning operating equipment.
   b. problems that do not require significant expenditure of funds.
   c. problems that affect safety.
   d. complaints that have to do with cleanliness.

132. Once a supervisor has verified that a minor infraction has occurred and the offending employee has been identified, which of the following is the correct next step to take?
   a. discussing the matter with the offending employee
   b. making a report of the alleged incident
   c. contacting the internal affairs unit
   d. starting a full investigation

133. The success or failure of a police department is determined primarily by
   a. its ability to suppress and respond to crime.
   b. its ability to win public support.
   c. the happiness of its employees.
   d. political approval.

134. Upon being notified that a (nonpolice) strike is about to take place, what would it be best for a supervisor to do?
   a. notify his or her superior
   b. begin planning for the strike
   c. begin ordering resources and see that sufficient personnel are available
   d. go to the scene of the strike

135. What is the best first step for a supervisor to take when he or she hears a call concerning a missing five-year-old boy dispatched to one of his or her officers?
   a. Respond to the scene to ensure that the responding officers have gotten a good description of the missing person from the complainant.
   b. Detail a subordinate to ascertain if the responding officers have gotten a good description of the missing person from the complainant.
   c. Oversee the job and critique it afterwards.
   d. Delegate all tasks in this instance.

136. Which type of hostage captor or barricaded person creates the greatest difficulty for law enforcement?
   a. the professional criminal
   b. the professional criminal who has his or her escape blocked
   c. the emotionally disturbed person
   d. the terrorist

137. Law enforcement officers, because of the nature of their job, are given a tremendous amount of discretion. In order to keep such discretion from becoming capricious and arbitrary, a police administrator should establish
   a. procedure.
   b. policies.
   c. guidelines.
   d. rules and regulations.

138. While at the scene of an unusual occurrence, Sergeant Levy is in charge of setting up a command post. A command post should normally be all of the following EXCEPT
   a. inside the area of the unusual occurrence.
   b. easy to find.
   c. in an area where personnel and equipment can be assembled.
   d. near telephone and electrical power lines.

139. You are the supervisor at the scene of an ongoing labor dispute. The most important concern for law enforcement personnel assigned to the dispute is
   a. logistics associated with the scene.
   b. proper placement of the command post.
   c. ensuring that impartiality is maintained.
   d. maintaining viable communications.

140. You, as the sergeant in charge of a squad, receive an order from upper management that is in your opinion incomplete, confusing, or unclear. Which of the following is the best course of action for you to take under these conditions?
   a. Relay the order down the chain of command without comment.
   b. Relay the order down the chain of command and then seek clarification from your superiors.
   c. Relay the order, see if it is understood by the workers, and if not, then seek clarification from the source of the order.
   d. Seek clarification at the source before passing the information along.

141. Which of the following is the least accurate statement concerning complaints received against the police?
   a. Only in the case of nontrivial complaints should the complainant be notified of the results of the inquiry or investigation.
   b. The line supervisor handles any necessary minor corrective action, such as employee counseling.
   c. Most agencies generally allow the line supervisor receiving the complaint to handle the reception of the information, the investigation of the facts of the incident, and the reporting on the findings of the inquiry.
   d. The line supervisor may become involved at the review and disposition end of any departmental inquiry into serious allegations (for example, an allegation of criminal activity) against any of his or her subordinates.

142. Sergeant Kowalski is giving a lecture about order giving. When she discusses requests for volunteers, she should highlight that these types of orders should
   a. be used most often.
   b. be reserved for distasteful assignments.
   c. be reserved for dangerous assignments.
   d. never be used.

143. Which one of the following goes a long way toward preventing problems and abuses often associated with police corruption, incompetence, or misuse of authority? Choose the best answer.

a. training of police personnel

b. maintaining open lines of communication

c. maintaining good discipline programs

d. selection of police personnel

144. It is generally agreed among experts that police corruption is

a. new to rural areas.

b. restricted to large cities.

c. not restricted to any particular part of the country.

d. most common in medium-sized suburban departments.

145. According to experts in the field of community policing, in order to supervise effectively in an agency practicing community policing, a supervisor must be able to shift his or her attention away from numbers and too-rigid rules and focus on his or her employees'

a. response time for calls for service.

b. quickness in handling a call and returning to service.

c. knowledge of their area, their citizens, and the problems to be found there.

d. consistency in keeping him or her briefed on their problems, plans, and whereabouts.

146. Sergeant Alvarado reports to the scene of a bomb threat at a shopping mall. Regarding the evacuation of the mall, Sergeant Waters should know that the decision to evacuate should be made by

a. a supervisor at the rank of captain or above.

b. the manager or owner of the facility.

c. Sergeant Alvarado.

d. the chief of police.

147. Which one of the following is the best course for the supervisor to take to assess the safety knowledge of his or her fresh-from-the-academy rookies?

a. listening to them

b. questioning them

c. carefully observing their functioning on the street

d. testing them in a classroom setting

148. Sergeant Pollock is giving a lecture about a technically difficult subject. Sergeant Pollock should gear the difficulty of the material to

a. the lowest level of understanding in the class.

b. the highest level of understanding in the class.

c. the average level of understanding in the class.

d. a level equal to her own level.

149. Assume you are a supervisor in charge of a squad. One of your workers is Officer Tyler. From many occasions past, you know him to be a liar. Now, you are being transferred to a new squad and will meet with the supervisor who is to take over your old squad. Which of the following is the best course of action for you to take under the circumstances?

- **a.** Brief the new supervisor regarding the potential problem.
- **b.** Make no mention of Officer Tyler's problem and have the new supervisor discover the problem for himself.
- **c.** Make no mention of Officer Tyler's behavior to the new sergeant, but bring the situation to the attention of the new sergeant's superior officer.
- **d.** Make sure everyone on the squad knows about Tyler's past behavior.

150. A leader who gives off an attitude of self-confidence and self-control under stressful surroundings is displaying

- **a.** common sense leadership.
- **b.** bureaucratic leadership.
- **c.** command presence.
- **d.** storm-trooper command.

▶ Answers

Section 1:
Supervision and Management

1. **b.** Unwilling obedience resulting in little loyalty and no desire to support the common cause is known as *yielding*. Willing obedience, when workers follow because they want to do what their leader assigns to them, is far preferable.

2. **c.** Training the raters is the key to the successful administration of a rating system and is also its most usual source of weakness. If the training of those who are to do the rating is neglected, then the entire system will fail.

3. **a.** This type of leadership is best used in situations calling for emergency action. Usually there is no time to indulge in dialogue. A continuation of this leadership style, however, can lead to nervous frustration for the subordinates. The secret to good leadership is using the right type of leadership in the right situation.

4. **c.** This interview is also an excellent device for discovering personal characteristics, such as behavior and judgment under varying pressure situations. Of secondary importance is the giving of information about the position and the employing agency.

5. **b.** The most common rating error is known as the error of leniency. This error is often the product of inexperience and can have a detrimental effect on the performance of high-performing officers.

6. **d.** The primary function of the supervisor is to preside over the process of delegation. This requires all of his or her judgment and much of his or her time. He or she must constantly attempt to provide, by delegation, the opportunity to train so that the employee can grow. Choice **c** would be a primary function at a higher level of management. The task of dividing the work effort is not usually a supervisor sergeant's mandate.

7. **c.** The technique of nondirective counseling can be extremely productive. An employee-centered counseling session should be nondirective and should allow the employee to reflect on his or her problems. The interviewer must be skilled in listening and, above all, must allow for the interviewee to express him- or herself.

8. **d.** Rhetorical questions such as "She was in danger, right?" are questions that suggest a certain response; factual questions call for a specific answer. Both types are useful in starting or stimulating discussion on a subject requiring emphasis or elaboration. They keep the discussion focused while still eliciting a response.

9. **a.** Compensatory damages are those awarded because of actual loss of wages, medical expenses, or pain and suffering.

10. **b.** Experts agree that the initial conversation should ordinarily be directed toward the subordinate's performance rather than toward him or her as an individual. This will help in maintaining a professional relationship and eliminate the undue pressure usually associated with a personal critique.

11. **d.** If the supervisor has determined that the employee must be removed, then he or she must have already tried reprimand, positive discipline, and counseling. With no alternative method of inducing improvement in the employee's work performance, the negative form of discipline (punishment) must be administered before the employee can be removed from the force.

12. c. While research by experts indicates that adherence to formal channels within the hierarchy facilitates communications, morale is better in systems involving informal channels. In other words, while there must be a formal channel of communications, overstructuring communication leads to frustration among subordinates and superior officers alike.

13. d. This type of question is known as an overhead question. Overhead questions are utilized when you need to assess the level of participant comprehension of the lecture material.

14. b. The best choice is to receive the transcript of the proceedings and include it in the investigation file on the incident. In most jurisdictions, the county prosecutor, not the local prosecutor, will have jurisdiction in this type of incident. Given the likelihood that you will not have time to attend the inquest yourself, the best plan is to get a transcript of the proceedings.

15. d. When this rating error occurs, the outstanding worker doesn't receive his or her due credit. At the same time, the worker who barely gets through the day is rewarded—and all because the rating officer did not have the ability or courage to properly and objectively perform his or her rating duties. One can readily see why this type of supervisor is covertly (secretly) disrespected.

16. b. A supervisor must intervene immediately in situations of possible misconduct, both minor and serious, or in situations where the departmental reputation may be negatively affected, regardless of unity of command concerns.

17. a. Remember, directing is giving orders. Here's how it works: The sergeant organizes his or her equipment and personnel in the best fashion he or she can in order to get the job done. He or she then plans what the order is going to be or what it is going to entail and who is best to carry out the order. He or she then gives the order and follows its progress in order to coordinate equipment and personnel as he or she goes.

18. d. The degree of orderliness is directly related to the conduct and performance of the workers, which is a direct consequence of discipline in the department. The most important factor in achieving a high level of discipline within the organization is the first line supervisors. Usually, these are sergeants.

19. d. A supervisor should intervene in an officer's personal problems only when the officer's performance at work is being negatively affected or when the officer asks the supervisor for assistance. Even when asked for assistance, a supervisor should avoid attempting to solve any problems or give any affirmative advice.

20. b. The exception principle states that the supervisor handles exceptions to everyday procedures, and if it is to work effectively, the supervisor must free him- or herself of everyday tasks by delegating them down the line. So the best answer is **b**, delegation.

21. d. The supervisor who upholds a platform of "Do as I say, not as I do" will eventually relinquish any respect he or she may enjoy among his or her workers.

22. c. A supervisor should intervene in an officer's personal problems only when the officer's performance at work is being negatively affected or when the officer asks the supervisor for assistance. Remember, when an officer's personal problem begins to affect his or her performance, it no longer remains a personal problem.

23. b. Other examples of work divided by purpose are public relations activities, homicide units, and the like. Youth activities or juvenile offenses are examples of work groups organized in terms of clientele. Crime and forensic laboratories, garages, and the like are examples of work groups organized in terms of function.

24. a. While autocratic orders are an excellent means of delivering an emergency order—because of their speed and directness—you must guard against making arbitrary autocratic orders. One should not use autocratic orders in everyday situations.

25. b. The use of instructional aids is most important in these stages since it is at these junctures that most opportunities for the student to learn or to misunderstand occur. Instructional aids should never take the place of solid instruction but can help reduce boredom and fix points of instruction in the students' minds.

26. d. This type of interview is extremely valuable in determining possible reasons for the separation, regardless of its kind. This information in turn helps a lot in recruiting and hiring.

27. c. While choices **a**, **b**, and **d** all have their places in the classroom, attention is necessary for learning even to begin.

28. a. Unity of command requires that each employee have only one direct supervisor. (During emergency situations, the principle can be disregarded or bypassed.) Choice **b** describes span of control, while choice **c** relates to the principle of authority commensurate with responsibility.

29. c. *Noise* is widely interpreted as referring to any distractions that block effective communication, among them both environmental distractions, such as sirens or screaming, and stress.

30. a. Choice **a** is a false statement. In fact, the free-rein style of communication delivers a minimum of contacts, leaving subordinates to operate with very little or no supervision and guidance.

31. a. A supervisor should not filter any information. This is as true for both positive and negative information and upward or downward communication.

32. b. The exception principle dictates that a supervisor should only retain those work tasks that subordinate officers cannot perform. Remember, when delegating work, you must delegate the authority to complete and you retain the responsibility for the task.

33. c. This type of question can also be used in taking a partial response from one person and then redirecting the question to another. By the way, it can also be used effectively to quiet an overly talkative person, especially if the question is designed in such a fashion that it would be almost impossible for the person to answer.

34. c. The *first* thing a superior officer should do is set an example by his or her own conduct.

35. a. Most experts agree that instruction should generally move from the simple to the complex and from the safe to the hazardous and from the known to the unknown; as part of this overall view, they agree that the learner's starting point should also be the starting point of the lesson.

36. b. Written orders should be used in situations where complex operations or numerous persons are going to be affected, not only to ensure that all receive the order, but to make the order available for everyone to examine at his or her own pace.

37. b. Supervisors must continually review this type of plan to check its effectiveness. This process will not waste time, effort, or money; if anything, it will help the department protect itself against costly lawsuits.

38. a. The higher and wider the channels of communication and the more intricate they are, the more detailed the communication must be, and the more follow-up is needed for clarity and understanding. The simpler the department, the less chance there is that communications will be misunderstood.

39. a. Direct authority of supervisors over subordinates working in the field is the only kind of authority in a straight-line organization. In functional organizations, which are rare, responsibility and authority are parceled out according to specialty—for example, there might be a commander for juvenile affairs with authority over any personnel handling a juvenile case. In a line-and-staff organization, line commanders have authority over personnel working in the field, while staff personnel generate new ideas and give advice (with the force of a command) to line supervisors. No departments have staff organization only, since all require line personnel.

40. b. Staff officers usually have authority only over personnel assigned to them. Occasionally, however, the chief may give more authority to the staff officer; for example he or she could be responsible for instructing line officers how to fill out reports properly. Ordinarily, however, he or she will not have authority over line personnel outside his or her unit.

41. b. This is a tough one. The *chain of command* helps define what hierarchy is, but it isn't a principle of management. What has been violated in the scenario is the principle of *unity of command*, which requires that there be only one commander (that is, one direct supervisor) for each employee. *Span of control* lays out the number of employees that a commander in a given position can supervise. *Authority commensurate with responsibility* is a principle stating that anyone given responsibility for a task has to also be given enough authority to carry it out.

42. c. When a delegated task is completed to the point where the person delegating the task approves it without further instruction or amendment, it is referred to as "completed staff work."

43. a. Training is a form of positive discipline. A well-disciplined unit is a well-trained unit.

44. a. Functional overlapping between units occurs where one unit's work effort creeps into the other unit's work boundaries, usually without their knowledge, or when one unit does not know where its work stops and the other unit's work begins. A duplication of efforts occurs, causing friction.

45. c. This style of leadership will succeed most often in normal order giving or communications mainly because this method allows for input and feedback from those who are to be affected.

46. b. Mirrors allow the searchers to look behind packages and under tables and chairs and other objects without disturbing them.

47. d. Morale can vary due to numerous reasons and is not directly tied to the morale level of supervisors. In many instances, a sergeant's morale can be high and their subordinate officers' may be low.

48. a. The primary function is to obtain and transmit field intelligence to headquarters so that relief and control plans can be implemented without unnecessary delay. Communications to headquarters will help not only in evacuations, but in the actions listed in choices **b** and **d** also. Furthermore, the actions in **c** and **d** are usually not performed by police; at most, the police assist other agencies in these tasks.

49. a. A supervisor should avoid filtering information.

50. d. Supervisors do not need to have advanced or superior knowledge of all tasks they supervise; they need only have a good working knowledge of those tasks so that he or she can inform and instruct subordinates.

51. b. Specific objectives are specific goals that are to be achieved in the various segments of the lesson or lessons. The general and primary objective of any training is to affect job performance positively.

52. b. This rating error must be prevented, since it destroys the validity of the rating system. Personal bias can be reduced if the rater keeps records of his or her subordinate's behavior throughout the rating period. In this way the rater can examine the motives behind his or her ratings and keep prejudice and bias from creeping in.

53. d. Leniency is the most common rating error; it happens when the rating supervisor wants to not rock the boat. A rating supervisor who places too great store in being liked by all also tends to make widespread errors of this kind in evaluating personnel. This is probably most unfortunate for the subordinates who are doing a great job, since their evaluations don't stand out from the crowd the same way their actual work does.

54. a. Captain Brassner retains responsibility over the report. Remember, you can delegate work away, but you cannot delegate away responsibility.

55. b. One-day suspensions, unlike the other options, result in a loss of pay. Such a loss will hurt the employee's family as much as it hurts the employee, and therefore it is to be used only after other types of discipline have failed.

56. d. The tasks in **a**, **b**, and **c** are principally the responsibility of the fire department, while the task in **d** is the responsibility of the police department. In the absence of special requests from the fire department, the rookie police officer should work on **d**.

57. c. Once again, this is an example of selecting the choice that is the most inclusive. Once you ensure that the fire department (the expert group in this situation) is on the way, you can do the rest as needed.

58. b. The defense mechanism of denial usually appears in the second, or intermediate, stage of alcoholism. The astute supervisor should be aware of all the symptoms of problem drinking.

59. a. The fact that orders that are written down exist as a permanent record will create the ability to follow up if an order isn't carried out and will enable the supervisor to establish accountability.

60. c. All of the risks listed can result from regression, but the greatest risk from the point of view of the supervisor is the employee not doing his or her job.

61. a. This method is widely recommended. The idea is that raters should rate all the employees on one characteristic (for example, punctuality), then rate them all on another (for example, community relations), and so on, rather than rating one employee completely and then the next employee and then the next. Individual-trait rating helps reduce the tendency to let an employee's good performance in one area bring about a high score in another, unrelated area.

62. c. *General orders* (also known as *department policies*) are those issued to establish policy (the broad rules describing the general objectives of the organization). *Rules and regulations* cover specifics, not broad policy. *Tactical plans* concern unusual, emergency situations. *Operational plans* lay out the procedures for accomplishing everyday tasks, such as the procedure for responding to a domestic violence call.

63. c. A supervisor derives his or her official authority from management (even if he or she derives his or her practical authority from his or her subordinates).

64. c. When called for, discipline should be prompt and fair. Supervisors should avoid delaying discipline.

65. d. Negative discipline may involve the mildest form of punishment. It can range from a slight admonishment or oral reprimand to arrest and termination from the service. As long as it is punitive in nature, it is to be considered negative. All other forms of training are considered positive discipline.

66. c. Any change in operating procedure should be fully explained to subordinates. This explanation should also discuss the reasons for the change.

67. b. This is one of several conditions that affect the learning rate of students. When the teacher is aware of these conditions, he or she can better adapt his or her teaching methods to the students' learning ability.

68. d. At the highest level of the organizational structures, policies are basic. As you move down the organizational structure, policies need to become more detailed, until you reach the lowest level. At the lowest level, policies need to be the most detailed and exhaustive because this level is where the work will be taking place.

69. c. People have a desire to perform their jobs. When a person does not possess the skills necessary to perform a task, frustration can set in. In order to avoid frustration, a supervisor needs to place officers in positions where they are best suited.

70. c. There are no specialists in this type of department (thus **a** and **b** are wrong). As a result, supervisors often end up doing the work that specialists would do in a line-staff organization. It is actually an advantage of the line organization that the functional overlap referred to in **d** is mostly eliminated.

71. a. The most inclusive answer is **a**, management. Choices **b**, **c**, and **d** are all part of management.

72. a. The majority of police organizations will take the form of line and staff organizations. Note: The smallest police organizations usually take the form of line organizations.

73. a. In the role of a conference leader, it is important for the supervisor to remain neutral, something like a referee in a ball game. He or she should not be overbearing, instructive, or demonstrative, three types of behavior that will stifle initiative and thus weaken the conference.

74. b. Coordination of effort is paramount to good supervision. Observing and inspecting people and things that are designed to do a job helps ensure that the job gets done. Seeing that both materials and people are not being wasted is coordination of effort.

75. a. It is at the lower levels of the organization that the plans are usually going to be executed. Since these are the levels most likely to be affected, they should provide the most detailed input. Workers on the line possess vital knowledge and must contribute to planning in central, substantive ways.

76. d. The most common reaction to failure in human beings is rationalization. Humans attempt to mitigate their frustrations and embarrassment by creating excuses, thereby nullifying their responsibility to successfully complete the task.

77. d. When the organization increases in size, it usually gets more personnel, more area to be covered by the organization, and bigger building space. All these things require more precise coordination.

78. d. The majority of complaints against police officers involve noncriminal conduct. Most complaints concern discourteous treatment of the public and profane language. These complaints often stem from a perceived lack of empathy and a failure to communicate properly.

79. b. Attempts by staff officers to extend their authority too far into line functions can cause a lot of friction. Remember that a staff officer has jurisdiction within his or her own unit only; he or she should not attempt to exercise authority outside this domain except in recognized emergency situations.

80. a. Always imposing the same punishment for the same actions doesn't work in practice, even if it sounds good in principle. If an errant officer commits a rule infraction but is otherwise a very good officer, he or she should not be made to suffer the same punishment as the officer who has just committed the same infraction for the fifth time.

81. d. *Unity of command* concerns those who are commanded and not those who command. *Chain of command*, on the other hand, applies to the actual chain in the hierarchy (that is, sergeant, lieutenant, captain, and so on). The other answer choices are not relevant.

82. d. Most complaints against police involve non-criminal misconduct.

83. d. Records should sometimes be purged, but not automatically. The department should purge an errant employee's record of negative reports only if he or she has mended his or her ways and should determine its own time frame for doing so.

84. d. If the officer lacked training in the area that he or she failed in, then the failure is not on the officer's part but on the police department's part. It is the sergeant's responsibility to ascertain whether the department was negligent before concluding that the officer was at fault.

85. a. Regardless of the reason for the supervisor's disciplinary cases being overruled, the result will most probably be the same. The supervisor will be reluctant to bring about future actions unless they are flagrant.

86. c. The organization should establish the policy and procedures to be followed in the disposing of complaints against personnel. This is not only due to the influence of civilian review boards and the like, but also in order to thwart avoidable legal action against the organization.

87. b. Employee performance interviews are conducted in order to get the employee to engage in active self-appraisal. The goal of this self-appraisal is to get the officer to be aware of areas where he or she needs improvement and to create a plan to make the improvements.

88. b. As managers, supervisors become accustomed to speaking rather than listening; they learn how to give orders, speak to citizens, speak to subordinates' families, give lectures, and speak at affairs. Listening well takes enormous skill, but opportunities to practice it present themselves more rarely.

89. d. Once the supervisor realizes the grievance is real to the employee, the supervisor can take steps to allow his or her employee to vent his or her feelings. The supervisor should attempt to have the employee see for him- or herself that the grievance is without merit or, if it has merit, correct it. The employee should never be forced to think of him- or herself as foolish, nor should he or she be humored.

90. b. The missing basic human drive is the drive for new experiences, including curiosity, adventure, and craving for excitement. This drive motivates people more strongly than the desire to prevent change.

91. a. Managers can be developed from among the rank and file, provided they are motivated to achieve the position. This can be accomplished by providing incentives. The other thing that is needed is training. The individual must be trained in management and supervisory principles right from the start of his or her promotion and throughout his or her career.

92. c. Informal lines of communication, often referred to as the grapevine, exist in every organization, including police organizations. Informal lines of communication can be used to the benefit of savvy supervisors to help transmit information and gain an understanding of the sentiment of subordinate officers.

93. c. Street miles are the most reliable indicator of the need for patrol time. A large patrol area that consists of multiple square miles may have less need for patrol time than a small area that consists of multiple street miles.

94. c. Anytime you, as a sergeant, receive an order from management to delegate downward, you must support it as though it were your order. If the order is not working out or for any other reason you think the order is wrong, discuss it with management, not the workers.

95. b. The ability to follow up effectively is a very important skill for the supervisor; however, it is not an interpersonal skill. Moreover, you must communicate before you follow up. And you cannot earn respect or make referrals if you communicate poorly.

96. b. Some experts in the field of management refer to actual authority as "real" authority. In any event, it is that authority that is granted to you by your subordinates. Management establishes official authority.

97. c. For a supervisor to keep abreast of the information needed in order to make decisions, avoid problems, get to know his or her workers, and apply basic human behavioral traits, he or she must not restrict him- or herself to the use of formal communications networks but must utilize informal ones as well.

98. a. Such a person gets fixated on a problem that he or she never deals with directly. This person is one who continues to make the same mistakes over and over again and on whom correction has no effect.

99. b. Examples are gathering and disseminating intelligence, providing communication functions, and developing legal research. The staff manager usually acts in this capacity as an advisor, usually to line managers. However, the line officer is not obligated to follow the advice of the staff manager unless, of course, the order comes from the chief administrator.

100. a. Operating level managers (usually sergeants) also perform these functions, but to a different extent.

101. b. In this situation, the manager is directing his or her own subordinate. The subordinate must comply, so this is a line function. Had the manager offered advice to another commander in another unit, then that commander of the other unit would not have had to comply, so this would have been a staff function.

102. c. The delegation task does not contribute to rote assignments. On the contrary, the process yields interesting new assignments that subordinates are usually eager to execute. Among other things, failure to delegate makes for boredom among subordinates.

103. d. During the conclusion, the rater should make it clear that he or she is always approachable and should also explain the appeals process.

104. a. An existing collective bargaining agreement is a contract. Saying that the terms of the contract have been violated is stating a grievance.

105. d. Once the supervisor has verified that the infraction occurred, he or she must then take pains to ascertain with certainty which officer is being accused before taking further action. The exception is when the errant employee was observed during the infraction by the supervisor him- or herself.

106. a. Complaints involving minor infractions are best handled by the offending officer's immediate supervisor.

107. c. When all forms of positive discipline fail, negative discipline must be administered. Again, remember that the term *discipline* covers two kinds of measures: positive and negative. Positive discipline is training, while negative discipline is punishment.

108. a. One must not resort to counseling only after a problem occurs; communicating and counseling subordinates are a continuing responsibilities of supervisors.

109. a. Shift training is also known as *roll-call* training. It is used to good effect in introducing or reviewing topics in a short period of time (not more than 15 minutes).

110. c. While the impressive rank of an officer might have the tendency to attract the trainee's attention, if the trainer does not appeal somehow to the trainee's own best interests, his or her attention will be short-lived. There is no better way to keep the attention of students than to show them how the material being taught can benefit them in a practical way.

111. b. Notes should be taken at every counseling session, but supervisors should be cautious not to take notes during the session, as it may cause officers to become less forthright or unnecessarily nervous. Therefore, notes should be taken at the end of these sessions.

112. c. Agencies should periodically review their policies with the intent of purging the outdated rules and regulations, many of which are already being ignored by the rank and file. Leaving such rules and regulations on the books can lead to a lack of control and loss of morale when some supervisors attempt to keep discipline by enforcing old rules that other supervisors ignore.

113. d. A businesslike discussion is an interpersonal exchange of thoughts, words, views, and ideas between people. The dictionary says its purpose is to "meet to get information"; managerial wisdom proclaims that it should "change attitudes."

114. c. A police agency can decide labor by numerous factors including the geographical area it conducts its work in, the clientele it serves, or the function or purpose it serves. In this example, choices **a**, **b**, and **d** all serve unique functions or purposes. Choice **c** most likely represents a division of labor by geography.

115. b. The first consideration in the distribution of patrol personnel must be their assignment to shifts. Data must be analyzed by hour of the day, how much and what kind of crime occurs, and what and how many services are needed within the hours of the day until proper shifts are outlined and staffed accordingly.

116. b. Where crime is currently occurring, **c** is one factor to consider when distributing the patrol force and the needs of the citizens is another. Notice that choice **b** covers both these factors. Assign personnel in proportion to the need for service and not in equal numbers for every time of the day; if nighttime is heavier in crime and more patrol services are needed, then the larger proportion of the patrol force has to be assigned to the night shift.

117. b. Experts agree that different weights should be assigned to different types of calls for police service in figuring out how to assign units. For example, responding to a burglary report might be weighted as a three in such a system, while giving a traffic summons might be weighted as a one. This method is clearly subjective, since one person could reasonably decide that a burglary should be weighted as a three, while another could, for equally good reasons, weight it as a two.

118. d. The supervisor must pay more attention to attitudes, emotions, and the mood of the persons involved than to the setting for communication.

119. b. Greater difficulty in achieving effective communication generally results when the difference in status or rank is great. There tend to be more inhibitions on the lower-ranking officer addressing the higher-ranking officer than on officers in the reverse order.

120. b. Extensive cognitive testing proves this point. There is little doubt that what the learner thinks is important gets his or her attention.

121. b. Principles of supervision and management require the supervisor to engage his or her personnel in matters that affect them. In matters where their expertise and experience can not only clear up the facts but also help with the solution, they surely should be consulted.

122. c. While **d** is a prerequisite for ascertaining the competence level of the employee, it isn't directly relevant to training for a new job. When you couple knowing the differences between the requirements of the job with the employee competence level, as suggested in **c**, you can determine the training needs.

123. c. The principle of control is included in supervision. Supervision is included within management. Pyramiding is included within management. Once again, the correct response is the biggest (most inclusive) answer choice given.

124. d. The giveaway here is a group of people interacting for a purpose: This is organization in action.

125. c. Lateral communication entails open discussion between members of associated units. This is key to coordination of effort, because each unit is informed about the operations of the other units.

126. c. Choice **d**, the sergeant, is too general. The sergeant in charge of records, the computer room, the jail, or any unit other than the line unit does not bear the burden described. The line unit is where the greatest responsibility for discipline lies. Therefore, the correct answer must refer to the line officer. In addition, remember that the first line supervisor could be a lieutenant or corporal as well as a sergeant.

127. a. It would be very difficult, if not impossible, to obtain any other skill as a police supervisor without the ability to engage successfully in interpersonal relations. They come second only to breathing!

128. c. In situational questions of this nature, most of the question is just filler. The important part is the question within the question, and that is, "How do I get subordinates to willingly do a good job?" Clearly, accomplishing that is a matter of human relations, not study and not necessarily native leadership ability or protracted listening.

129. a. Assumptions in police work definitely have their place, considering that investigations would not get along too well without assumptions. Assumptions are rooted in criminal analysis, traffic accident reconstruction, and the like; however, they have no place in training. One should not assume that anyone knows anything.

130. d. It is the agency that is ultimately responsible for internal discipline, even though the agency does not expect the immediate supervisors to ignore their responsibility if they initiated the charge. Only when the matter is taken outside the department do the criminal or administrative courts take over.

131. c. Should safety problems continue after calling them to the attention of higher authorities, supervisors are obligated to lodge their own complaints. Remember that safety hazards in the workplace can be a violation of federal law, and a complaint can be lodged against the police agency under OSHA (the Occupational Safety and Health Act).

132. a. A prompt, private, and relatively informal discussion of the incident should be conducted between the offending officer and his immediate supervisor. As with almost any other employee interview, the supervisor should start the meeting by giving the employee some positive response to his performance and then introducing the specific matter at hand. The ultimate goal is to bring about improved performance in the future and not to inhibit or insult the employee.

133. a. The core responsibility of any police agency is to respond to and suppress criminal activity. Police agencies that are able to meet this responsibility effectively can be considered to be functioning properly. Next is the agency's ability to win the support of the public that it serves.

134. d. You never want to act before you get the facts. In this instance, before you would take any of the actions suggested in choices **a**, **b**, and **c**, you would want to get a good idea of the goings-on at the strike.

135. a. Some may feel that this is a routine enough complaint, where the supervisor can delegate a subordinate to handle the complaint and obtain a good description. But when a child this young is involved, the supervisor should respond personally to oversee the complaint. Complaints of missing children may be the results of serious criminal acts, and they should be treated as such until determined to be otherwise. Accuracy of physical description is critical when children are involved.

136. d. Once the professional criminal understands that he or she is "finished," he or she will usually surrender peacefully. The emotionally disturbed person can usually be talked into surrendering peacefully. Terrorists are different, because creating a dangerous or deadly situation is often their objective and, in such cases, they have little or no interest in having the situation resolved peacefully.

137. c. Discretion is a critical element of police work. It is not possible to enforce every law on the books all the time. However, in order for discretion not to become whimsical, guidelines must be promulgated and, preferably, made available in writing. In this way, the police and citizens know what to expect from each other. This will also put in place a system of checks and balances among agency personnel. The other answers do not concern discretionary situations.

138. a. If the site is dangerous, the command post should be set up outside of it. Furthermore, if the occurrence is a strike or demonstration of some sort, the command post should be set up outside in order to give the appearance of neutrality.

139. c. Answer **c** is crucial since even the appearance of partiality can lead to a needlessly dangerous situation. Toiletries, coffee machines, and the like should not be used by police officers unless the police force supplies them. Conversely, no one but police personnel should be allowed to use the police accommodations.

140. d. Contrary to popular belief, it is the duty of the person receiving an order to always make certain that it is, above all, legal, and then understood.

141. a. Whether the complaint is serious or trivial, the complainant must be notified of the result of the inquiry or investigation. More serious allegations, such as allegations of criminal acts by police employees, may be reported in writing by the line supervisor for a more detailed investigation by other members of the department, such as investigators from the internal affairs unit.

142. c. Requests for volunteers should be reserved for dangerous assignments. Other than this, these orders should be used rarely and should never be used to deflect distasteful work assignments.

143. d. This is another example of the test makers offering four good choices among which you must choose. However, a closer look reveals that choices **a**, **b**, and **c** address corrections of employees already on the job. Only answer **d** points to the original selection of police personnel. The idea is to pick the right person from the start, avoiding selecting a person with a propensity to be corrupt or incompetent or to misuse his or her authority.

144. c. Contrary to popular belief, police corruption is not restricted to any part of the country, nor is it restricted to major metropolitan police agencies. It may be rampant in a tiny rural or a medium-sized suburban department, while a nearby big city department remains quite clean.

145. c. Community policing does not reduce the line officers' accountability to their supervisor, but it does mean that they may be given extra time away from handling regular calls to try to find ways to reduce repeat calls for police service for the same problems.

146. b. The ultimate decision to evacuate a building or facility, such as a mall, rests with the owner or manager of the facility. Once the decision is made, the police will assist in any way possible with the evacuation process.

147. c. Once again, you must choose the best from a group of good answers. The best way to determine safety knowledge is to assess it personally. You can listen to your rookies tell you what they know about safety knowledge, or ask them if they know, or even test them in the classroom to see if they know, but that does not equate to putting safety knowledge into action where it can be inspected empirically.

148. c. When giving a lecture, the complexity of the material should be geared toward the average student in the class. If you make the information too complex, the lower performers will not gain any knowledge. If you make the information too simple, the high performers in the class may not be challenged by the information.

149. a. Being an effective supervisor is not a popularity contest. Whenever a problem with a subordinate is even suspected, it should be discussed with the officer's new supervisor so that the new supervisor can correct the problem. If you neglected to give information to the new supervisor, you would be held responsible if the problem grew to a point where someone were injured or worse.

150. c. The leader who stays cool under all conditions has command presence. He or she achieves a reputation that affords him or her great prestige among his or her personnel.

▶ Section 2: Criminal Procedure and Constitutional Law

1. Which of the following constitutional amendments is violated if counsel's performance is so inadequate that the defendant is denied a fair trial?
- **a.** Fourth
- **b.** Fifth
- **c.** Sixth
- **d.** Seventh

2. The Court has recently ruled that a dog sniff of luggage is not a search under the Fourth Amendment to the Constitution. Which of the following is required before a dog is allowed to sniff someone's luggage on an airport carousel?
- **a.** reasonable suspicion
- **b.** probable cause
- **c.** articulable suspicion
- **d.** nothing

3. With regard to a *Terry* frisk, which one of the following statements is least accurate?
- **a.** The officer need not be absolutely certain that the individual is armed.
- **b.** The issue is whether a reasonably prudent person in the circumstances would be warranted in the belief that his or her safety or that of others was in danger.
- **c.** In determining whether or not the officer acted reasonably in such circumstances, due weight must be given to vague but strong suspicions that something is wrong.
- **d.** In determining whether or not the officer acted reasonably, due weight must be given to the specific reasonable inferences from past experiences.

4. The following is a statement made by the Supreme Court in *Terry v. Ohio*:
> *It is intended to vindicate society's interest in having its law obeyed, and it is inevitably accompanied by future interference with the individual's freedom of movement, whether or not trial or conviction ultimately follows.*

What does this statement refer to?
- **a.** a frisk
- **b.** a full-blown search
- **c.** an arrest
- **d.** a stop

5. The courts have held that evidence or contraband found because of an unconstitutional search may be inadmissible in any court proceedings against the possessor of the material. This is known as the
- **a.** inadmissibility rule.
- **b.** good faith rule.
- **c.** constitutional rule.
- **d.** exclusionary rule.

6. If a state treats a class of indigent defendants differently for purposes of offering them the opportunity to appeal, which of the following is most seriously violated?
- **a.** Fifth, Sixth, and Fourteenth Amendments
- **b.** the due process clause of the Fifth and Fourteenth Amendments
- **c.** the due process clause of the Fourteenth Amendment
- **d.** the equal protection clause of the Fourteenth Amendment

7. According to the Constitution, no search warrant shall be issued except on a showing of
   a. reasonable suspicion.
   b. mere suspicion.
   c. probable cause.
   d. factual knowledge.

8. A provision in the Occupational Safety and Health Act (OSHA) that empowered agents to search, without a warrant, the work area of any employment facility within OSHA's jurisdiction for safety hazards was
   a. illegal, since a warrant is required under these circumstances.
   b. illegal, since particular exactitude is required to obtain a warrant, and none existed.
   c. legal, since this is considered an administrative search and a warrant is not required.
   d. legal, since the balancing test can be applied, balancing the needs of society against such minor intrusions.

9. Read the following very closely and choose the best answer. Which of the following most certainly requires Miranda warnings?
   a. a motorist being arrested for bank robbery and asked about the crime
   b. a motorist questioned at the roadside about a bank robbery
   c. a motorist suspected of driving while intoxicated being asked at the roadside how many drinks he or she had
   d. a motorist arrested at the roadside for bank robbery

10. In the landmark case of *Terry v. Ohio*, the Supreme Court applied which of the following tests?
   a. fear test
   b. reasonable suspicion test
   c. balancing test
   d. frisk test

11. According to the Supreme Court, which of the following may not issue an arrest warrant?
   a. court clerks
   b. nonlawyer magistrates
   c. judges
   d. prosecutors

12. Sergeant Vitry is at the scene of a homicide in the residence of Mrs. Couvillion. The body of Mr. Couvillion was taken out of the house by the medical examiner. Sergeant Vitry tells Mrs. Couvillion that other officers will be coming to set up a crime scene. Mrs. Couvillion tells Sergeant Vitry that she does not want the officers in her home anymore and that they are not allowed in unless they have a warrant. Sergeant Vitry should
   a. explain to Mrs. Couvillion that there is no need for a warrant due to the crime scene exception to the Fourth Amendment.
   b. explain to Mrs. Couvillion that there is no need for a warrant due to exigent circumstances.
   c. secure the scene and get a warrant.
   d. call her supervisor to the scene.

13. Which of the following is an example of a search within the meaning of the Fourth Amendment to the Constitution?
   a. use of a trained dog to sniff for narcotics
   b. use of a magnetometer to detect weapons at an international airport
   c. use of ultraviolet light to detect wrongdoing
   d. entering an unlocked apartment building and, through an imperfectly hung door, hearing conversations inside an apartment

14. Of the following, select the one that a defendant may choose to represent him or her at his or her criminal trial.
   a. his or her accountant
   b. a disbarred attorney who is a friend of the defendant
   c. the defendant him- or herself
   d. a prison inmate who has served time with the defendant

15. Police officers undertook a decoy operation in a high-crime area where young gang members were thought to have been snatching purses from passersby. An officer posing as an inebriated indigent smelling of alcohol and pretending to drink wine from a bottle plainly displayed $150 in currency. Two suspects then stole the money from the officer. The courts ruled that the decoy operation was
   a. legal, since the high-crime-rate area gave the police the right to use decoys.
   b. illegal, since the decoy situation did not match the method of operation used by the perpetrators of the unsolved crimes in the area, making it entrapment.
   c. legal, since the suspects were predisposed to commit the crime.
   d. illegal, since the Fifth, Sixth, and Fourteenth Amendments were violated in this situation.

16. The standard of proof required for conviction at a criminal trial is
   a. probable cause.
   b. preponderance of evidence.
   c. mere suspicion.
   d. beyond a reasonable doubt.

17. Which one of the following is considered to be "evanescent evidence"?
   a. a person's blood type
   b. a person's fingerprint type (whorls, arches, or loops)
   c. dried blood under a person's fingernails
   d. evidence

18. The primary legal advisor to the grand jury is
   a. the Constitution.
   b. the assignment judge.
   c. the prosecutor.
   d. the grand jury foreperson.

19. The touchstone of *reasonableness* under the Fourth Amendment is sufficient
   a. proof.
   b. particularity.
   c. probability.
   d. warranty.

20. The sergeant in charge of the detective squad had an eyewitness view two separate lineups. The witness was told that the suspect might or might not appear in the room being viewed. The suspect was not in the first lineup but was in the second. The sergeant wanted to guard against the possibility of the eyewitness simply being inclined to accuse someone, whether the eyewitness really recognized him or her or not. The lineup the sergeant used is referred to as a(n)

a. blank lineup.

b. reverse lineup.

c. bifurcated lineup.

d. exclusion lineup.

21. A police officer went to the home of Mr. Rupert to arrest him for the crime of burglary. During the search for the defendant, the detective observed a pair of shoes. He lifted the shoes up to observe the heels to see if they matched shoe prints found at the scene of the burglary. The detective's actions in lifting and examining the shoes were

a. legal, since probable cause existed to arrest the suspect, making it legal for the detective to search for "mere evidence."

b. legal, since the shoes were in the province of intimate personal control.

c. illegal, since such an examination goes beyond the scope of the Chimel rule.

d. illegal, since a warrant for such a search is required under the Fourth Amendment.

22. Which of the following describes the process by which the criminal justice system operates?

a. modulation effect

b. sieve effect

c. de facto effect

d. absorption effect

23. Sometimes an automobile can be searched without a warrant. Which of the following best describes the scope and limits of such warrantless searches?

a. when the officers have probable cause and know the nature of the container in which the contraband is secreted

b. when the officers know the object of the search and have probable cause for believing it is in the vehicle

c. when the officers are experienced, have probable cause, and know the type of vehicle to be searched

d. when the totality of the circumstances favor such a search

24. The court uses certain methods for appointing counsel. Which of the following is not one of the three systems used for the appointment of counsel to assist the indigent?

a. the assigned counsel system

b. the public defender system

c. the accepted counsel system

d. the mixed system

25. Under which of the following circumstances is a police officer required to give Miranda warnings to a suspect?

a. post-custody, post-interrogation

b. pre-custody, post-interrogation

c. post-interrogation, pre-indictment

d. post-custody, pre-interrogation

26. Which of the following searches is NOT a recognized exception to the Fourth Amendment warrant requirement?
  a. consent search
  b. movable vehicle search
  c. inventory search
  d. crime scene search

27. The advantage of the grand jury over conventional police investigations is seen in all of the following EXCEPT
  a. its ability to use the subpoena authority of the court that empanelled it.
  b. the control of the grand jury by knowledgeable prosecuting attorneys.
  c. grants of immunity.
  d. secrecy requirements.

28. Police officers were called to a hotel room after a maid saw a sawed-off shotgun there while cleaning. The room was not abandoned and was still under rental. The police in this instance could
  a. seize the weapon under the exigency rule as quoted in *Rochin v. California*.
  b. seize the weapon, since the gun posed an immediate danger to the community in general.
  c. not seize the weapon without a criminal search warrant.
  d. not seize the weapon without an administrative search warrant.

29. Under which of the following circumstances would Miranda warnings be required most?
  a. The police question a person at headquarters who is suspected of committing a crime.
  b. The police arrest someone and bring him or her to headquarters.
  c. The police stop someone on the street and question him or her.
  d. The police question a person about the crime they arrested him or her for.

30. A subpoena requiring the party who is summoned to appear in court to bring with him or her some document, piece of evidence, or other thing to be used or inspected by the court is most accurately referred to as a(n)
  a. writ.
  b. subpoena *duces tecum*.
  c. order to produce.
  d. subpoena *ad testificandum*.

31. Probable cause for arrest most nearly means
  a. evidence going beyond a mere hunch but less than that a crime has been or is being committed.
  b. evidence that would warrant an experienced police officer to believe that a person or persons unknown committed a crime.
  c. evidence that would warrant a prudent and reasonable person to believe that a particular person has committed or is committing a crime.
  d. a hunch that a particular person has committed a crime.

32. A police officer stopped a motorist who was weaving. The officer approached the vehicle in question and asked the driver to step out of the vehicle. Noticing that the driver had difficulty standing, the officer concluded that he would be charged with a traffic offense and not allowed to leave the scene. The officer did not tell the driver this. The officer administered a field sobriety test to the driver. The driver failed. The officer then asked the driver whether he had been using intoxicants. The driver replied that he had consumed two beers and smoked marijuana a short time before. In keeping with this, his speech was slurred. The officer then formally placed the driver under arrest. At no time during this sequence of events did anyone give the driver the Miranda warnings. The Supreme Court held that

a. the arrest was lawful based upon the officer's observations; any statement made in response to the officer's questioning must be suppressed without the benefit of a Miranda waiver.

b. both the arrest and the statements made by the defendant were inadmissible; the driver was seized when the officer's intentions to charge and not let the driver leave the scene became clear in his mind; Miranda warnings should have been given before any questioning.

c. both the arrest and the statements were admissible and Miranda warnings were not required under these circumstances.

d. the arrest and subsequent statements could not stand based on the fact that the arrest was the result of the fruits of the poisonous tree doctrine and not the Miranda application.

33. Mike Johnson is a 33-year-old man who resides with his elderly parents in their home. The police suspect that Mr. Johnson has illegal contraband stored in his room. The police go to his residence and speak with his father. The elder Mr. Johnson explains that his son is not home, but he gives the police permission to break into his son's locked room in order to search it. The elder Mr. Johnson further explains that he does not know if drugs are in his son's room, because he is not allowed to go in there. The police do so and find a kilogram of cocaine. The search by the police was

a. constitutional; the officers did not need a search warrant because they had the homeowner's consent.

b. unconstitutional; Mr. Johnson had an expectation of privacy in his room, so the police needed a warrant to search it.

c. constitutional; the police had exigent circumstances.

d. unconstitutional; Mr. Johnson was not present.

34. Patricia Clofer is a 20-year-old woman who resides with her sister in her sister's home. Her sister suspects that Ms. Clofer has illegal drugs in her room. The sister breaks into Ms. Clofer's room and finds the drugs in the middle of Ms. Clofer's bed. She brings the drugs to the police. At any subsequent trial for the possession of the drugs, the drugs will be

a. inadmissible; the sister did not have a search warrant.

b. admissible; the drugs were in plain view, so no warrant was needed.

c. inadmissible; the sister broke into the room to find the drugs.

d. admissible; constitutional protections do not protect citizens from actions of other citizens.

35. Police officers obtained a warrant to search the living room of the home of the defendant to seize three marijuana plants. The police entered the home and immediately found the three plants in the living room. The police officers then searched the rest of the house for more plants and discovered several more in the kitchen and basement. The courts ruled that the search and seizure were

    a. legal for the first three plants but illegal for the additional plants.

    b. legal for all of the plants.

    c. illegal for the first three plants but legal for the additional plants.

    d. legal for the first three plants under the search warrant, and legal for the additional plants under the doctrine of plain view.

36. Which of the following is most relevant to the question of whether a warrant is required for the routine inventory search of an impounded vehicle?

    a. the Carroll Rule

    b. the protective property rule

    c. the community caretaking function

    d. the purpose of the search

37. Which of the following is considered to be the linchpin in determining the admissibility of witness identification testimony?

    a. experience

    b. reliability

    c. subjectivity

    d. objectivity

38. The purpose of the exclusionary rule is to

    a. deter searches by nongovernment officials.

    b. deter police from using tainted evidence.

    c. deter verdicts based on the fruit of a poisonous tree.

    d. deter unreasonable searches by government officials.

39. The principal objective of the Fourth Amendment is the protection of

    a. privacy.

    b. citizens.

    c. places.

    d. property.

40. Officers were called to the scene of a possible burglary. They found the rear door open and entered. Inside, they found no evidence of a burglary, but the officers did find numerous boxes containing expensive televisions. The officers suspected that the televisions were stolen. One of the officers opened a box, pulled out the television, and wrote down the serial number. The officer called headquarters, ran the serial numbers, and determined that the televisions were indeed stolen. Just then, the owner of the house walked in and was placed under arrest for possession of the stolen televisions. The trial judge should determine that the televisions are

    a. admissible; the officers were lawfully in the house and the televisions were in plain view.

    b. inadmissible; the officers were in the house lawfully and the televisions were in plain view, but the officers illegally seized the televisions before they know they were stolen.

c. admissible; the officers needed no search warrant because they were lawfully investigating a burglary.

d. inadmissible; the officers had no lawful right to be in the apartment.

41. When a police detective has applied for a search warrant, which of the following determines whether or not there is sufficient probable cause for the warrant?

a. the judge only

b. the detective only

c. the judge and the detective

d. the judge, the detective, and any other person named in the affidavit

42. Brett Clayton is running a crystal meth lab out of a hotel room. The police suspect that he is conducting this operation out of this room. When he is not there, they go to the hotel owner and ask him if he would consent to a search of his property and open the room. He consents and gets his extra key to open the room. Upon opening the room, the police find large quantities of crystal meth inside. Mr. Clayton is later arrested for possession of the drugs. At his trial, the drugs would be

a. inadmissible; the hotel owner had no right to consent to a search of the room.

b. admissible; the hotel owner is the only person with a right to privacy to the room.

c. inadmissible; the hotel owner needs a warrant to consent to the search.

d. admissible; you sign away your rights when you fill out the hotel rental agreement.

43. The crux of the Supreme Court's ruling in *Terry v. Ohio* was

a. the propriety of the officer taking steps to investigate the suspects' suspicious behavior.

b. whether there existed probable cause for the original stop and subsequently fear to frisk.

c. whether there was justification for the police officer's invasion of Terry's personal security by searching him for weapons.

d. whether there was reasonable suspicion for the original stop based on the experience of the officer coupled with fear to frisk for weapons.

44. Which of the following statements is most accurate concerning the power to frisk?

a. It is founded upon a reasonable suspicion, which in turn is founded upon the officer's experience.

b. It is not considered to be a search within the meaning of the Fourth Amendment.

c. It is not an exception to the probable cause rule in search and seizure.

d. Facts must be established from which an inference that the suspect is armed and dangerous can be made.

45. Which of the following is a recognized exception to the Miranda rule?
- **a.** good faith
- **b.** public safety
- **c.** inevitable discovery
- **d.** the exclusionary rule

46. In which type of area would the courts in the United States relax the particularity requirement when the police apply for search warrants?
- **a.** urban areas
- **b.** rural areas
- **c.** suburban areas
- **d.** depressed areas

47. When a police officer fails to administer a legally required Miranda warning, what is created?
- **a.** a presumption of *mens rea*
- **b.** a presumption of compulsion
- **c.** a presumption of innocence
- **d.** a presumption of misunderstanding

48. Two police detectives responded to Mr. Park's house armed with an arrest warrant for him for burglary. Mr. Park's mother let them in and led the officers to Mr. Park's room. Without telling him that the police had a warrant for his arrest, one of the detectives stated he "felt" Mr. Park was involved in the burglary in question. Mr. Park replied, "Yes, I was there." Mr. Park was then transported to police headquarters and, approximately an hour later, one of the detectives advised Mr. Park of his Miranda rights for the first time and then took a written statement detailing Mr. Park's involvement in the burglary. The Supreme Court held that
- **a.** the first statement, "Yes, I was there," was admissible at trial since it was not coerced and was considered voluntary; the second statement was also admissible.
- **b.** the first statement was not admissible at trial, since it was a violation of Miranda rights; the second statement was inadmissible at trial because it was tainted by the first statement.
- **c.** the first statement, "Yes, I was there," was not admissible at trial; the second statement was admissible, since it was not an outgrowth of the coerced first statement.
- **d.** the first statement, "Yes, I was there," was not admissible because it was considered a fruit of the poisonous tree; the second statement was admissible, since it was a rebuttable presumption.

49. Does a person actually have to die in order to have his or her dying declaration admitted into the courtroom proceeding?

   a. No, a dying declaration is admissible as long as the declarer believed he or she was going to die.

   b. Yes, a dying declaration is admissible only if the person is deceased.

   c. No, a dying declaration is presumed to be the truth.

   d. Yes, or else it would just be a *res jeste* statement.

50. Two police officers approach Mr. George, who is wanted for murdering his wife. They apprehend him. While they are transporting him to headquarters for arrest processing, Mr. George begins to cry and says, "I need to get this off of my chest; I killed my wife . . . I should be punished." Mr. George was in custody at the time he made the statement, but the officers had not advised him of his right against self-incrimination as required by Miranda. Is the statement admissible for evidentiary purposes at Mr. George's subsequent trial?

   a. Yes; Mr. George was not officially in custody for the purposes of Miranda until he reached a police department facility.

   b. No; Mr. George was in custody and not advised of his rights; therefore, the statement is not admissible.

   c. Yes; though Mr. George was in custody, he was not questioned by the police, so his statements were spontaneous utterances.

   d. No; Mr. George did not make a formal confession.

51. Of the following, what would NOT be considered as "suppressible fruit" under the Constitution?

   a. an illegally arrested defendant

   b. narcotics seized in violation of the Fourth Amendment

   c. a weapon seized as a result of an invalid consent search

   d. a dead body as evidence in a murder

52. A police officer is called to the scene of a burglary in progress. As the officer approaches the home, the burglar runs out of the home and runs toward the backyard in order to get away. The officer can see that the burglar has some jewelry in his hands, but the burglar has no weapons. The officer yells, "Stop, or I'll shoot." For the officer to shoot the burglar to prevent his escape would be

   a. constitutional; the person committed a felony.

   b. unconstitutional; at this angle he would shoot the burglar in the back.

   c. constitutional; the person had proceeds from the crime.

   d. unconstitutional; this would be an unconstitutional seizure.

53. Officer Walker sees a vehicle that he believes is transporting drugs. Officer Walker would like to stop the vehicle to question the driver, but he has no independent reason to do so. Officer Walker follows the vehicle and observes the vehicle cross a lane of traffic without signaling. Officer Walker stops the vehicle based upon the traffic violation, with the intent of questioning the driver about the transportation of drugs. Regarding this pretext stop, the court has ruled that pretext stops are

a. unconstitutional, because the motivation for the stop is to discover contraband, not enforce traffic law.

b. constitutional, regardless of the motivation of the officer.

c. unconstitutional, because no probable cause exists that contraband is located in the vehicle.

d. constitutional, and the vehicle can be subsequently searched based upon the violation of the traffic law.

54. A police officer suspects that an illegal sports betting ring is being conducted out of a home. The police officer stakes out the house and observes the homeowner bringing a large quantity of trash out to the curb. The officer drives up, loads the trash into his car, and brings it back to headquarters, even though he does not have a warrant to search through the trash. He searches through the trash and finds used betting slips and other evidence of illegal betting. At the trial, the evidence found because of this warrantless search would be

a. admissible; it was in plain view.

b. inadmissible; it was not in plain view, so a warrant was needed.

c. admissible; you do not need a warrant to search through trash.

d. inadmissible; the officer needed a search warrant.

55. A man was arrested and taken to police headquarters. He was given Miranda warnings and waived his rights. While being interrogated, unbeknownst to the interrogating officers, an attorney from the public defender's office called police headquarters. The attorney stated that the suspect's sister hired her on her brother's behalf to handle the case. The police officer who received the phone call failed to notify the interrogating officers; subsequently, a confession was obtained from the suspect. The suspect was never mistreated in any way. The court ruled that the confession was

a. legal, because there was no bad faith on the part of the interrogating officers and the suspect voluntarily waived his rights.

b. legal, because a trustworthy waiver under Miranda was obtained.

c. illegal, because the defendant's Fifth Amendment privilege against self-incrimination was violated.

d. illegal, because the defendant's Sixth Amendment right to counsel was violated.

56. Two police officers are transporting a suspect accused of kidnapping and murdering a young girl. The suspect has just been taken into custody pending an investigation, but the girl's body has not been located. The subject is uncooperative and has not been notified of his rights under Miranda, so the detectives instruct the officers not to question him regarding the crime. The officers begin to talk to each other. One officer says, "It's a shame that the family will not get to bury their young girl." The other officer agrees and says, "Yeah, that girl should at least have the decency of a good burial." Upon hearing this, the suspect says, "I did it . . . and I'll tell you where the body is so she can have a good burial." The suspect's statement would be

a. admissible; it was a spontaneous admission.

b. inadmissible; he was in custody and was not yet read his rights.

c. admissible; he does not need to be read his rights until he is arrested.

d. inadmissible; it was in violation of his right to avoid self-incrimination.

57. The term *critical stage* as used by the Supreme Court most accurately refers to

a. the point at which the right to counsel first arises.

b. the point at which the police first supply the suspect with an attorney.

c. the point at which the right to counsel attaches.

d. the point at which counsel is first requested by the suspect.

58. A man is arrested and taken to police headquarters; he is about to be questioned regarding the crime for which he was arrested. The suspect is given his Miranda warnings and indicates that he wants an attorney. Select the statement that is most accurate regarding this situation.

a. All questioning must cease and the suspect can never be questioned again regarding the crime surrounding this particular arrest.

b. The police can question the suspect if they readvise him of his Miranda rights.

c. All contact with the suspect must cease until an attorney arrives.

d. The police can discuss the crime in question with the suspect if the suspect initiates the conversation.

59. The right to counsel first arises at what stage of the criminal justice process?

a. arrest and interrogation

b. reasonable suspicion

c. appearance before a magistrate

d. indictment

60. A police officer is called to respond to the scene of a robbery in progress. Upon arrival, the officer observes the suspect with a large gun in her hand, and a shootout ensues. The officer shoots and injures the suspect. The suspect runs down an alley, hides the gun, and falls to the ground. The officer runs up to the suspect, handcuffs her, and informs her that she is under arrest. The officer then asks the suspect where she hid the gun. The suspect tells her the location, and the officer retrieves the gun. At her trial, the suspect points out that the officer never read her rights to her and moved to suppress the gun. At trial, the gun would be

a. admissible; it was in plain view.

b. inadmissible; the officer conducted an interrogation of an arrested suspect without reading her rights to her.

c. admissible; the court has held that this type of questioning is allowable under a public safety exception to Miranda.

d. inadmissible; it was fruit of a poisonous tree.

61. A man is arrested and taken back to police headquarters. Shortly thereafter, the suspect is read his Miranda rights. The suspect states that he will not talk to the police until he has an attorney present. The police decide not to talk to the suspect, and they process him and put him in the local jail. The next day, he is arraigned. The police now decide they want to question him. The suspect did not make bail, so the police go to the jail to begin the interrogation of the suspect. At what present stage of the criminal justice process are we?

a. Fifth Amendment setting, critical stage

b. Sixth Amendment setting, critical stage

c. interrogation stage, Fifth Amendment setting, critical stage

d. Sixth Amendment setting, noncritical stage

62. Sergeant Everly suspects Conrad Hilmer of possessing illegal drugs. His wife gives consent to the police to search her and her husband's bedroom for the illegal drugs. Regarding the consent search, Sergeant Everly should know that

a. the suspect's wife cannot give consent to search the room.

b. both Mr. Hilmer and his wife must consent to the search before it can take place.

c. regardless of consent, a warrant is still needed.

d. the suspect's wife can consent to a search, because they both have a right to privacy in the shared room.

63. A person is arrested and shortly thereafter put before witnesses in a corporal lineup for identification purposes. Which of the following is the most accurate statement?

a. The suspect is entitled to have an attorney present before the lineup commences but not during the lineup procedure.

b. The suspect is not entitled to have an attorney present before or during the lineup procedure.

c. The suspect is entitled to have an attorney present during the lineup, but the attorney must act only as an observer and cannot interfere with the lineup process.

d. The suspect is entitled to have an attorney present before and during the lineup procedure and the attorney can act as counsel by giving legal advice to his or her client before and during the process.

64. The police arrest a man for armed robbery. The suspect is taken to police headquarters and shortly thereafter given his rights as contained in the Miranda warnings. The suspect attaches his rights not to talk with police and also states that he wants his lawyer present. The police decide they do not need to question the suspect, so they process him without questioning. Several days later the suspect is indicted for armed robbery. Subsequently, the police conduct a postindictment photographic identification proceeding whereby witnesses pick out the suspect's photograph as being that of the robber. Choose the most accurate statement.
   a. The police violated the suspect's Fifth Amendment rights by not affording him an attorney at the photographic array.
   b. The police violated the suspect's Sixth Amendment right to counsel by not affording the suspect an attorney to be present at the photographic array.
   c. The suspect's rights were not violated and he did not have the right to have an attorney present during a postindictment photographic array.
   d. The suspect's rights were not violated because he did not ask for an attorney to be present, in spite of the fact that this procedure is considered a critical stage.

65. The Supreme Court has concluded that a person has been "seized" within the meaning of the Fourth Amendment only if certain circumstances existed. Under which of the following circumstances would the court most likely find that a seizure has taken place?
   a. a reasonable person would believe that he or she was not free to leave
   b. a reasonable and prudent police officer would believe that the suspect was not free to leave
   c. a police officer intended to place the person under arrest
   d. two police officers asked a person on the street to explain his or her reason for being there

66. A man is approached on the street by police officers. The police officers have a reasonable suspicion that the person they are talking to might be the one who robbed a bank the previous week. They do not have probable cause that he robbed the bank in question. The police inform the suspect that he is a suspect in the robbery. The suspect states that there is no problem and that he will be glad to help. The police then inquire as to whether or not the suspect participated in the bank robbery. The suspect says, "No." In this scenario, which of the following statements is most accurate?
   a. The suspect has been seized within the meaning of the Fourth Amendment to the Constitution.
   b. The suspect has not been seized within the meaning of the Fourth Amendment, since the police have a right to make an inquiry without more than a reasonable suspicion.
   c. Not only did the police seize this suspect within the meaning of the Fourth Amendment, but any questioning should have been preceded by Miranda warnings.
   d. The suspect was not seized within the meaning of the Fourth Amendment, since the police were armed with reasonable suspicion.

67. Two police officers stop a man on the street who they have reasonable suspicion committed a bank robbery. The police approach the suspect and tell him that they suspect him in the bank robbery. The suspect says that he wants to leave and starts walking away. The police order him to stay, and the suspect does so, but against his will. One police officer asks the suspect, "Did you participate in the bank robbery?" The suspect replies, "Yeah, I did it." The suspect is then placed under arrest. Select the statement that is most accurate.

a. The police seized the suspect within the meaning of the Fourth Amendment once they ordered him to remain for an investigation into the bank robbery, but any questions asked after that seizure required Miranda warnings.

b. The suspect was not seized within the meaning of the Fourth Amendment, and since the suspect was not in custody, his statement, "Yeah, I did it," is admissible against him.

c. The police did not seize the suspect within the meaning of the Fourth Amendment, and Miranda warnings were necessary before they questioned him.

d. The police seized the suspect within the meaning of the Fourth Amendment when they ordered him to remain, but Miranda warnings were not necessary, and the statement, "Yeah, I did it," can be lawfully used against him.

68. The police are armed with a reasonable suspicion that a particular man shoplifted a CD player. They have occasion to stop the suspect in order to conduct a *Terry* investigation or a *Terry* stop. The purpose of the stop, or "field investigation," as it is sometimes called, is to determine, insofar as is possible, whether or not the suspect stole the CD player. The police tell the suspect that he is not free to leave and that they may frisk him. Based on this scenario, which one of the following statements is most accurate?

a. The police have a reasonable suspicion that a crime has occurred and that the suspect did it, so they can immediately frisk the suspect for weapons.

b. The police can lawfully pat-down the suspect's outermost garments to find evidence.

c. In order to lawfully frisk the suspect at all, the police need to establish a separate and distinct reasonable suspicion that the suspect is armed and dangerous and must conduct the pat-down for weapons only.

d. The police, having a reasonable suspicion that a crime has occurred and that the suspect did it, are free to conduct a stop and frisk.

69. Which one of the following statements is most accurate with regard to the *Terry v. Ohio* frisk or pat-down?

a. The *Terry* frisk is not considered a search within the meaning of the Fourth Amendment, but only a limited pat-down of the outermost garment.

b. The *Terry* frisk is for the purpose of searching for any dangerous or contraband material and requires probable cause to be justified.

c. The *Terry* frisk is allowed by the Supreme Court for the purpose of preventing the imminent destruction of evidence, for the protection of the officer against weapons use, and to prevent an escape, and only requires reasonable suspicion.

d. The *Terry* frisk requires reasonable suspicion that the suspect is armed and dangerous and is considered a search within the meaning of the Constitution.

70. The *Terry* stop is considered a seizure within the meaning of the Fourth Amendment just as the frisk is considered a search. Which of the following statements most accurately further describes the *Terry* stop?

a. The stop requires only a reasonable suspicion that the suspect is armed and dangerous.

b. The stop requires probable cause to believe that a crime has been committed, is being committed, or will be committed and that the suspect is involved.

c. The stop requires a reasonable suspicion that the suspect has committed, is committing, or will commit a crime.

d. The stop requires a reasonable suspicion that the suspect has committed, is committing, or will commit a crime and that the suspect is armed and dangerous.

71. A police officer makes a stop of a motor vehicle after observing the driver go through a red light. The officer approaches the vehicle and recognizes the driver as a man wanted for a burglary that occurred about a month before. The officer informs the driver, who is the only occupant of the car, that he is under arrest for burglary. The officer places the man in handcuffs and escorts him to the rear of the patrol vehicle, which is parked about 10 feet behind the suspect's car. The officer then sees you, his sergeant, approach the scene. He asks you if and how he can lawfully search the suspect's vehicle. What should you tell him?

a. He can search the suspect and the entire motor vehicle as a search incidental to a lawful arrest.

b. He can search the suspect and the entire vehicle as a search based on probable cause.

c. He can search the suspect and the passenger compartment as a search incidental to a lawful arrest.

d. He can search the suspect only, since once the suspect is secured in handcuffs, the search of the vehicle is not allowed as a search incident to a lawful arrest.

72. Choose the statement that most accurately describes rules regarding a search incidental to a lawful arrest.

a. The search may occur immediately before the arrest.

b. The search may not occur until the arrest is complete.

c. A warrant is required for the search to be legal.

d. The suspect must consent to being searched.

73. The extent of a lawful search of the passenger compartment of a motor vehicle incidental to a lawful arrest depends upon
   a. the accessibility of the driver.
   b. the seriousness of the crime for which the driver is being arrested.
   c. the object of the search.
   d. whether the driver is secured or not.

74. Which one of the following is most accurate with regard to a search incidental to a lawful arrest?
   a. It is designed to block a successful escape by the suspect, and for the discovery of weapons but not evidence.
   b. It is designed to inventory the suspect's belongings, and for the prevention of weapons use against the arresting officers and others.
   c. It is designed to protect against escape, the destruction of evidence, and the use of weapons against the arresting officers or others.
   d. It is designed to protect against escape, destruction of evidence, the use of weapons, and for inventory of the suspect's belongings to protect against unfair claims.

75. One of your officers makes an arrest of a suspect who is operating a motor vehicle at the time. The arrest is lawful and the suspect is handcuffed and placed in the rear of the officer's patrol car. The suspect is then transported to police headquarters and the vehicle is searched some 15 minutes later (while the suspect is at police headquarters). The most accurate conclusion that can be drawn from the above scenario is that
   a. the search is lawful because the arrest is lawful.
   b. the search is unlawful because too much time elapsed between the arrest and the search.
   c. the search is lawful; it is an inventory search, not a search incidental to a lawful arrest.
   d. the search is unlawful due to the handcuffing.

76. When a police officer has probable cause to search a moving motor vehicle on a highway, then he or she may lawfully search
   a. only the passenger compartment of the vehicle and any containers found therein, whether open or closed.
   b. only the passenger compartment of the vehicle, but not those compartments of persons who are not in control of the vehicle.
   c. the entire vehicle for the object that is being searched for.
   d. none of the vehicle's contents; a warrant must be sought.

77. Assuming the police have probable cause that a particular container is located within the trunk of a motor vehicle, which one of the following statements is most accurate?
   a. The police may lawfully search the trunk and seize the object; however, a search warrant must be obtained to open the package.
   b. The police may lawfully search the entire vehicle, starting with the passenger compartment and then leading the search to the trunk, where the object, if seized, may be opened without first obtaining a search warrant.
   c. Because of the particularity clause of the Fourth Amendment, a search warrant must be obtained.
   d. The police may lawfully search the trunk of the vehicle, seize the object of the search without a search warrant, and open it without first obtaining a search warrant.

78. Officer Juniper suspects that Jim Selma is about to commit a crime. Officer Juniper does not have probable cause, but she has very strong reasonable suspicion. Officer Juniper approaches Mr. Selma, stops him so he is not free to go, and begins to question him. During the questioning, Officer Juniper sees a large bulge in Mr. Selma's jacket pocket. Officer Juniper frisks the jacket and feels a gun. Officer Juniper seizes the gun and places Mr. Selma under arrest. Officer Juniper's actions were
   a. proper; she is allowed to conduct a limited search in this situation.
   b. improper; she conducted a search without a warrant.
   c. proper; she had probable cause to believe Mr. Selma had a gun.
   d. improper; Mr. Selma did not commit a crime yet.

79. Which of the following is always needed in order to lawfully conduct a search of a readily movable motor vehicle on a public highway?
   a. a lesser expectation of privacy
   b. reasonable suspicion that there is evidence of a crime inside
   c. a search warrant
   d. probable cause

80. If the police wish to search a readily movable motor vehicle that is located on private property, which of the following is needed for the search to be lawful?
   a. an arrest warrant
   b. probable cause
   c. reasonable suspicion
   d. a search warrant

81. Sergeant Santos has made numerous drug arrests on a particular highway that is known for vehicles transporting cocaine. Sergeant Santos instructs his officers to set up a roadblock in order to find drug traffickers, just as they do for people driving under the influence of alcohol. This type of roadblock is
   a. constitutional; the courts have approved it.
   b. unconstitutional; the court has ruled that it is unreasonable.
   c. constitutional; the police can always set up roadblocks.
   d. unconstitutional; you need a warrant for a roadblock.

82. According to recent Supreme Court decisions, which of the following criteria are needed for the plain view doctrine to apply?
   a. officers lawfully in the viewing area, incriminating nature of the evidence immediately apparent
   b. officers lawfully in the viewing area, incriminating nature of the evidence immediately apparent, inadvertent discovery
   c. officers lawfully in the area, officers cognizant, incriminating nature of the evidence immediately apparent, inadvertent discovery
   d. police officer there legally, incriminating nature of the evidence immediately apparent, probable cause for search

83. The "immediately apparent" prong of the plain view doctrine means that, upon viewing the object, the police must immediately have a reasonable suspicion that the item they are viewing
   a. is associated with contraband or is otherwise evidence of a crime.
   b. is in danger of being displaced before the police will have an opportunity to get a warrant.
   c. presents a clear and present danger either to the police themselves or to people in the vicinity.
   d. was instrumental in carrying out a crime.

84. With regard to the plain view doctrine, which one of the following statements is most accurate?
   a. The plain view doctrine is considered by the Supreme Court to be a recognized exception to the written-warrant requirement.
   b. If the viewing in the plain view doctrine is lawful, then it rightfully follows that seizure would also be lawful.
   c. The plain view doctrine is considered a prior justification supplementation.
   d. According to the Supreme Court, there are three prongs that must be lawfully fulfilled in the plain view doctrine: the "lawfully present" prong, the "immediately apparent" prong, and the "inadvertent" prong.

85. Officer Martinez pulls over Matt Santos. As Officer Martinez approaches the vehicle, he peers into the back window of the car and sees a large quantity of marijuana on the backseat. Officer Martinez arrests Mr. Santos. At trial, the marijuana would be
   a. admissible; it was in plain view.
   b. inadmissible; the officer searched the vehicle without a warrant.
   c. admissible; upon stopping a vehicle for a traffic violation, an officer can search the entire vehicle.
   d. inadmissible; the stop was improper.

86. Which of the following has the Supreme Court indicated regarding contraband objects already in plain view?
   a. Observation of the objects is legal but seizure without a warrant is illegal.
   b. Observation and seizure are legal as long as the viewer is independently justified in being in a position to see and seize the objects.
   c. Testimony based on such viewing is to be considered hearsay evidence.
   d. If the objects are inside the confines of a private home, no testimony about the objects will be admitted as evidence.

87. A police officer is walking on the sidewalk on his beat. He observes a plant in a second-story window of a private house. The police officer is an expert in narcotics, and he has no difficulty whatsoever in categorizing the plant in question as an adult marijuana plant. Based on this information, which one of the following statements is most accurate?

a. The officer's viewing is illegal and the officer may not even request a search warrant.

b. The officer clearly has all the necessary prongs needed for the lawful viewing of the marijuana plant, but he needs a search warrant to seize the plant.

c. The officer's viewing is illegal and seizure of the plant would also be illegal.

d. The officer is lawfully in the viewing area, the plant is immediately apparent as contraband, and he can seize the plant without a warrant.

88. The government made a warrantless naked-eye aerial observation, at an altitude of 1,000 feet, of marijuana plants growing in a person's fenced-in backyard curtilage (the *curtilage* is the area immediately adjacent to a home). The Supreme Court ruled the action in this case to be

a. legal, since in this case the person had no expectation of privacy from commercial air space, observed from 1,000 feet.

b. illegal, since a person has a reasonable expectation of privacy within the curtilage of his or her home regardless of the distance of air-space observation.

c. legal, because the person took no effort to conceal the plants in question.

d. illegal, because a search warrant should have been secured for the viewing and the seizure of the marijuana plants.

89. There is a constitutional protection against coerced statements obtained from a police officer that prohibits use of these statements in a subsequent criminal proceeding if the statements were obtained under threat of removal from office. Which of the following cases explicitly establishes that this protection exists?

a. *Garrity v. New Jersey*

b. *Miranda v. Arizona*

c. *Ohio v. Rendez*

d. *Michigan v. Summers*

90. A police officer suspected of wrongdoing may be compelled to respond to administrative questions

a. only if he or she is advised of his or her Miranda rights.

b. even if he or she is not advised of his or her Miranda rights as long as he or she is not in custody.

c. about the performance of his or her duties.

d. about his or her duties if his or her answers are not used against him or her in criminal proceedings; if he or she refuses, he or she can be terminated.

91. Consider this hypothetical scenario: There is a special grand jury sitting for the United States. The jury is investigating unlawful organized crime transactions. The jury subpoenas a woman to testify in a murder case about which she has information. The woman complains that if she speaks before the grand jury she will almost certainly be killed. Which one of the following statements is most accurate?

a. If it can be proved by a preponderance of the evidence that the woman will be seriously injured or killed as a direct result of her testimony, then she can be excused from testifying.

b. If it can be proved that the woman will be at risk of injury or death by clear and convincing evidence, then her subpoena to testify will be annulled.

c. The woman will have to testify regardless of any threats or evidence that she will be injured or killed.

d. If it can be proved that the witness will be in jeopardy, her testimony will be secret and sealed and her identity withheld.

92. A basic principle of Fourth Amendment law is that searches and seizures inside a home without a warrant are

a. conclusively unreasonable.

b. conclusively reasonable.

c. presumptively unreasonable.

d. presumptively reasonable.

93. What does a police officer in the United States need in order to conduct a lawful, valid, and thorough search?

a. probable cause

b. reasonable suspicion

c. knowledge of a serious crime

d. a search warrant

94. One of your officers asks you, "Hey, Sergeant, we have an arrest warrant for Mr. Lamb. We are going to his friend's house to serve it because Lamb likes to hang out there. Are we OK with this idea?" How should you respond?

a. Tell the officers they are OK and the arrest warrant authorizes them to go wherever Lamb is located within the jurisdiction of the state in order to arrest him.

b. Inform your officers that in order to go to the house of anyone not named in the arrest warrant, absent consent or an exigency to enter, they will need a search warrant.

c. Tell your officers that regardless of the circumstances, when they arrive at the house in question, they will need a search warrant.

d. Inform your officers that they should obtain a telephonic warrant before trying the house in question.

95. Grand juries for all practical purposes are an investigative arm of

a. the judicial branch of government.

b. the executive branch of government.

c. the legislative branch of government.

d. all three branches of government depending upon the circumstances for which they are convened.

96. Which one of the following statements is least likely to be considered an "open field" for Fourth Amendment purposes?
  a. those areas immediately adjacent to a house but lacking in fencing or any other manifestation of an expectation of privacy
  b. a thickly wooded area with no trespassing signs
  c. a sparsely wooded area with no trespassing signs clearly manifesting an expectation of privacy
  d. an open field with no trespassing signs and a fence with barbed wire to ward off trespassers

97. Which of the following is true with regard to probable cause?
  a. Probable cause is an objective good-faith belief.
  b. It is sufficient to prove that guilt is more probable than innocence.
  c. It is only necessary that the information lead a reasonable officer to believe that guilt is more than a possibility.
  d. It is less than clear and convincing evidence of guilt but more than a preponderance of proof.

98. Airport screening searches of potential passengers for weapons and explosives are held to be reasonable under the Fourth Amendment provided
  a. probable cause exists for the search.
  b. reasonable doubt exists for the search.
  c. prospective boarders receive warning before the search begins.
  d. the prospective boarder retains the right to leave rather than submit to the search.

99. The only question about detaining an arrested person pending further proceedings is
  a. whether counsel has been provided.
  b. whether compulsory process for witnesses has been afforded.
  c. whether there is probable cause.
  d. whether or not the state required a full preliminary hearing.

100. Which of the following is most accurate? The Constitution is
  a. what the legislatures say it is.
  b. what the judges say it is.
  c. what the executive branch of government determines it to be.
  d. a rigid instrument.

▶ Answers

Section 2: Criminal Procedure and Constitutional Law

1. c. When counsel is not afforded, it is a violation of the Sixth Amendment's right to counsel. It is implicit in this that a defendant has the right to the assistance of effective counsel.

2. d. The dog is an extension of the police officer. If the police officer needs a reasonable suspicion to stop and investigate, then the dog needs the same. However, if the officer isn't required to meet any standard, for example at the public carousel at an airport, then the dog isn't either.

3. c. The officer's suspicions must be specific. In determining whether or not the officer acted reasonably in such circumstance, due weight must be given by the court to the officer's particularized suspicion or hunch that the suspect is armed and dangerous.

4. c. Remember that for an arrest, the court requires the government to have probable cause. For an investigatory stop or a frisk, the court requires the police to have a quantum of belief equated to a reasonable suspicion.

5. d. The exclusionary rule dictates that any evidence or contraband found as the result of an unconstitutional search may be inadmissible in any trial or proceeding against the possessor of that material.

6. d. When the rights of a class of individuals are violated, the equal protection clause of the Fourteenth Amendment is violated. The Fourteenth Amendment is commonly referred to as the "civil rights amendment."

7. c. The Fourth Amendment of the Constitution specifically requires there be probable cause before any search warrant can be issued. In addition to probable cause, the warrant must describe the place to be searched and the articles or people to be seized.

8. a. In the case of *Marshall v. Barlow's, Inc.*, 436 U.S. 307 (1978), the court held that in order for inspections of employment facilities within OSHA's jurisdiction to be undertaken, there must be a warrant based on probable cause. The court stated that to allow otherwise would frustrate the provisions of the Fourth Amendment. This kind of warrant is commonly referred to as an "administrative warrant."

9. a. Miranda warnings are required only when two things are happening: arrest and interrogation. If the situation does not involve both arrest and interrogation, Miranda is not required. The only choice above that contains both prongs, arrest and interrogation, is answer **a.**

10. c. The Court balances intrusion on the individual's privacy against the interests of society in effective law enforcement.

11. d. The Court in *Shadwick v. City of Tampa*, 407 U.S. 3455 (1972) rejected the notion that all warrant authority must reside exclusively in a lawyer or judge and noted that even within the federal system warrants were until recently widely issued by nonlawyers. The court concluded that an issuing magistrate must meet two tests: He or she must be neutral and detached, and he or she must be capable of determining whether probable cause exists for the requested arrest or search. The clerk or magistrate possesses the requisite detachment and can in principle determine if there is probable cause. Prosecutors are not neutral and detached.

12. c. According to the Supreme Court, there is no crime scene exception to the Fourth

Amendment. In order to search the home of Mrs. Couvillion, the police would need a warrant barring any exigent circumstances. Because the body of Mr. Couvillion had already been removed, the exigency was over and a warrant would be needed.

13. b. The use of the magnetometer to detect weapons is a search, and so is the use of an X-ray machine.

14. c. A defendant can represent him- or herself at his or her own criminal trial provided the judge holds a hearing to determine that the defendant is mentally sound. The defendant must abide by the rules of evidence as an attorney. The court can, however, appoint a standby attorney over the objections of the defendant.

15. b. The courts throughout the United States are not in agreement with respect to the objective and subjective tests for an entrapment defense. For the most part, the objective test focuses on whether the government acted properly and not on the predisposition of the suspect. The subjective test is the defendant's predisposition to commit the crime.

16. b. In order to convict a person on criminal charges, it must be demonstrated beyond a reasonable doubt that a crime was committed and that the accused committed it. In a civil trial, the standard of proof is a preponderance of evidence, a lower standard.

17. c. *Evanescent evidence* is that which "lasts or stays only a short time." Typically, it is evidence that is easily destroyed. This phrase is important because the court will determine if an exigency exists by analyzing whether or not the evidence is evanescent. (*Exigency* means "a situation requiring immediate action.")

18. c. In most jurisdictions, the grand jury foreperson is in charge of the grand jury, but the legal advisor is the prosecutor assigned to the case.

19. c. Probable cause is determined by a probability of guilt. It is a judgement call that should be made on the premise that there is a reasonable belief that guilt is more than possible. It is not necessary to prove that it is more probable that the subject is guilty than that he or she is innocent.

20. a. The purpose of the blank lineup is to guard against the danger that an eyewitness will assume that the suspect is present in the lineup and thus tend to identify the person who most nearly resembles the person he or she saw. For these reasons, most commentators have urged the use of the blank lineup; note that it is very difficult for defense counsels to discredit evidence from blank lineups.

21. b. In hearing a case like this, the court explained that since the police were lawfully present to arrest the defendant and the shoes were in plain view, "to view the heels of shoes was within the province of intimate personal control."

22. b. Experts in the field of criminal justice explain that if one were to draw a diagram of the criminal justice process, charting the number of people processed in each state, the shape of the diagram would resemble a funnel. As the caseloads move through the system, it sifts out cases. (Note: A *sieve* is a strainer or sifter.)

23. b. The Supreme Court held that the scope of a warrantless search of an automobile "shall be defined by where the object may be found," not by the nature of the container in which the contraband is secreted. The officers are legally obligated to limit their search to the areas where there is probable cause to believe that the object of the search will be found.

24. c. Under the assigned counsel system, an individual attorney is selected by the court to represent a particular indigent defendant. The public defender system relies upon a state-funded legal office. The mixed system uses elements of both of the other systems.

25. d. Remember that generally Miranda is applicable when two criteria are met: (i) the suspect has been rendered into custody, and (ii) prior to interrogation. Both criteria must be met; if one is missing, Miranda is not applicable.

26. d. There is no crime scene exception to the Fourth Amendment warrant requirement. All the searches in answer choices **a**, **b**, and **c** are recognized exceptions.

27. b. The prosecuting attorneys do not control grand jury investigations. In most jurisdictions, the people sitting on the jury cannot only disregard the prosecutor's advice, but even go off on their own, repudiating the prosecutor altogether. (This is referred to as a "runaway grand jury.")

28. b. In this case, the D.C. District Circuit Court stated that the presence of a sawed-off shotgun posed an immediate danger to the safety of the community in general and more particularly to the police who had responded to the management's call. *United States v. McKinney*, 477 F. 2nd 1184 (D.C. Cir. 1973).

29. d. Remember the two prongs necessary for Miranda warnings to generally apply: custody and interrogation. Custody is when a person's freedom of movement has been curtailed in any significant way. Interrogation is questioning designed to elicit statements from a person that can be used against that person in a criminal matter. Note the difference between *questioning* and *interrogation*. If one is questioned about one's height, weight, age, and the like,

this is just questioning. If one is questioned and one's statements can be used against one in a criminal matter, that is interrogation.

30. b. The term *duces tecum* is Latin for "bring with you." A subpoena *ad testificandum* is the technical term for the ordinary subpoena to testify.

31. c. Against **b**, the Court does not restrict its definition to an experienced police officer, but to a prudent person. (Remember that in some instances a judge establishes probable cause.) Choice **b** also lacks the particularity clause of the Fourth Amendment to the Constitution.

32. c. The Court stated that although technically the driver was seized when the police officer had stopped his car and detained him, he had not been taken into custody for Miranda purposes until he had been formally arrested. Thus the statements made by the driver prior to his arrest were admissible against him. Again, remember that two criteria are required for Miranda to trigger: custody and interrogation. In this instance, custody was missing. *Berkemer v. McCarty*, 468 U.S. 420 (1984).

33. b. Mr. Johnson had an expectation of privacy in his room. His father could not consent to a search of his son's room, even though he was the owner of the home. The father had proprietary right to his son's room, as evidenced by the fact that he stated that he was not allowed in the room. The police would need a warrant or consent to search from Mr. Johnson.

34. d. The protections outlined in the Constitution do not protect citizens against the unconstitutional actions of other citizens. They protect citizens only against the unconstitutional activities of the government or governmental agents, such as police officers.

35. a. When a search warrant is issued, it commands the police to search the area particularly described in the warrant for the items particularly described in the warrant. Once the object of the search is discovered and lawfully seized, the search is over. The exception is that if, during the course of the lawful search, the police view contraband or other evidence of a crime, they may seize it under the plain view doctrine.

36. d. Inventory searches are not conducted in order to discover evidence of crime. For that reason, there is no need to establish probable cause and no warrant is involved.

37. b. This is evaluated by considering the witness's opportunity to see the criminal at the time of the crime, the witness's degree of attention, the accuracy of his or her prior description of the criminal, the level of certainty demonstrated at the confrontation, and the time between the crime and the confrontation. The corrupting effects of any suggestive evidence must be weighed against those factors.

38. d. The exclusionary rule was created by the Supreme Court to deter official misconduct. It is a prophylactic rule to protect the constitutional rights of individuals. It operates to deter not only police misconduct, but misconduct by any government official. It does not pertain to private citizens.

39. a. The Supreme Court made a very simple statement on this subject: The principal object of the Fourth Amendment is the protection of privacy, rather than property. The question, then, is what society is prepared to accept as private.

40. b. The officers were lawfully in the house, because they were investigating a possible crime in progress. The televisions were in plain view, but the officers did not readily recognize them as being contraband. In addition, the officer seized the televisions without a warrant when they exercised control to open the box and read off the serial number. This is not a plain view exception to the requirement for a search warrant.

41. a. Whether a warrant is issued depends on whether a detached and neutral magistrate determines that the facts presented establish probable cause for the search and/or seizure. The police, who are in the business of continuously stamping out crime, are not in a position to be neutral or detached.

42. a. For legal purposes, when Mr. Clayton paid for the room, he became the sole occupant and the sole person with a right to privacy concerning the contents of the room. Although the hotel owner has sole proprietary rights to the entire complex, when he rented the room to Mr. Clayton, he deeded away his right to that room for the period of the rental agreement. Therefore, the owner could not consent to a search of Mr. Clayton's room.

43. c. The court was admittedly concerned not only with the government interest in investigating the crime but with the immediate interest of the police officer in taking steps to assure himself that the person with whom he was dealing was not armed with a weapon to use against him.

44. d. Choice **a** is true with regard to stopping suspects but not with regard to frisking them. Remember that the stop and the frisk are separate actions and a particularized articulable suspicion must be established for each. In other words, for the stop, a police officer must be able to articulate his or her reasonable suspicion that the person he or she stopped was involved in criminal activity. For the frisk, the officer must be able to point to particular facts that led him or her to believe the person he or she had stopped was armed and dangerous. *Terry v. Ohio*, 392 U.S. 1, 88 Sup. Ct. 1868, 20 L. Ed. 2d 889 (1968).

45. b. In a landmark case, the police had a rape suspect in custody and subsequently asked the suspect where his gun was. The suspect responded by pointing out where his gun was located. This was an incriminating statement, and for that reason the State of New York excluded the statement. The Supreme Court admitted the statement and established the public safety exception to the Miranda warnings. The Court concluded that overriding considerations of public safety justified the officer's failure to provide Miranda warnings before he questioned the suspect in this case. *New York v. Quarles*, 104 Sup. Ct. 2626, 81 L. Ed. 2d 550 (1984).

46. b. Courts in the United States have held that less particularity is required for rural premises; for example, description of a farm by name of the owner and general direction for reaching the farm is adequate. The Supreme Court has stated that "it is enough if the description is such that the officer with a search warrant can, with reasonable effort, ascertain and identify the place intended."

47. b. When police ask questions of a suspect in custody without administering the required warning, Miranda dictates that the answers received be presumed to be compelled and that they be excluded from evidence at trial in the state's case-to-be. Also, the court stated that the presumption is irrebuttable, meaning that when Miranda is violated there is a bright-line rule that the answers were compelled.

48. c. Remember, when a person is rendered in custody and is going to be interrogated, Miranda warnings are applicable. If they are not forthcoming, the court will presume that any answers the police receive were compelled. In this case, the first statement was compelled but not coerced to the point where it nullified or tainted the second statement.

49. b. A dying declaration is considered hearsay, but it is an exception to the hearsay rule. Therefore, a dying declaration is admissible only if the person is deceased. If the person is not deceased, the person will be available to give actual testimony and be subjected to cross-examination; the declaration would not be needed.

50. c. Mr. George was under arrest and therefore in custody, but the police did not question him. Instead, he made a voluntary statement sometimes called a "spontaneous utterance," or *res jeste* statement. Miranda attaches only when a person is in custody and is subjected to a police interrogation or questioning. Mr. George's statements would be admissible in the case against him.

51. a. Although an illegal arrest or other unreasonable seizure of a person is itself a violation of the Fourth and Fourteenth Amendments, the exclusionary sanction comes into play only when the police have obtained evidence as a result of the unconstitutional seizure. The Supreme Court has held that an illegally arrested defendant "is not himself a suppressible fruit and the illegality of his detention cannot deprive the Government of the opportunity to prove his guilt through the introduction of evidence wholly untainted by the police misconduct in his illegal arrest." *United States v. Crews*, 445 U.S. 463 (1980).

52. d. The Supreme Court, in *Tennessee v. Garner*, ruled that the use of deadly physical force to apprehend an unarmed, non-dangerous fleeing felon is an unconstitutional seizure; therefore, it is barred by the Fourth Amendment.

53. b. In *Wren v. United States*, the Supreme Court ruled that the motivation of a police officer conducting a pretext stop is irrelevant under the Constitution as long as there is probable cause to believe that a traffic violation has occurred.

54. c. The court has ruled that there is no expectation of privacy to trash once it is brought to the curb of a home. The reason for this is that you are now placing it in the public domain for all to see, including trash collectors. (Note: This is not true of trash still on your property that has not yet been put out for collection.) Therefore, a warrant is not needed and the evidence is admissible.

55. c. It is a provision of the Fifth Amendment that people cannot be forced to incriminate themselves; during the interrogation stage described in the example, the suspect had the right to protection from self-incrimination by virtue of this amendment. It is a consequence of the Sixth Amendment that after a suspect has been formally charged, or after the courts have become involved in some other way, the right to counsel attaches: That is, the suspect must be given the opportunity to retain counsel before being questioned. That stage had not been reached in the present example, since the suspect hadn't been formally charged and hadn't yet appeared before a magistrate.

56. a. The suspect was in custody for Miranda purposes, but the officers did not interrogate him. They were talking with each other and never addressed any statements to the suspect. Had they questioned him, his statements would not be admissible.

57. c. As noted in the comments on question 55, it is a consequence of the Sixth Amendment that after a suspect has been formally charged, or after the courts have become involved in some other way, the right to counsel attaches—that is, the suspect must be given the opportunity to retain counsel before being questioned. The critical stages in the judicial process are arraignment, indictment, formal charge, and first appearance before a magistrate. Formal charges and/or appearance before a magistrate trigger the right to counsel.

58. d. Once counsel is requested, all questioning must stop and the police have two options: (i) get the suspect an attorney before any resumption of questioning occurs, or (ii) resume questioning if the suspect initiates the conversation.

59. a. The time of arrest is the commencement of the adversarial judicial process, and it is at this time that the court recognizes a Fifth Amendment setting. It is also at this juncture, prior to any questioning that could elicit incriminating statements from the suspect, that Miranda rights must be given, and it is at this stage that the right to counsel first arises. (It does not attach at this point.)

60. c. The gun would be admissible under the public safety exception to Miranda. The court has allowed this type of question when it deems that the threat to public safety far outweighs the constitutional violation.

61. b. The right to counsel has attached and the suspect must be given an attorney at this stage or his or her Sixth Amendment (not Fifth Amendment) right to counsel will be violated.

62. d. When two people share a room, either person can give the police consent to search the room without a warrant.

63. b. This is not a critical stage; therefore, the right to an attorney has not attached. The suspect is not entitled to have an attorney present during a preindictment lineup.

64. c. The Supreme Court has held that a photographic display conducted after adversary proceedings have begun is not considered a critical stage. The court has stated that the Sixth Amendment right to counsel has always been limited to "trial-like confrontations" between prosecuting authorities and the accused, where the lawyer acts as a spokesperson for or advisor to the accused.

65. a. The subjective intention of the police is not of the same value as the "objective" conduct of the police. The court will review whether actions by the police would have made a reasonable person feel that he or she was not free to leave. This is referred to as the *objective test of custody*.

66. b. The court has established that when the police approach someone and that person's freedom of movement has not been restricted, and the actions of the police do not lead that person to believe he or she is not free to leave, then that person is not seized within the meaning of the Fourth Amendment. The questions posed to the suspect are a mere inquiry and do not have to be preceded by Miranda warnings, since the suspect is not in custody.

67. d. Once the suspect was ordered to remain against his will, he was seized. It was legal for the police to detain him against his will because they had reasonable suspicion that he committed a bank robbery. Even though this was a seizure within the meaning of the Fourth Amendment, it was not custody for Miranda purposes and no warnings were necessary. The suspect in this scenario is distinguished from the one in question 66 because in this scenario, the police had to use a command to make the suspect remain.

68. c. In order to conduct a stop of a person to investigate criminal activity, the government needs an articulable reasonable suspicion that a crime has occurred and that the individual is involved. This does not, however, give the government the right to frisk the suspect. In order to conduct a frisk or pat-down of the suspect lawfully, a separate, individualized reasonable suspicion that the suspect is armed and dangerous is required. Furthermore, the frisk or pat-down of the suspect is allowed only to uncover weapons.

69. d. The frisk is allowed by the court only for the purpose of finding weapons. However, if during the lawful frisk of a suspect, the officer becomes immediately certain through the sense of touch that there is probable cause to believe the suspect has contraband in his or her possession, then the officer is allowed to retrieve the contraband as well.

70. c. Be sure to notice that the reasonable suspicion the police need to stop someone is different from what they need to frisk him or her. Even if the police have a reasonable suspicion that the suspect is involved in criminal activity (and that therefore they can stop him or her), it doesn't follow that the suspect can be lawfully frisked. The frisk requires the separate and distinct reasonable suspicion that the individual is armed.

71. c. The search of the passenger compartment and any containers, whether open or closed, within the passenger compartment is lawful as "a search incidental to a lawful arrest."

72. a. The search can be lawfully accomplished before the arrest as long as the search is "contemporaneous" to the arrest. In other words, when probable cause exists for the arrest, the search can lawfully occur just prior to the arrest. (*Contemporaneous* means "existing or occurring at the same time; concurrent.")

73. a. If the arrest is lawful, the search is contemporaneous with the arrest, and the suspect is located within a motor vehicle, then the extent of the area to be searched depends on accessibility. In other words, how far can the driver reach prior to and after the arrest?

74. c. The "search incidental to a lawful arrest" is a recognized exception to the written warrant requirement and is for the purpose outlined in choice **c.**

75. b. The search in this instance was not contemporaneous in time with the arrest. Furthermore, too much distance was put between the suspect and his or her vehicle.

76. c. This is the doctrine laid down by the Supreme Court in *Chambers v. Maroney* and *United States v. Carroll*. The court allows the search of a motor vehicle without a search warrant in circumstances where the vehicle is in public and readily mobile.

77. d. The law in this area was set down by the Supreme Court in 1991 in *California v. Acevedo*. When probable cause exists, the police may search for the object of the search, seize it, and open it without obtaining a warrant. In the above scenario, the police would have to restrict their search to the trunk, because that is where they have the probable cause to search.

78. a. Officer Juniper's actions were proper. She conducted a *Terry* stop. According to that

case, an officer who reasonably suspects that someone is engaged in criminal activity may stop that person and may further search that person for any weapons.

79. d. The question asks about a vehicle that is readily movable and on a public street; such a situation creates the exigency, meaning that the only further thing needed is probable cause.

80. d. In this instance, the vehicle is on private property, and therefore its owner enjoys the constitutional right to privacy. Probable cause in this instance is not enough. Absent probable cause and an exigency or consent to search, a search warrant is needed.

81. b. The court has ruled that roadblocks carried out for drug interdiction are unreasonable, but they are allowed for DWI interdiction and random vehicle safety checks.

82. a. The "inadvertent discovery" prong that was necessary in the past is no longer necessary. Now it is required that the discoverer be on the premises lawfully and that the incriminating nature of the evidence be immediately apparent.

83. a. The "immediately apparent" prong means that the police must have probable cause to associate the item with contraband or reasonable suspicion that it is evidence of a crime.

84. c. In spite of a very popular yet erroneous belief, the plain view doctrine is not an exception to the written-warrant requirement. The police must have a prior justification for lawfully being in the viewing area, that is, a warrant for another object, hot pursuit, search incident to a lawful arrest, or some other legitimate reason for being present in the viewing area. *Horton v. California*, 496 U.S. 128 and 466 (1990).

85. a. The marijuana was in plain view. The court has ruled that the action of peering into a car window by a police officer does not constitute a search; therefore, no warrant was needed.

86. b. The person making the observation and seizure of an article must have a legitimate justification for being able to view and seize it. For an example, try the next question.

87. b. This question is not only an actual case scenario but a good illustration of a difficult and rarely known concept of procedural law. In this case, even though the police officer is lawfully within the viewing area and has the "immediately apparent" prong (probable cause to associate the item with contraband), he cannot seize the plant, because it is located in an area where there is an expectation of privacy. The police officer does not have a prior justification for being there. So the viewing of the plant is legal, but the seizure, without a consent, exigency, or search warrant, would not be.

88. a. In this case, the court stated, "in an age where private and commercial flight in the public airways is routine, it is unreasonable for a person to expect that his marijuana plants growing within his fenced-in-back-yard curtilage were constitutionally protected from being observed with the naked eye from an altitude of 1,000 feet." *California v. Ciraolo*, 476, U.S. 207 (1986).

89. a. When in an administrative questioning session a law enforcement officer is ordered to give a statement of the facts under threat of discharge, that statement may not thereafter be used against the officer in a criminal proceeding.

90. d. This case is *Lefkowitz v. Turley*, 414 U.S. 70 (1973). If the officer is advised of his Miranda rights and voluntarily waives them, his statements can be used against him administratively and criminally. If, on the other hand, he chooses to remain silent after being read his rights, then he can lose his job for failure to speak about his duties when ordered to do so.

91. c. The only way the witness can be excused from testifying is if it is ruled by the administrative judge that her testimony could be incriminating to her in a criminal matter. Even then, if the court grants her immunity, she will have to testify.

92. c. Simply stated, if the police have occasion to enter the home without a search warrant, the court will look at the police action, right from the start, as unreasonable and the state will have the heavy burden of proving that the search was reasonable. In contrast, if the police enter with a warrant, the entry will be presumed to be reasonable.

93. d. Probable cause isn't good enough. The best choice by far is **d**, a search warrant. Only with probable cause and an exigency can you circumvent the warrant requirement. Remember, if you act without a warrant, you are presumed to have acted unreasonably until you prove otherwise. You cannot search with reasonable suspicion alone either. If you're thinking of a pat-down search, you must recall that a pat-down search is allowed by the courts only for weapons.

94. b. For Fourth Amendment purposes, an arrest warrant founded on probable cause implicitly carries with it the limited authority to enter a dwelling in which the suspect lives when there is reason to believe he is inside. Absent consent or exigent circumstances, however, law enforcement officers may not legally search for the subject of an arrest warrant in the home of a third party without first obtaining a search warrant.

95. a. Federal grand juries are called into existence by order of the district court. They are for all practical purposes an investigative and prosecutorial arm of the judicial branch of government. There are basic and general similarities among state grand juries and some subtle differences. You are encouraged to check with your local police advisers for the rules governing your particular state grand jury procedures.

96. a. The curtilage is the area immediately adjacent to a home. Technically, it is the area to which the intimate activity associated with the sanctity of one's home and the privacies of life extends. It is considered part of the home itself for Fourth Amendment purposes. Choices **b**, **c**, and **d** describe areas that are not constitutionally protected; they are considered "open fields." *Oliver v. United States*, 104 Sup. Ct. 1735 (1984).

97. c. Probable cause to arrest refers to that quantum of belief which would lead a police officer, acting as a reasonable person, to believe that the defendant probably committed a crime. It is a judgment call based on a common sense analysis.

98. d. Now that all passengers and their carry-on luggage are checked, airline passenger searches are upheld as a form of administrative search.

99. c. The Supreme Court holds that the Fourth Amendment requires a judicial determination of probable cause as a prerequisite to extended restraint on liberty following arrest. Grand jury determination to indict would provide such a judicial determination.

100. b. As Chief Justice Charles Evans Hughes of the Supreme Court (CJ 1930–41) wrote, "We are under a Constitution, but the Constitution is what judges say it is." It is the courts that interpret the meaning of the Constitution, whether through case law or legislative recommendations.

► Section 3: Criminal Investigation

1. An investigator should know that criminal investigation is best characterized as a(n)
   a. art.
   b. science.
   c. job.
   d. talent.

2. A spent shell found at the scene of a murder should be marked by the collecting officer by placing a mark on the
   a. base of the shell.
   b. primer of the shell.
   c. rim of the shell.
   d. side of the shell.

3. Which of the following is the best way to submit a firearm found loaded at the scene of a crime to the lab?
   a. in the very condition in which it was found
   b. unloaded
   c. with the firing pin removed
   d. inside a plastic bag

4. Bullets should be marked for evidence on the
   a. open end.
   b. nose or base.
   c. base only.
   d. side.

5. According to the experts in the field of criminal investigation, a crime in which the testimony of an eyewitness is usually insufficient to convict is
   a. robbery.
   b. assault.
   c. battery.
   d. forgery.

6. What is the primary reason a finished sketch is made from a rough sketch?
   a. to improve accuracy and clarity
   b. for courtroom presentation
   c. for future use
   d. to reproduce scale and proportion

7. The system of searching a crime scene that is generally most effective is the
   a. zone method.
   b. wheel method.
   c. double-strip method.
   d. spiral method.

8. What is the most common purpose for the use of video recordings, according to criminologists?
   a. narcotics buys
   b. auto theft
   c. drunken drivers
   d. political corruption

9. The latent fingerprints of a criminal suspect found at the scene of a crime most accurately establish
   a. proof of guilt.
   b. probable cause the suspect committed the crime.
   c. the suspect's presence at the scene.
   d. the *corpus delicti*.

10. According to sound criminal investigation procedures, a sample of blood should be kept
   a. refrigerated.
   b. at room temperature.
   c. in boiling water until purified, then refrigerated.
   d. frozen.

11. Of the following, the compound that prolongs the preservation period of a sample of blood the longest is
    a. baking soda.
    b. table salt.
    c. sodium fluoride.
    d. silver nitrate.

12. When collecting evidence, the majority of mistakes are committed
    a. during transportation.
    b. during the collection of samples.
    c. while in the laboratory.
    d. in the identification process.

13. Each person who handles an item of evidence from the time of its discovery until presentation in court must take certain safeguards. This safeguarding of the evidence from person to person is most accurately termed
    a. standards of comparison.
    b. control of evidence.
    c. chain of custody.
    d. integrity of evidence.

14. One of your officers is investigating a hit-and-run fatality. A large green paint smear is found on the motor vehicle of the deceased, apparently from the hit-and-run vehicle that caused the victim's death. You observe the officer carefully removing this paint smear for forensic analysis by the laboratory. Which of the following must you also advise your officer to do to be most correct?
    a. Advise the lab of the direction of the striking vehicle in relation to the victim's car.
    b. Provide a paint sample from near the smear and from a distance of about one foot away.
    c. Provide the crime lab with photographs of the skid marks.
    d. Give the lab details of the deceased: age, height, weight, and any marks on the body.

15. Bloodstains found on a piece of linoleum are best collected for analysis by
    a. removing all of the affected linoleum.
    b. scraping the affected area with a sterile knife.
    c. scrubbing a sterile cotton swab onto the affected area.
    d. using a syringe to draw a sample of blood.

16. According to experts in the field of criminal investigation, the type of crime in which the perpetrator is least likely to leave evidence at the scene is
    a. murder.
    b. robbery.
    c. burglary.
    d. arson.

17. Which one of the following does the novice investigator during an interrogation usually overlook?
   a. the more refined techniques of modern crime detection
   b. making the suspect feel comfortable
   c. allowing the suspect to talk
   d. asking the suspect if he or she committed the crime in question

18. It is agreed by experts that a confession is most plausible when
   a. it is reduced immediately to a written form.
   b. it is given without coercion.
   c. its details could not be known by someone who is innocent.
   d. it establishes a motive for the crime.

19. Which of the following areas would most help a police investigator improve in the art of criminal interrogation?
   a. practical psychology
   b. the ability to speak well
   c. the ability to listen well
   d. patience

20. The identity of a criminal suspect can be determined through multiple means, including
   a. confession.
   b. eyewitness testimony.
   c. circumstantial evidence.
   d. all of the above

21. What must the prosecution prove early in a criminal trial to prevent the case from being dismissed?
   a. the guilt of the defendant
   b. the method used to execute the crime
   c. the fact that a crime was committed
   d. prior knowledge on the part of the defendant

22. You are the sergeant in charge of an investigation unit and one of your detectives is seeking advice on a recent case that has the squad baffled. It appears as though an unknown person has been not only very active in the community burglarizing houses but also extremely successful at it. The entire squad feels the burglar is a professional. There is some trace evidence left at some of the burglary scenes at the point of entry, but that is about all the significant evidence available at this time. Which of the following is the best advice to give your detective?
   a. Look for a person who does not reside in the community where the burglaries are being committed.
   b. Look for a person who does reside in the community where the burglaries are being committed.
   c. This is probably a person who is committing these burglaries due to the exceptional opportunities that are being made available to him.
   d. This person is probably under the influence of narcotics when committing the burglaries.

23. Chain of evidence is an extremely important aspect of a criminal investigation. In order to establish the chain of evidence, most solid evidentiary items should be clearly marked with the initials of the
   a. assigned investigator.
   b. victim.
   c. patrol supervisor.
   d. officer who discovered them.

24. When an investigator is interrogating a subject who is obviously telling a string of lies, the investigator should
   a. stop the interview immediately.
   b. allow the person to continue talking.
   c. instruct the person that he or she knows that his or her story contains lies.
   d. ask the person yes and no questions.

25. An investigator is interrogating a murder suspect. The investigator holds up a videotape and says to the suspect, "You know that you were caught on tape committing the act, so just come clean." In reality, the tape is blank and the investigator is telling a lie. The actions of the investigator are
   a. permissible; an investigator is allowed to use trickery and deception to obtain a confession.
   b. not permissible; the investigator is lying.
   c. permissible; the investigator did not play the tape and could not know that it was blank.
   d. not permissible; it violates the subject's rights under Miranda.

26. With regard to the term *homicide*, which one of the following statements is least accurate?
   a. Homicide is the killing of one human being by another.
   b. The police should not assume all homicides to be murder until determined otherwise.
   c. Most homicides are cleared by arrest within the first 24 to 48 hours of discovery.
   d. Homicide is justified in certain circumstances.

27. Positive identification of a deceased person can at times be difficult due to factors such as severe decomposition, burning beyond recognition, or the necessity to make identification from the remains of only partial body parts. Which one of the following would be least likely to yield a positive identification of an unknown deceased?
   a. teeth
   b. blood
   c. scars and deformities
   d. laundry marks on clothes

28. When a person is going to commit suicide with a knife, history has shown that the person will generally select the region of the heart, the throat, or the
   a. wrists.
   b. stomach.
   c. face.
   d. skull.

29. You, as the sergeant in charge of a squad, are summoned to the scene where your subordinates found a man lying in the bathroom of his one-family house. He appears to have a knife wound in his right side and several small slash wounds on both his palms. The best preliminary conclusion to draw from these facts is

a. homicide.

b. suicide.

c. suicide made to look like a murder.

d. murder.

30. Which one of the following statements is least accurate with regard to homicides?

a. They occur most frequently during nonleisure hours.

b. Over half are committed over the weekend.

c. The majority involve alcohol.

d. Most occur in areas which have the highest delinquency rates.

31. It is important for an investigator to understand some of the statistics of homicide. Males commit more than three-fourths of the homicides and also make up more than three-fourths of the victims of homicide. It is said that in over one-fourth of homicide cases the victim is

a. a complete stranger.

b. a family member.

c. a lover.

d. someone the victim knew casually.

32. When a male kills a female, the victim is usually

a. his wife or girlfriend.

b. a robbery victim.

c. a rape victim.

d. a stranger.

33. The length of skid marks at an accident scene gives some clues about the movement of the vehicle that left them. By knowing the length of the skid marks and the coefficient of friction of the roadway, an expert can reasonably determine the

a. minimum speed at which the vehicle was traveling before the brakes were applied.

b. minimum speed at which the vehicle was traveling at the time of impact.

c. maximum speed at which the vehicle was traveling before the brakes were applied.

d. maximum speed at which the vehicle was traveling at the time of impact.

34. Which of the following is not a low-explosive substance?

a. gunpowder

b. carbon monoxide

c. gasoline

d. dynamite

35. Evidence is divided or classified into three major categories. Which of the following is not considered one of these categories?

a. associative evidence

b. real evidence

c. circumstantial evidence

d. direct evidence

36. When creating a crime scene sketch, the scale of the drawing should be

a. the largest possible.

b. a one-to-one scale.

c. the smallest possible.

d. of no concern.

37. Ms. Kozlov is passing by a bar when she observes Mr. Li and Mr. Samson enter the bar. Ms. Kozlov hears a gunshot and sees Mr. Li exit the bar with a smoking gun in his hand. When Ms. Kozlov immediately enters the bar to call the police, she observes Mr. Samson lying on the barroom floor, apparently shot. This scenario is, most accurately, an example of
  a. admissible evidence.
  b. a competent witness.
  c. direct evidence.
  d. circumstantial evidence.

38. A competent witness is one who is eligible to testify. Generally, the competency of a witness over thirteen years of age is presumed. Regarding competency, which one of the following refers to the ability to see, recall, and relate?
  a. mental competency
  b. moral competency
  c. legal competency
  d. emotional competency

39. To be admissible, evidence must be
  a. weighted and clear.
  b. material and relevant.
  c. competent and clear.
  d. truthful and relevant.

40. If the fact which the evidence tends to prove is part of an issue of the case, then the evidence is said to be
  a. credible.
  b. relevant.
  c. material.
  d. admissible.

41. Evidence that tends to prove the truth of a fact at issue is
  a. relevant.
  b. competent.
  c. material.
  d. admissible.

42. Certain facts need not be proven by formal presentation of evidence since the court is authorized to recognize their existence without such proof. This recognition is most accurately referred to as
  a. court acceptance.
  b. rule circumvention.
  c. judicial notice.
  d. judicial apperception.

43. A statement that tends to incriminate the utterer, but does not prove that the utterer in fact committed a crime, is called
  a. a confession.
  b. evidence.
  c. circumstantial evidence.
  d. an admission.

44. The best evidence of recent narcotic use is
  a. the discovery of narcotics in the subject's pocket.
  b. the discovery of paraphernalia on the person of the subject.
  c. a positive blood or urine narcotic screening.
  d. dilated pupils.

45. From the hair of a victim, it can usually be established
  a. whether the victim is male or female.
  b. what the victim's race is.
  c. what the victim's age is.
  d. what the victim's occupation is.

46. Which one of the following is considered to possess the greatest number of identifying characteristics?
a. fibers
b. fingernail clippings
c. animal hair
d. human hair

47. Which of the following is widely considered to be the best form of identification in firearm ballistics (because the bullet diameter is greater than the groove diameter of the barrel that fired it)?
a. tattooing
b. peppering
c. symbioses
d. striations

48. It is important for all police officers to understand the value associated with latent fingerprints found at crime scenes. They are unparalleled as a means of positive identification. The search for fingerprints should be conducted before anything at the crime scene is moved. Which of these four kinds of fingerprints is of least value to an investigator?
a. latent fingerprints
b. smudge fingerprints
c. plastic fingerprints
d. visible fingerprints

49. The element of surprise tends to minimize the possibility of the surprised person lying; if the person speaks before he or she has time to reflect or to fabricate a lie, it is presumed that he or she will speak the truth. This statement most nearly refers to
a. a dying declaration.
b. the best evidence rule.
c. spontaneous exclamation.
d. *res* gesture.

50. In the body of a deceased person, the stiffening of the limbs and joints known as *rigor mortis* usually begins about ten hours after death and subsides after
a. 12 hours.
b. 24 hours.
c. 30 hours.
d. 36 hours.

▶ Answers

Section 3: Criminal Investigation

1. **b.** Criminal investigation is a science. The investigator has multiple tools available as he or she proceeds through the investigatory process.

2. **d.** Expended shells should be marked on the side in order to preserve the firing pin markings for later comparison to a suspected weapon.

3. **b.** The danger of a loaded weapon takes precedence over preservation of evidence. Furthermore, if the weapon is unloaded carefully, little or no destruction of evidence will result. If the weapon is a loaded revolver, a diagram should be made of the position of the cartridges in relation to the firing pin before unloading the weapon.

4. **b.** In marking bullets, caution should be taken to avoid damaging an area that contains rifling imprints (striations). Therefore, the best place to mark bullets is not on the side, as many believe, but on the nose or base.

5. **d.** In some crimes, such as robbery or assault, the eyewitness testimony may provide all of the elements needed for conviction. However, more complicated crimes, such as forgery, burglary, fraud, and embezzlement, ordinarily require more than the evidence of eyewitnesses.

6. **b.** It is recommended that the finished drawing be drawn by a person skilled in either mechanical or architectural drawing. This not only makes a professional appearance in court presentation, but also offers less grounds for attack by the defense team.

7. **c.** This method is where three searchers traverse a rectangle first in a parallel motion to the base and then parallel to a side.

8. **c.** Video cameras are used in practically every phase of police work. The most common purpose for them is to videotape drunk drivers.

9. **c.** The latent prints at the scene of the crime do not prove anything other than the fact that the suspect left them there. It does not provide probable cause that he or she committed the crime, because he or she could have a legitimate right to be at the scene.

10. **a.** A blood sample that is not refrigerated may lose some of its grouping properties, especially if subjected to heat. Refrigeration also significantly delays the putrefaction process. (To *putrefy* means "to undergo or to cause to undergo destructive changes.")

11. **c.** Sodium fluoride will preserve the blood sample for approximately one week at room temperature and indefinitely if added to a sample of refrigerated blood. It should be noted that anytime an investigating officer intends to add any preservative to blood, experts should be consulted first.

12. **b.** Insufficient sample collection, a failure to supply samples for comparison with control samples, and a failure to collect control samples are the most common errors.

13. **c.** Sometimes referred to as *continuity of evidence*, this chain of custody must be completely clear in order to preserve the integrity of the evidence. The process from the discovery of the evidence to courtroom presentation depends on each person in the chain being able to testify and show his or her

receipt pattern and his or her responsibility in the chain of custody.

14. b. The second paint sample is called a control sample. The laboratory will be able to ascertain from the control sample any impurities that could affect the evidence sample containing the suspect's paint smear. The lab technician can also determine any difficulties the background substances will add to the analysis. Remember that failure to do this is among the most common errors in evidence collection.

15. a. Removing the linoleum itself is accepted by experts as the best possible method to get this bloodstain to the laboratory. Similarly, laboratory scientists agree that if a door is stained with blood from a crime, it is best to bring the whole door to the lab for forensic analysis and serology process.

16. b. Perpetrators of a robbery usually are busy taking things, not leaving them behind. In contrast, murderers, burglars, and arsonists often unintentionally leave evidence of their presence at the scene.

17. d. This lesson is so elementary that it is frequently neglected by beginners in their eagerness to use the more refined techniques of modern crime detection. The guilty person is in possession of most of the information necessary for a successful prosecution. If he or she is questioned intelligently, he or she can usually be induced to talk.

18. c. It has been said that the most egregious error on the clever criminal's part is answering questions. Whether the answers are truthful or not, the fact that criminals love to talk is of great value to the skillful investigator because he or she is receiving information, the first and most important of the three Is of investi-

gation (information, interrogation, and instrumentation). A district attorney in New York City once stated that in 16 years of dealing with homicide cases, he encountered only two defendants who would not talk to the investigators. Those two were acquitted.

19. a. Patience is a good choice, as are the abilities to speak well and to listen well, but what better way can the investigator learn these important skills than by knowing practical psychology? The biggest (most inclusive) choice is the best answer. Practical psychology will enable the investigator to establish an understanding of a vast array of individual personalities.

20. d. Investigators use multiple methods to identify criminal perpetrators. These means include seeking the identity through a confession, the interviewing and gathering of eyewitness testimony, and the analysis of circumstantial evidence, which can tie a person to a crime.

21. c. Early in a criminal trial the prosecution must prove the fact that a crime was committed (the *corpus delicti*). Unless an offense can in fact be shown to exist, the court may dismiss the case. (*Corpus delicti* is Latin for "body of the crime.")

22. a. The professional criminal does not operate near his or her residence. The amateur, on the other hand, usually commits a crime because of the exceptional opportunity that is made available to him or her and he or she is often under the influence of some habit-producing drug. However, amateurs are rarely as successful as the burglar described in the paragraph.

23. d. The first step in establishing the chain of evidence is the marking of the evidentiary item. This should be done by the officer who finds the item. The mark should consist of the officer's initials, but extreme care should be taken not to destroy the item or alter its evidentiary value.

24. b. The investigator should allow the subject to continue the story, including the lies. Even a story full of lies may contain some truth that can later be used to compare future renditions of the events of the incident.

25. a. An investigator may resort to trickery and deceit in order to obtain a confession. In any event, the courts will rely on a "totality of the circumstances" test to review the voluntariness of a confession.

26. b. Assume for a moment that the police come to the scene of a deceased body. If the investigating officers are spending a lot of time attempting to prove crimes less than murder and later determine that the victim was in fact murdered, they will very likely have let the trail grow cold.

27. d. Just a few years back, the answer would have been blood. DNA testing has changed that. In fact, any bodily fluid sufficient for ascertaining DNA schematics is an excellent means of identification. Laundry and dry cleaning marks are a good source of identification, but they pale in comparison with the other choices. While the garment can be positively identified and traced, its history can't necessarily be linked to the body that is currently wearing the garment.

28. a. Suicides are prone to select the front of the body for attack. With a knife, they will select the throat, wrists, or heart region. With a gun, the choice is usually the temple, forehead, mouth, heart, or center of the back of the head.

29. a. On these facts alone, it is very reasonable to assume the person was killed by someone else. The strongest evidence for this presumption is the slash wounds on both palms, which are not consistent with suicide but instead suggest that the dead man tried to defend himself from attack. It is possible, given what you know so far, that the killing was in self-defense. Therefore, you can safely draw the preliminary conclusion that the man was the victim of a homicide (the killing of one human being by another) but not that he was murdered (which would require intent).

30. a. Most homicides are committed during leisure hours, that is, between 8:00 P.M. and 2:00 A.M.

31. b. In over three-fourths of the cases, the victim knows his or her assailant. In over one-fourth of the cases, the victim is a member of the family.

32. a. Statistics show that when a man kills a woman, she is more likely to be his wife or girlfriend than a stranger or acquaintence.

33. a. The evidence-gathering method is photographing the skid marks on the roadway. Photographs should be made of the tire tracks with the camera lens at a distance of approximately five feet and with the plate parallel to the surface of the road. A ruler should be included in the field to provide a reference scale for later measurements on the photograph.

34. d. Low explosives are characterized by the relatively low velocity with which the energy wave is transmitted, a few thousand feet per second, and the sound of a pop or boom. High explosives have velocities as high as 25,000 feet per second and are accompanied by a shattering high-frequency sound. These sounds often make it possible to identify the character of the explosion even though no traces of the explosives remain.

35. a. Associative evidence links the suspect to the crime scene or the offense. An example is broken glass particles found in the suspect's pant cuff that match the broken window found at the point of entry at a burglary. This evidence could be real, circumstantial, or direct, depending on the context.

36. c. The scale of a crime scene should be the smallest scale possible. If a large scale is used, the drawing may not be detailed enough. A one-to-one scale would require a sketch to be the same exact size as the actual crime scene.

37. d. No one can say at this juncture whether Ms. Kozlov will be considered a competent witness or whether her testimony will be admissible; that is up to the judge to decide. Circumstantial evidence is evidence that establishes something from which the court may infer another fact at issue. In the above scenario, Ms. Kozlov did not see the actual event, but the facts are so closely associated that it may reasonably be inferred that Mr. Li shot Mr. Samson.

38. a. Mental competency refers to the ability to see, recall, and relate, while moral competency implies an understanding of the truth and the consequences of a falsehood.

39. b. The rules of evidence may differ slightly from jurisdiction to jurisdiction, but they are generally concerned with the admissibility and pertinence of the facts and not with their weight or the clarity of their presentation. The weight of evidence is a question of fact for the judge or jury to determine.

40. c. Evidence that proves something that is not at issue is immaterial. To be material, the evidence must affect an issue of the case significantly.

41. a. Most students find the distinctions among types of evidence difficult to grasp, but they are very important. Evidence is *relevant* when it concerns facts the jury or judge have to consider. It is *material* when it is nontrivial. It is *competent* when nothing in the rules of evidence would exclude it. It is *admissible* when it meets all three of these criteria and furthermore would not be excluded by rule or law.

42. c. The general rule prescribes (dictates) that the court will not require proof of matters of general or common knowledge, such as historical and geographical facts, a state's own laws, weights and measures, and the like.

43. d. An admission is a statement that tends to incriminate the person who said it, but falls short of a confession. An admission can be introduced into the court proceedings and can help to establish proof of guilt.

44. c. A positive blood or urine screening is the best evidence of recent narcotic use. In the majority of cases, if proper guidelines are followed, this evidence will be directly admissible in court.

45. b. This is accomplished primarily by a study of pigment distribution, cross-section analysis, and other physical characteristics.

46. a. Since fibers vary widely in composition, source, color, and shape, they possess many more identifying characteristics than hair or fingernails.

47. d. The firing of the gun sends the bullet passing through the barrel, causing it to be in contact with the entire inner surface of the barrel during passage. Rifling impressions are thereby inscribed into the projectile, causing striations (scratches or grooves) that are of great value for ballistic evidence.

48. b. *Smudges* are of little value because they have no discernable ridge characteristics. *Latent* prints are hidden or relatively invisible and must be developed by one of several special methods. *Plastic* prints are impressions that are depressed below the original surface and may be found on such objects as soap, butter, putty, and melted wax. *Visible* prints are left by fingers covered with a colored material, such as paint, blood, grease, ink, and dirt.

49. c. Anyone who heard it can testify to a spontaneous exclamation. The spontaneous excla-

mation can be used either in favor of or against the person who made it. This is an exception to the hearsay rule.

50. d. The existence or absence of rigor mortis can help the investigator narrow down the time of death. It begins in the joints of the neck after about ten hours and moves on to the limbs a few hours later. After about 36 hours, rigor mortis subsides and the body's joints begin to flex once again.

► Section 4: Patrol Practices

1. When responding to a burglary-in-progress call, it is important for you as a sergeant to guide your personnel in correct procedure. What is the least appropriate move to make when responding to a burglary call?
   a. Assume that the burglar is still inside until you establish otherwise.
   b. Immediately enter the building and begin searching for the suspect(s).
   c. Know that you have the advantage from the outside; the burglar has the advantage when you go in.
   d. Look for point of entry and point of exit.

2. The appraisal made of the police by the general public is brought about in large measure by the encounters between citizens and the police during traffic stops. The police sergeant should emphasize to his or her subordinates that the police officer's salutation to the violator should NOT be
   a. polite.
   b. condescending.
   c. free of familiarity.
   d. advisory.

3. Supervisors at the scene of an unusual incident, such as a riot, should know that their initial responsibility is to
   a. ensure that they have enough patrol officers.
   b. seek out the leader of the group.
   c. set up a command post.
   d. evaluate the incident and report back to superior officers.

4. Most jurisdictions in the United States allow for traffic warnings in lieu of traffic citations. This practice brings about good public relations and at the same time educates the violator without punishment. When should the police officer make his or her decision about whether to write a traffic summons or give a warning?
   a. at the time the officer observes the violation
   b. before any violation is observed; it should be clear in the officer's mind what actions he or she will take if an anticipated traffic violation occurs
   c. subsequent to the violation and subsequent to talking to the violator
   d. each violation must be treated separately and individually evaluated

5. Should a command post set up at the scene of a large natural disaster, such as a forest fire, suddenly become compromised by approaching danger, the command post should
   a. remain at its original location.
   b. be disbanded.
   c. move to a safer location.
   d. be abandoned.

6. Throughout your tour of duty, you should be alert for any activity that seems out of the ordinary and arouses your suspicions. Of the following, the most important life that you, as a police officer, are charged to protect is
   a. the suspect's.
   b. the victim's.
   c. the citizenry.
   d. your own.

7. Photographing the exterior of a building where a crime occurred, a hallway leading to the exact location of the crime, and the exact location itself is most accurately referred to as
   a. sequencing.
   b. broadening.
   c. phasing.
   d. orientation.

8. The number of police officers at the scene of an armed and dangerous barricaded person should be kept to the minimum amount necessary. The main reason for this is to
   a. assist with communication.
   b. avoid confusion.
   c. regulate the span of control.
   d. ensure safety.

9. Generally, at the scene of a crime, after caring for the injured or wounded, the field officer's primary responsibility is to
   a. locate and interview witnesses.
   b. take statements from victims.
   c. locate and arrest offenders.
   d. protect the crime scene.

10. When conducting a frisk, the best course of action is to
   a. handcuff the subject prior to the frisk.
   b. maintain your own balance by remaining flat-footed.
   c. conduct the frisk with two hands.
   d. avoid making your commands ambiguous and verbose.

11. As a police officer, it is important to understand that your most frequent source of information is generally
   a. the underworld informant.
   b. the paid informant.
   c. those you arrest for petty offenses who bargain information for leniency.
   d. those in whom you have cultivated a feeling of pride and respect by keeping their neighborhood crime-free.

12. Reserch indicates that a burglar would rather enter a building through
   a. the rooftop.
   b. a front door.
   c. a rear door.
   d. a window.

13. When it becomes necessary to handcuff a suspect behind his or her back, the best course of action is to
   a. not use the double lock because this increases the chances of the cuffs tightening.
   b. use the double-lock position and have the suspect's palms in an inward position.
   c. handcuff the suspect in the hands-over-head position, double-lock the cuffs, and have the suspect's palms in an outward position.
   d. use the double lock to prevent the cuffs from tightening and have the suspect's palms in a outward position.

14. When two officers are transporting a prisoner in a police vehicle equipped with a screen or shield separating the driving compartment from the rear of the vehicle, what is the proper seating arrangement?

   a. One officer drives while the other officer sits in the rear, immediately behind the driver with the prisoner to his or her right.

   b. One officer drives while the other officer sits in the rear, diagonally from the driver with the prisoner to his or her left.

   c. Both officers sit in the front with the prisoner in the rear.

   d. One officer drives, the prisoner sits in the front passenger seat, and the second officer sits directly behind the prisoner.

15. One excellent method for developing a closer working relationship with the community is to assign officers on a permanent basis to designated districts. In this approach, the department is broken down into smaller units, if possible in such a way that most police activities (including juvenile, detective, traffic, and patrol) are all handled by this "neighborhood police force." The desired result is that the people in each district have the feeling that they have their own police department. This concept is most accurately referred to as

   a. neighborhood watch.

   b. district policing.

   c. community policing.

   d. community relations.

16. A hostage negotiator at the scene of a hostage situation should know that the hostage taker's demands should

   a. be denied.

   b. be initially denied, then met.

   c. be met, regardless of type.

   d. be met, except when more weapons or ammunition are demanded.

17. Care must be exercised by the police when called to the scene of a large strike in order to not antagonize or inflame the crowd and to remain neutral. Officers should generally not make arrests for

   a. destruction of company property.

   b. destruction of public property.

   c. littering.

   d. assaultive behavior.

18. Which of the following is the least accurate statement or directive regarding being fired upon?

   a. If fired upon, jump to your left.

   b. Most people are right-handed, so assume the shooter is right-handed if you can't see him or her.

   c. When a left-handed person fires a gun, there is usually a sharp pull to his or her right.

   d. If you see the gun in the suspect's left hand, jump to your right.

19. Which one of the following is considered by experts to be an extremely effective weapon for short-range person-to-person assault?

   a. 9-mm automatic pistol

   b. 45-cal automatic pistol

   c. 12-gauge shotgun with 00 buckshot

   d. mini-14 automatic rifle

20. On a burglary-in-progress call, once you have searched a particular room or portion of the building, what is the best way to "clear" the searched area?

    a. Close the door and place available furniture in strategic locations so it would have to be moved for someone to pass through that area.

    b. Place officers at strategic locations to guard "cleared" areas (if the area is small enough).

    c. Tape the area with barricade tape.

    d. Execute a preplanned signal; for example, one of the searching officers could shine his or her flashlight through an opened window to others outside the structure to indicate a cleared area.

21. Assume that you are a training sergeant in charge of training new recruits in the correct procedure in burglary-in-progress calls. Which one of the following should you probably NOT include in your training instructions to the recruits?

    a. Open any doors in the suspect's building as quietly as possible while looking through the opening of the hinge side to observe anyone inside.

    b. As you prepare to leave a lighted area for a dark area, turn on all the lights that you can before entering.

    c. As you move about the premises, leave all the lights on.

    d. Be aware that the time it takes for the human eye to adjust from darkness to light is usually between five and fifty seconds.

22. While searching for a suspect in a building, how should the flashlight be held?

    a. away from your body and preferably with your weak hand

    b. away from your body and preferably with your strong hand

    c. as close to the weapon as possible

    d. as close to the body as possible

23. While in the courtroom, an officer should

    a. appear to be overly interested in what is taking place.

    b. appear to be totally disinterested in the case.

    c. sit attentively with a stoic expression.

    d. shake or nod his or her head when disagreeing or agreeing with the testimony being given.

24. There are five basic objectives in the interview or interrogation process. Which of the following encompasses the five basic objectives most completely?

    a. Ascertain the truth, whatever it is; secure complete information in detail; distinguish fact from fantasy; have a target objective (the truth); and proceed according to plan.

    b. Obtain the truth; understand the subject; distinguish fact from lies; have a target objective (a confession); and make a friend.

    c. Obtain the truth; secure complete information in detail; distinguish between importance and trivia; attempt to remain calm; and don't attempt to proceed to action at the expense of interrupting the interview or interrogation.

    d. Ascertain the truth; keep calm; listen; speak only to keep the conversation flowing; and make the subject feel comfortable.

25. Experts agree about the importance of interviewing (or interrogation) in criminal investigation. Which of the following should a police interviewer do first?

a. Adapt his or her personality to the various situations and the personalities of the people whom he or she questions.

b. Study and know him- or herself—flaws, temperament and personality, strengths and weaknesses.

c. Develop a style that is distinctive, and improve on it with study and experience.

d. Have an intense interest in human nature, a desire to develop the skill, and the ability to learn from each interview experience.

26. At the scene of a bomb threat inside a building, an officer should do all the following EXCEPT

a. locate the owner or manager of the building.

b. transmit a description of the explosive device over his or her handheld radio.

c. assist in any evacuation plans.

d. retrieve a mirror out of the patrol car.

27. One of your subordinates approaches you, his or her sergeant. The subordinate asks you, "What is the main purpose of a crime report?" Which of the following is the best answer?

a. to establish jurisdiction of the case

b. to reflect all elements of the *corpus delicti* (body of the offense)

c. to support the successful prosecution of the alleged perpetrator

d. to require data to serve as a base for the investigator

28. A report should have an introduction, a body, and a conclusion. When the author of the report includes recommendations for further action or a statement that this particular case requires no further action, this should most accurately be included where?

a. in the conclusion

b. in the introduction

c. in the body

d. in the synopsis

29. When first receiving a call concerning an "in-progress" situation, all units in the area should be alerted as to the nature of the event. Once the alert is broadcast, the units in the immediate vicinity should acknowledge receipt of the call and give their respective locations. Which of the following is it best to assign to handle the call?

a. the unit assigned to that particular district

b. the unit with the officers who are most experienced with the type of situation at hand

c. the unit that is closest to the event

d. the unit that requests to respond to the event

30. There are several indicators that a person is driving a motor vehicle while under the influence of drugs or alcohol. Which of the following is NOT usually considered one of those indicators?

a. The driver has the windshield wipers on for no apparent reason.

b. The driver remains in one lane of traffic continuously without changing lanes.

c. The driver maintains a fixed stare straight ahead with apparent disregard for peripheral sightings, such as passing vehicles.

d. The suspect vehicle has a wide-open window on a very cold night during a rainstorm or blizzard.

31. In a large percentage of cases, adult missing persons are
a. the victims of amnesia.
b. confused.
c. missing by choice.
d. the victims of violence or kidnapping.

32. According to many experts in the field, which one of the following is most critical to the success of an interview?
a. the art of questioning
b. getting answers
c. hearing what is said
d. listening to what is said

33. If you are in a well-lit business area or an industrial complex with high fences and buildings with few open driveways, what would be the best place for you to attempt to make the contact for a field interview?
a. near a street light in the middle of the block
b. in a lighted area near one side of a high fence
c. between two buildings
d. in a darkened area on the inside of a high fence

34. Officers have chased a dangerous criminal into a high-rise building. The officers have formed a perimeter and have requested additional officers respond in order to conduct a building search. Once backup arrives, it is determined that the building has five floors. The officers should begin their search
a. in the basement.
b. on the fifth floor.
c. on the roof.
d. on the first floor.

35. What is generally considered to be the final step in the police investigation process?
a. the prosecution of the offender
b. a determination of guilt
c. testifying in court
d. submission of admissible and reliable evidence

▶ Answers

Section 4: Patrol Practices

1. b. The correct procedure in a burglary-in-progress call is to not enter any building alone before assistance has arrived. Rather than immediately enter and begin to search for suspect(s), you should notify headquarters, apprise them of your findings, and wait for backup units to arrive. Do not enter the building in question until it can be surrounded and all escape routes protected.

2. b. Your salutation to the traffic violator should be polite and advisory in nature (that is, any questions with regard to court appearances and the like should be answered). The encounter should be free of familiarity, and the police should not be condescending toward the violator. (*Condescending* means "speaking down to.")

3. d. Before all else, supervisors at these types of scenes should appraise the scene and report to superior officers. With the proper information, superiors can begin to make plans for additional patrol officers and roll out a command post.

4. a. The purpose of the warning is to educate the traffic violator in the event the violation is not so serious that a traffic summons is in order. At the time of the observation of the event, the officer should be clear in his or her mind whether a summons or a warning is called for. Other procedures could result in the appearance of prejudicial or biased action on the part of the police. Not only must impropriety of this kind be scrupulously avoided, but even the appearance of it must be avoided.

5. c. Care should be taken to locate a command post in a safe location outside the perimeter of the disaster area. When circumstances change and the threat endangers the command post, it should be relocated to a safer area.

6. d. Contrary to a widely accepted belief, police officers are to take anticipated, controlled risks, not suicidal ones.

7. d. Photographs such as those described are taken so that they take the viewer on a pictorial journey from a peripheral view to the place of the crime. Such photographs are also sometimes referred to as *background* or *condition* photographs.

8. d. Barricaded subjects are extremely dangerous situations. The number of officers in the primary incident area at this type of scene should be kept to the minimum needed to end the incident safely. Supervisors should avoid endangering additional officers by assigning them to take positions in the danger zone.

9. c. Generally, the duty order at the crime is (i) aid the injured, (ii) locate and arrest offenders, (iii) protect the scene, and (iv) locate witnesses and record statements from victims and/or witnesses. It is important to note that there may be times when the initial duty of the police at the crime scene is to subdue and arrest the offenders, especially when they are a danger to police or others.

10. d. Just as in the arrest situation, police actions in the frisk or pat-down should be without confusion and directions should be stated in such a way that they cannot be misunderstood. The officer must be professional and exhibit command presence. The more dangerous the situation becomes, the calmer the officer becomes.

11. d. The most frequent source of valuable information for everyday common crimes are people who have come to respect and admire the police. Among the more specific sources of information regarding particular crimes, it is usually the paid informant who will supply information that leads to successful arrest and conviction, since the paid informant has access to the criminal.

12. c. The modern-day burglar does not prefer to enter through a window, a method that can cause him or her to be cut and leave blood as evidence. Entering through a rear door creates less noise when the door is jimmied, since no glass breaks and the main entrance appears to be normal.

13. d. This method takes a little more time, but it can prevent the handcuffs from tightening to the point of causing serious injury to the suspect. If the double lock is not used, the suspect can complain that the cuff has tightened, causing extreme pain. The officer might then adjust the cuffs out of sympathy and inadvertently allow the suspect to try to escape.

14. c. If the vehicle does not have a shield or screen, place the prisoner in the right portion of the rear seat and the second officer immediately behind the driver. If there is one officer and one prisoner, and the police car is not equipped with a screen between the front and rear compartment, consider placing the arrestee in the front seat with the seat belt securely fastened and his or her hands cuffed behind his or her back.

15. c. This concept is also referred to as *team policing*. The people are constantly reminded by their regular police officers that crime prevention and the apprehension of criminal offenders depend on the citizens and the police working together.

16. d. Hostage situations are one of the most serious types of incidents that police deal with. The demands made by the hostage taker should generally be met, except when the demand is for more weapons.

17. c. Labor disputes can be tense situations. Officers attempting to enforce all laws strictly may inflame the crowd. Therefore, officers should avoid making arrests for minor incidents, such as littering.

18. c. When a right-handed person fires a gun, there is usually a sharp pull to his or her left.

19. c. This is not only an extremely effective weapon but also standard equipment in many departments. The weapon has a dramatic effect on suspects, and it is extremely effective when used by an officer with meager marksmanship skills. There is also less danger to surrounding neighborhoods than with the other weapons listed because of its limited range.

20. a. The question presupposes that there is time to conduct a protracted search. The method detailed in **a** is useful in this situation not only because it inhibits a suspect's movement if he or she tries to escape, but also because it makes it likely that he or she would be heard if he or she tried to leave (because of the noise he or she would make moving the objects).

21. a. Each time you enter a room, push the door hard to the door stopper or the wall to make sure there is no one hiding behind the door. This enables you to stand a distance from the door in the event the hiding suspect decides to assault you from the crack in the hinged side of the door.

22. a. Most inexperienced shooters have a strong tendency to shoot directly at the light source, assuming it is close to the body of the holder. This method is also advantageous because such a shooter will be unlikely to hit your body and because it leaves your strong shooting hand free to return fire if necessary.

23. c. An officer sitting in the courtroom either before or after testifying should avoid any expressions or shaking or nodding disapproval or agreement because any such behavior might indicate to the jury or judge that the officer has a personal rather than impersonal involvement in the case.

24. a. Whenever possible, arrange to have a private area for the interview. The best location is a room at police headquarters designated for that purpose. Set aside enough time to conduct the interview or interrogation without being interrupted. If you are interrogating a suspect, be sure to ascertain as many facts as possible concerning the crime in question, in order to be able to ascertain the truthfulness of the suspect's responses.

25. b. "Above all know thyself." That's a famous adage that applies here. The behaviors in **a**, **c**, and **d** are important for conducting successful interviews or interrogations, but choice **b** is the most fundamental.

26. b. At the scene of a bomb threat, officers should avoid transmitting over their handheld radios because the radio transmissions can detonate the explosive device. Officers should instead seek out a hardwired telephone and phone in all pertinent information.

27. c. The main purpose of the report is to support the successful prosecution of the actor. While the other answers contribute to reaching this ultimate goal, they are not broad enough to be good answers to the question asked.

28. a. Most reports demand that the officer recount the information in ordinary language and in longhand. As in any essay or other form of written communication, the report should have an introduction, body, and conclusion. The introduction usually consists of a synopsis of the report and an announcement of what the reader may expect to find in the body of the report. The conclusion consists of a reiteration of the body in capsule form and some recommendation regarding further action.

29. c. In the event there is a department policy that requires the district unit to be assigned the call, a reassignment can be made after the closest unit has responded. The primary concern should be getting a police officer to the crime scene as quickly as possible. After the initial unit is detailed, consideration of backup units must be made.

30. b. On the contrary, weaving or changing lanes without apparent reason is a sign of a driver under the influence of drugs or alcohol.

31. c. If there is some evidence or probable cause to believe that the missing person has met with forced absence or violence, then an immediate investigation should be undertaken. It should not automatically be assumed that the person missing is missing by choice, in spite of the statistics suggesting that this is likely.

32. d. All of the choices are recommended for good interviewing, but the most critical of all is the ability to listen to what is said. It is important to remember that the interviewer must have as many facts as possible concerning the subject of the interview in order to be able to ascertain the truthfulness of the interviewee's responses.

33. **a.** If the officer is in a residential area where there are many driveways and open areas, then he or she should choose an intersection for the contact. The reason for selecting these contact locations is to make it easy for the officer to pursue the suspect if he or she should decide to run. It is easier to chase a subject down a street than through backyards and alleyways.

34. **c.** Building searches should begin on the roof in an attempt to flush the subject out of the building and into the custody of perimeter officers.

35. **c.** The responsibility of the police officer is to present evidence and testimony factually, objectively, and without prejudice. The final determination of guilt or innocence is the responsibility of the judge or jury. The prosecution of the offender is the responsibility of the state.

▶ Section 5: Community Relations

1. Most community relations experts believe that the primary mission of a police force is
   a. promotion and maintenance of order in the community.
   b. arresting violators of the law.
   c. law enforcement.
   d. protection of property.

2. Read the following paragraph and choose the answer it best describes:

   Attitude adapted without sufficient exploration of the facts results in prejudging, that is, making a judgment before or independently of the relevant facts in the matter.

   a. symbolism
   b. scapegoating
   c. zeal
   d. prejudice

3. Read the following paragraph and choose the answer it best describes:

   It is related to prejudice, but it is not the same as prejudice. It entails the unequal treatment of different people depending on the group to which they belong.

   a. racism
   b. hatred
   c. discrimination
   d. fascism

4. According to experts in the field of human relations and police-community relations, there is more than one type of prejudice. One type is firmly embedded in the personality makeup, making it extremely difficult to banish. This type of prejudice is most accurately referred to as
   a. character-conditioned prejudice.
   b. culture-conditioned prejudice.
   c. race prejudice.
   d. gender prejudice.

5. In reference to influence on police/community relations, the most influential level in any police agency is the
   a. patrol level.
   b. first line supervisory level.
   c. investigatory level.
   d. chief executive level.

6. With regard to racial and ethnic traits, which of the following statements is most accurate?
   a. Racial and ethnic traits are sharply different in nature.
   b. Racial and ethnic traits are rarely confused and are actually the same.
   c. Racial and ethnic traits contribute to most criminal motives.
   d. Racial and ethnic traits are unimportant.

7. The police action that tends to have the greatest effect on public perception of the police is
   a. criminal investigations.
   b. mass demonstrations.
   c. traffic enforcement.
   d. use of force.

8. Which of the following is the main barrier to communication when the police deal with citizens?

a. treating citizens as children

b. treating citizens without empathy

c. withholding vital information from citizens

d. failing to be strict with citizens

9. Occasionally, the press works at cross-purposes with the police, and this sometimes hinders law enforcement. This is particularly true in

a. organized crime cases.

b. rape cases.

c. kidnapping cases.

d. juvenile cases.

10. When citizens feel that a police officer has treated them improperly, they sometimes initiate complaints. Officers should know that the majority of complaints concern

a. use of force.

b. criminal behavior.

c. serious misconduct.

d. noncriminal conduct.

11. For police officers, the importance of understanding human relations can never be overstated. Knowing what binds people together is paramount to understanding human relations. What binds people together the most is their

a. color.

b. nationality.

c. politics.

d. culture.

12. The police are considered to be the street interpreters of the law through the use of

a. their discretion.

b. their expert knowledge.

c. their interpretation of case precedents.

d. their impartial enforcement of the law.

13. It has been stated that people entering the criminal justice profession need to posses a very special communication quality. Unlike the development of voice or listening skills, this concept has a rather vague nature. Experts also maintain that those entering police-oriented professions need to have large amounts of this. The statement just made most nearly makes reference to

a. the capacity for human empathy.

b. the capacity for human sympathy.

c. the ability to clearly understand the law.

d. impartiality without emotion.

14. The most extreme form of unexpressed inward aggression is

a. suicide.

b. depression.

c. repression.

d. frustration.

15. Generally, the rules that regulate our use of personal space are implied. For example, business interactions call for a different amount of distance than do interactions between close friends. Experts identify four basic personal space zones: intimate distance, personal distance, social distance, and public distance. Which calls for a distance of one and one-half feet from the body?

a. intimate distance

b. personal distance

c. social distance

d. public distance

▶ Answers

Section 5: Community Relations

1. **a.** Community relations experts contend that law enforcement is only a small part of the task of the police. They feel that if the police promote order and maintain it by a continual dialogue between the police and the community they serve, what will follow is the lessening of the other police tasks of arresting violators and protecting property. It is certainly true today is that only a small portion of the police duties involve law enforcement activities and the greater portion is the maintenance of order.

2. **d.** Think of prejudice as judging without sufficient cause or without sufficient facts. If one has ill will toward another only because he or she belongs to a group, that is prejudging and must scrupulously be avoided. The police have too much power to indulge in service with prejudice.

3. **c.** When one prejudges a group and consequently treats that group differently from other groups, that is *discrimination*. *Racism* is defined as the prediction of decisions based on considerations of race.

4. **a.** A person who has a *character-conditioned* prejudice is psychologically prejudiced and is considered to be a very dangerous person. *Culture-conditioned* prejudice is primarily learned or acquired in the process of social interaction and is easier to "unlearn."

5. **a.** Patrol officers are the most visible level of any police organization. To the public, they embody what the police department is. This has led many police and community relations experts to contend that the patrol level is the most influential level of any police organizations in terms of public relations.

6. **a.** When people confuse racial and ethnic traits, they are confusing what is given by nature with what is acquired through learning. Racial traits are hereditary, while ethnic traits are absorbed during social and cultural experiences.

7. **c.** Most citizens interact with the police through normal traffic enforcement. Officers should be courteous during these interactions, because most citizens will frame their perceptions of the police based upon these limited interactions.

8. **a.** Inherent in police organizational methods of problem solving is an institutionalized parent/child authoritarian role model. If police officers attempt to apply this model in their interaction with the public they are sworn to serve, then communication blocks result. When the police officer treats the citizen like a child, the citizen may respond with verbal or physical attacks, show resentment, refuse to cooperate, and withhold information that is vital to the police.

9. **c.** The relationship between the press and the police is most critical in kidnapping cases; the safety of the victim often depends upon the cooperation given by the press to the police.

10. **d.** The majority of complaints against the police entail noncriminal conduct, such as rude treatment and the use of obscenities. Serious misconduct and criminal misconduct are much rarer, but they require a more serious response by the police organization.

11. **d.** *Culture* is the learned and shared behavior of a group of people together with their cultural artifacts (art, music, and traditions). The basis

of culture is the ideas and the standards people have in common. Effective police-community relations are easiest to achieve in a community that is relatively culturally integrated.

12. a. According to the experts in the fields of social psychology and community relations, discretion occurs at every stage of the justice process. However, it is difficult to find any court in the land that will give countenance to police discretion. The view of the courts is that the law is to be enforced equally, without prejudice or bias. That suggests there is no discretion as to which laws the police will enforce and which they may ignore. Yet in practicality, for all but the most serious crimes, police discretion does exist.

13. a. It is a caring attitude, the developed capacity to understand another and to comprehend another's feelings, attitudes, and sentiments.

It is being capable of "putting yourself in the other person's shoes"—empathy.

14. a. Aggression is necessary to human development, especially to the development of a sense of self-worth, self-importance, and self-assertiveness. Repressing aggression can have unfortunate results. Aggression that is not directed outward is often misdirected inward, leading to self-doubt, self-hatred, depression, and, in the most extreme cases, suicide.

15. b. Intimate distance extends to about 18 inches from the skin, social distance is about four to 12 feet from the body, and public distance is more than 12 feet. Police officers must remember not to invade another's distance without understanding that the person might instinctively pull away.

Police Sergeant Practice Exam 2

You have come a long way since you began studying for the police sergeant exam, and now is the time to demonstrate that fact to yourself—and to catch yourself in the areas that remain difficult. There are 100 questions on this test, just as there were on the first one. It's a good bet that you will face a similar number of questions on your department's exam.

ou may have chosen to take your time with the exam in Chapter 4, since at that point you had a lot of studying still to do. Now, time should become a factor. Time yourself strictly while you take this test, giving yourself the same amount of time as you will have in your own department on test day. (Remember to practice the antianxiety techniques recommended in Chapter 2 of this book if you find yourself getting nervous with the element of time added.)

Like the other practice material in this book, this exam comes supplied with an answer key and thorough answer explanations. After you finish the exam, score your test. If you still had problems with some of the questions (and nearly everyone will have had some), study the answer explanations to those questions carefully.

Finally, compare your results with this chart. Do the questions that gave you trouble fall into any one area? If so, you know just where to focus your efforts in the weeks remaining before test day.

QUESTION RANGE	TOPICS COVERED
Questions 1–10	Patrol Practices
Questions 11–15 and 89–100	Constitutional Law and Criminal Procedure
Questions 16–56	Supervision and Management
Questions 57–76	Criminal Investigation and Forensic Science
Questions 77–88	Community Relations

ANSWER SHEET

Section 1: Reading Comprehension

1.	ⓐ	ⓑ	ⓒ	ⓓ
2.	ⓐ	ⓑ	ⓒ	ⓓ
3.	ⓐ	ⓑ	ⓒ	ⓓ
4.	ⓐ	ⓑ	ⓒ	ⓓ
5.	ⓐ	ⓑ	ⓒ	ⓓ
6.	ⓐ	ⓑ	ⓒ	ⓓ
7.	ⓐ	ⓑ	ⓒ	ⓓ
8.	ⓐ	ⓑ	ⓒ	ⓓ
9.	ⓐ	ⓑ	ⓒ	ⓓ
10.	ⓐ	ⓑ	ⓒ	ⓓ
11.	ⓐ	ⓑ	ⓒ	ⓓ
12.	ⓐ	ⓑ	ⓒ	ⓓ
13.	ⓐ	ⓑ	ⓒ	ⓓ
14.	ⓐ	ⓑ	ⓒ	ⓓ
15.	ⓐ	ⓑ	ⓒ	ⓓ
16.	ⓐ	ⓑ	ⓒ	ⓓ
17.	ⓐ	ⓑ	ⓒ	ⓓ
18.	ⓐ	ⓑ	ⓒ	ⓓ
19.	ⓐ	ⓑ	ⓒ	ⓓ
20.	ⓐ	ⓑ	ⓒ	ⓓ
21.	ⓐ	ⓑ	ⓒ	ⓓ
22.	ⓐ	ⓑ	ⓒ	ⓓ
23.	ⓐ	ⓑ	ⓒ	ⓓ
24.	ⓐ	ⓑ	ⓒ	ⓓ
25.	ⓐ	ⓑ	ⓒ	ⓓ
26.	ⓐ	ⓑ	ⓒ	ⓓ
27.	ⓐ	ⓑ	ⓒ	ⓓ
28.	ⓐ	ⓑ	ⓒ	ⓓ
29.	ⓐ	ⓑ	ⓒ	ⓓ
30.	ⓐ	ⓑ	ⓒ	ⓓ
31.	ⓐ	ⓑ	ⓒ	ⓓ
32.	ⓐ	ⓑ	ⓒ	ⓓ
33.	ⓐ	ⓑ	ⓒ	ⓓ
34.	ⓐ	ⓑ	ⓒ	ⓓ
35.	ⓐ	ⓑ	ⓒ	ⓓ

36.	ⓐ	ⓑ	ⓒ	ⓓ
37.	ⓐ	ⓑ	ⓒ	ⓓ
38.	ⓐ	ⓑ	ⓒ	ⓓ
39.	ⓐ	ⓑ	ⓒ	ⓓ
40.	ⓐ	ⓑ	ⓒ	ⓓ
41.	ⓐ	ⓑ	ⓒ	ⓓ
42.	ⓐ	ⓑ	ⓒ	ⓓ
43.	ⓐ	ⓑ	ⓒ	ⓓ
44.	ⓐ	ⓑ	ⓒ	ⓓ
45.	ⓐ	ⓑ	ⓒ	ⓓ
46.	ⓐ	ⓑ	ⓒ	ⓓ
47.	ⓐ	ⓑ	ⓒ	ⓓ
48.	ⓐ	ⓑ	ⓒ	ⓓ
49.	ⓐ	ⓑ	ⓒ	ⓓ
50.	ⓐ	ⓑ	ⓒ	ⓓ
51.	ⓐ	ⓑ	ⓒ	ⓓ
52.	ⓐ	ⓑ	ⓒ	ⓓ
53.	ⓐ	ⓑ	ⓒ	ⓓ
54.	ⓐ	ⓑ	ⓒ	ⓓ
55.	ⓐ	ⓑ	ⓒ	ⓓ
56.	ⓐ	ⓑ	ⓒ	ⓓ
57.	ⓐ	ⓑ	ⓒ	ⓓ
58.	ⓐ	ⓑ	ⓒ	ⓓ
59.	ⓐ	ⓑ	ⓒ	ⓓ
60.	ⓐ	ⓑ	ⓒ	ⓓ
61.	ⓐ	ⓑ	ⓒ	ⓓ
62.	ⓐ	ⓑ	ⓒ	ⓓ
63.	ⓐ	ⓑ	ⓒ	ⓓ
64.	ⓐ	ⓑ	ⓒ	ⓓ
65.	ⓐ	ⓑ	ⓒ	ⓓ
66.	ⓐ	ⓑ	ⓒ	ⓓ
67.	ⓐ	ⓑ	ⓒ	ⓓ
68.	ⓐ	ⓑ	ⓒ	ⓓ
69.	ⓐ	ⓑ	ⓒ	ⓓ
70.	ⓐ	ⓑ	ⓒ	ⓓ

71.	ⓐ	ⓑ	ⓒ	ⓓ
72.	ⓐ	ⓑ	ⓒ	ⓓ
73.	ⓐ	ⓑ	ⓒ	ⓓ
74.	ⓐ	ⓑ	ⓒ	ⓓ
75.	ⓐ	ⓑ	ⓒ	ⓓ
76.	ⓐ	ⓑ	ⓒ	ⓓ
77.	ⓐ	ⓑ	ⓒ	ⓓ
78.	ⓐ	ⓑ	ⓒ	ⓓ
79.	ⓐ	ⓑ	ⓒ	ⓓ
80.	ⓐ	ⓑ	ⓒ	ⓓ
81.	ⓐ	ⓑ	ⓒ	ⓓ
82.	ⓐ	ⓑ	ⓒ	ⓓ
83.	ⓐ	ⓑ	ⓒ	ⓓ
84.	ⓐ	ⓑ	ⓒ	ⓓ
85.	ⓐ	ⓑ	ⓒ	ⓓ
86.	ⓐ	ⓑ	ⓒ	ⓓ
87.	ⓐ	ⓑ	ⓒ	ⓓ
88.	ⓐ	ⓑ	ⓒ	ⓓ
89.	ⓐ	ⓑ	ⓒ	ⓓ
90.	ⓐ	ⓑ	ⓒ	ⓓ
91.	ⓐ	ⓑ	ⓒ	ⓓ
92.	ⓐ	ⓑ	ⓒ	ⓓ
93.	ⓐ	ⓑ	ⓒ	ⓓ
94.	ⓐ	ⓑ	ⓒ	ⓓ
95.	ⓐ	ⓑ	ⓒ	ⓓ
96.	ⓐ	ⓑ	ⓒ	ⓓ
97.	ⓐ	ⓑ	ⓒ	ⓓ
98.	ⓐ	ⓑ	ⓒ	ⓓ
99.	ⓐ	ⓑ	ⓒ	ⓓ
100.	ⓐ	ⓑ	ⓒ	ⓓ

► Police Sergeant Practice Exam 2

1. Activities performed by officers on patrol that are directed toward keeping violations of the law from happening are most widely known as
   a. community service.
   b. selective patrol.
   c. proportional enforcement.
   d. crime prevention.

2. An officer deciding whether or not to issue a traffic citation to a motorist should consider all of the following factors EXCEPT
   a. the seriousness of the offense.
   b. whether the law being violated is fair or unfair.
   c. whether a warning would better serve the interests of justice.
   d. the nature of the offense.

3. As an officer responding to a call that a group has assembled for what appears to be an unlawful purpose, you should
   a. stop at a strategic location away from the immediate scene, evaluate the situation, and notify the dispatcher.
   b. act quickly and decisively to disperse the group.
   c. request backup assistance, then tell the group to disperse while you are waiting for backup to arrive.
   d. announce to the group that they will have to disperse.

4. At the scene of a homicide, what is the medical examiner or coroner normally responsible for?
   a. planning the course of the investigation and assigning officers to various tasks
   b. obtaining the names and addresses of witnesses
   c. determining the cause of death and identifying any possible suspects
   d. securing the body of the deceased, as well as all associated clothing and personal property

5. You are required to administer a sobriety test to a motorist to determine if the motorist is intoxicated. During the test, the motorist experiences difficulty maintaining equilibrium. This is known as
   a. the Romberg sign.
   b. Fournier's test.
   c. Frankel's test.
   d. the intoxolyzer test.

6. In order to allow for accurate and complete reconstruction of an accident scene, it is important for an officer to measure skid marks to
   a. the nearest inch.
   b. the nearest foot.
   c. the nearest yard.
   d. the nearest half-yard.

7. Foot patrol by police officers is most effective in combating
   a. organized crime.
   b. robberies and street muggings.
   c. domestic abuse.
   d. white-collar crime.

8. More and more enterprising police departments are beginning to use bicycle patrols. Officers riding bicycles are especially effective in preventing crime that occurs on streets, in alleys, and in public areas where automobiles cannot patrol. In addition, bicycles are used to patrol large areas such as parks and beaches and have much the same impact as foot patrol. They are also excellent in operations where silence is desirable. What have experts recognized as the main disadvantage of bicycle patrols?
- **a.** Officers on bicycles are not equipped with long-range communications equipment.
- **b.** It is expensive to train bicycle officers and to maintain the bicycles.
- **c.** Administrators find it difficult to recruit officers for bicycle patrol.
- **d.** Bicycles are plagued with frequent mechanical failures and become obsolete quickly.

9. You are patrolling at 3:00 A.M. in an area that has been the target of numerous burglaries in the past week. You notice one of your subordinates paying special attention to a man apparently attempting to hide in a doorway. In a moment, the rookie officer comes to you and tells you that the man resembles the description of one of the burglary suspects. What is the best way to advise the rookie officer?
- **a.** Tell the officer to draw his or her gun and have the suspect assume the wall-search position.
- **b.** Remind the officer to frisk the suspect before questioning him.
- **c.** Direct the officer to explain his or her suspicions to the suspect and then question him.
- **d.** Have the officer transport the suspect to the station house for questioning.

10. You are a sergeant who has arrived at the scene of what your patrol officers originally thought was a robbery-in-progress call. You see three patrol cars on the scene. The lead officer tells you that the suspects fled over an hour ago. What should you have the other two officers do?
- **a.** assist in interviewing witnesses
- **b.** report back to service
- **c.** begin an immediate search of the vicinity
- **d.** resume general patrol in their assigned areas

11. The purpose of criminal investigation is to identify the perpetrator of a particular crime by gathering information from witnesses and suspects. Which of the following is of least concern to the police?
- **a.** who
- **b.** what
- **c.** why
- **d.** how

12. The Constitution and the rights expressed in it are directed at protecting citizens against the improper actions of which of the following?
- **a.** the military
- **b.** other citizens
- **c.** corporations
- **d.** the government

13. Which of the following is the highest court in the nation?
- **a.** the Court of Appeals
- **b.** the Federal District Court
- **c.** the Supreme Court
- **d.** the Criminal Court

14. The United States has determined that free speech is protected under the First Amendment of the Constitution. Which of the following situations would not be protected under the First Amendment?

   a. yelling "the president is corrupt"

   b. yelling "fire" in a crowded theater where there is no fire

   c. yelling at a police officer

   d. yelling in a ballpark during the national anthem

15. Under the Constitution, citizens are protected from double jeopardy, or being tried twice for the same crime. The Supreme Court has held that none of the following situations amounts to double jeopardy EXCEPT

   a. when a jury fails to get a unanimous verdict and a defendant is tried again.

   b. when a mistrial is granted by the court to protect the defendant's rights.

   c. when a defendant is acquitted and then tried again because new evidence is found.

   d. when a defendant is tried twice for the same act, once under state statutes and once under federal statutes.

16. Citizens periodically feel the need to make complaints against officers. One of the most important aspects of management is the organization of a solid civilian complaint system. Persons outside the department may file one of two different kinds of complaints against officers, depending on the status of the person making the complaint. What are the two kinds of complaints against an officer that may be filed by people outside the department?

   a. external or secondary

   b. secondary or primary

   c. internal or external

   d. internal or primary

17. The understanding of human behavior is paramount to good supervisory practices. A variety of barriers may get in the way of the ability of personnel to perform at their peak. When the barrier is an inadequate salary, this would be called a

   a. physical barrier.

   b. human barrier.

   c. psychological barrier.

   d. situational barrier.

18. According to experts in the field of law enforcement, when searching for a lost child, which of these areas should be searched first?

   a. the house of the lost child

   b. the immediate area of the lost child's home

   c. the immediate area from which the child disappeared

   d. all of the above

19. What is the result of psychological problems that go unaddressed and untreated?
   a. The problems become repressed.
   b. The problems grow in severity and become worse.
   c. The problems begin to affect other people.
   d. The problems usually lessen in severity.

20. Under most standard regulations for dealing with complaints, at what point in the process does a complaint officially become a grievance?
   a. when the supervisor first receives the complaint
   b. when the supervisor fails to resolve the complaint and refers it to the next level of management
   c. when the second level of management fails to resolve the complaint and refers it to the chief of police
   d. when the chief of police fails to resolve the complaint and refers it to arbitration

21. Which of the following conditions is most likely to result from a failure to plan and organize teaching material properly?
   a. a sense of aimlessness in the class
   b. rigidity of the teacher
   c. oversimplification of important points
   d. a fear of failure on the part of individual students

22. It is agreed among present-day industrial psychologists that there several steps in the teaching process. These include the "introduction step," the "presentation step," the "application step," and the "test step." Problem solving or role playing should be used during which of these steps?
   a. the introduction step
   b. the presentation step
   c. the application step
   d. the test step

23. You are the sergeant in charge of a squad. One of your officers recently suffered the death of a loved one. The mourning by the employee is beginning to affect his performance on the job. To be consistent with sound supervisory practices, all of the following might be appropriate responses to the officer EXCEPT
   a. encouraging the employee to take a vacation.
   b. diverting the employee's grief toward some physical activity.
   c. helping the employee focus energy on helping someone else.
   d. showing understanding, patience, and tact.

24. When a police manager uses the "charm-school approach," it is said that he or she is using which of the following leadership styles?
   a. the *laissez-faire* method
   b. the command-presence method
   c. the environmental method
   d. the democratic method

25. A conference that consists of persons with widely differing ranks is most accurately referred to as
   a. a horizontal conference.
   b. a vertical conference.
   c. a structured conference.
   d. a spontaneous conference.

26. It has been said that without a particular ingredient of supervision, each individual in an organization will do what he or she wants, when he or she wants, and any integrated activity is impossible. The ingredient referred to is
   a. direction.
   b. leading.
   c. controlling.
   d. organizing.

27. The ability to use appropriate questions during an employee interview allows the interviewer to elicit accurate and helpful responses. Which of the following statements is most accurate with respect to the kinds of questions that are effective in employee interviews?
   a. Questions framed in negative terms have a tendency to elicit accurate responses.
   b. Questions should lead the prospective employee to the expected answer.
   c. Questions that can be answered simply "yes" or "no" provide sufficient information for an employee interview.
   d. Questions framed in positive terms tend to elicit accurate responses, because positive terms are less suggestive than negative terms.

28. To be most effective at deterring rule-breaking in the future, punishment for serious infractions must be
   a. fair.
   b. impartial.
   c. swift.
   d. certain.

29. The principal responsibility for maintaining an appropriate level of discipline in a unit rests with the
   a. chief of police.
   b. immediate line supervisor.
   c. middle-level supervisors.
   d. first line sergeants.

30. In which situation would it be appropriate for a supervisor to violate the principle of unity of command?
   I. when efficiency is endangered
   II. when safety is endangered
   III. when the organization's reputation is endangered
   a. I only
   b. III only
   c. II and III
   d. I, II, and III

31. Which one of the following would be considered an example of "positive discipline"?
   a. A sergeant mildly admonishes one of his or her officers after observing a patrol function weakness.
   b. A sergeant reprimands one of his or her officers for being tardy too often.
   c. A police officer is fired after being convicted of a criminal offense.
   d. A sergeant offers an officer extra training on a particular skill or procedure.

32. You are the sergeant in charge of a unit. One of your officers, Officer Thomas, approaches you and informs you that she is concerned about Officer Suki, who is also in your unit. Officer Thomas tells you that she thinks Officer Suki has a drinking problem. She tells you that Officer Suki is beginning to physically deteriorate. If what Officer Thomas is telling you is true, Officer Suki would be at what stage of problem drinking?
   a. the early stage
   b. the intermediate stage
   c. the acute stage
   d. the final stage

33. Certain rating errors seem to occur more often in supervisors that exhibit certain traits. A supervisor who attaches a high degree of approval to static employees who don't "rock the boat" is probably engaging in which rating error?
   a. the error of personal bias
   b. the halo effect
   c. the error of related traits
   d. the error of leniency

34. A friend of yours has just been appointed to the rank of sergeant. She knows you are a highly respected sergeant and that you know your workers well. Your friend tells you that she realizes a skillful supervisor learns about her officers by various means, but she wants to know the most important way to learn about the employees in her unit. To be most consistent with sound supervisory practices, what would you tell the new sergeant?
   a. You get to know your employees by hearing others talk about them.
   b. You should analyze their work thorough the inspection process.
   c. You need to talk with your employees.
   d. You get to know your employees best by reviewing their reports.

35. Under which situation should a supervisor intervene into the personal problems of an officer under his or her direct supervision?
   a. when the problem is affecting the officer's family
   b. when the problem becomes known to the organization
   c. when the problem is serious
   d. when the problem begins to affect the officer's performance

36. When using which of the following types of orders is a supervisor often left without the ability to follow up?
   a. direct commands
   b. requests
   c. suggestions
   d. specific orders

37. During an employee-centered interview, the wise interviewer should adopt what approach?
a. "big heart, little mouth"
b. "big ears, little heart"
c. "big heart, big mouth"
d. "big ears, little mouth"

38. A supervisor is seeking to establish strict liability for employee compliance with a new order. What is the best method for the supervisor to communicate the order to his or her subordinates?
a. oral communication
b. demonstration
c. written communication
d. implied communication

39. Which one of the following workers would be most likely to accuse a supervisor of partiality in rating the employee on a service rating?
a. the outstanding worker
b. the marginal worker
c. the poor worker
d. the average worker

40. Upon observing a breach of discipline, a supervisor should usually call the matter to the attention of the employee promptly and privately. In which of the following situations may chastisement in the presence of fellow employees or the public be justified?
a. when the employee has made several mistakes
b. when other employees also observe the breach of discipline
c. when it is necessary to stop a continuing breach of order
d. it is never appropriate to discipline an employee publicly

41. The essence of participatory management is
a. delegation of authority and all that it entails.
b. involving employees in decision making.
c. training and motivating employees to realize their goals.
d. complete democratic participation by employees.

42. In which of the following four steps of the five-step teaching method may a teacher have the opportunity to evaluate the effectiveness of his or her teaching and the learner's comprehension of the subject matter?
a. the introduction
b. the presentation
c. the application
d. the test

43. When a supervisor investigates complaints against personnel, the ultimate purpose of the investigation is
a. to arrive at the truth.
b. to keep the public from hearing of the matter.
c. to determine the appropriate punishment.
d. to understand why an officer behaved a certain way.

44. There are occasions where the supervisor must conduct a separation interview. Which of the following is most accurate concerning this important interview?

    a. It is usually desirable to prepare notes as the interview progresses.

    b. The taking of notes during such an interview should be avoided.

    c. One should never supplement notes after the interview is over.

    d. The best time to prepare notes is upon completion of the interview so as not to inhibit the officer.

45. In most police agencies, the single most important training activity is

    a. teaching new employees to perform their basic duties.

    b. rating supervisors on job performance.

    c. conducting continuous training of all personnel.

    d. to have training start at the top of the hierarchy and "trickle down."

46. When a supervisor must take disciplinary action against a subordinate, there should be no hesitation. Failure to act decisively may result in the supervisor

    a. lowering the morale of the derelict employee.

    b. abdicating his or her position of leadership.

    c. increasing the feeling of retribution within the command structure.

    d. using fear as a tool of management to gain conformity.

47. Which type of communication is most effective in coordinating the efforts of an organizational unit?

    a. upward

    b. downward

    c. lateral

    d. circular

48. Of the following, what is considered to be the prime duty of a police sergeant?

    a. directing his or her subordinates

    b. leading his or her subordinates

    c. controlling his or her subordinates

    d. supervising his or her subordinates

49. Which of the following is inseparable from the principle of delegation?

    a. training

    b. the exception principle

    c. development of subordinates

    d. order giving

50. People react to failure in multiple ways. Of the following, which choice should supervisors recognize as the most common reaction to failure?

    a. fear

    b. aggression

    c. projection

    d. rationalization

51. While training subordinates, it can be helpful to ask questions of the trainees. Asking questions effectively leads to group involvement. Therefore, questions should be

    a. controversial, to arouse emotions.

    b. asked in a manner that suggests an answer.

    c. addressed to the entire group at the start of the discussion period.

    d. addressed to a particular trainee.

52. How should supervisors treat all subordinate officers?
a. fairly
b. equally
c. as they would want to be treated
d. consistently

53. As the sergeant in charge of a unit, you have discovered that one of your officers has been intentionally withholding information from you in an effort to show you that he is displeased with your leadership. According to management experts, this officer is practicing
a. reversed discipline.
b. upward discipline.
c. calculated block.
d. projection.

54. Under which of the following leadership styles would morale, discipline, efficiency, and production all begin to deteriorate?
a. the autocratic leader
b. the democratic leader
c. the *laissez-faire* leader
d. the hands-on leader

55. Many types of questions can be used with effective results while the supervisor is instructing subordinates during a training session. However, experts agree that the most commonly used questions in teaching situations are
a. reverse questions.
b. relay questions.
c. rhetorical questions.
d. overhead questions.

56. Which of the following actions by a supervisor would be most effective in generating control of the unit?
a. observation and inspection
b. direction and planning
c. planning and training
d. planning and organizing

57. Sergeant Kosova is rating Officer Sawyer. Sergeant Kosova recalls that Officer Sawyer has many of the same political beliefs that she has, and respects that. She therefore rates Officer Sawyer's performance as excellent. Which rating error has Sergeant Kosova committed?
a. leniency
b. related traits
c. halo effect
d. personal bias

58. The slang term used to denote a mixture of heroin and cocaine injected into the bloodstream by the user is
a. hot shot.
b. brown man.
c. speedball.
d. H and C.

59. According to experts in the fields of criminal investigation and forensic science, which of the following is NOT true about conducting interviews?
a. Middle-aged persons are considered to be among the worst witnesses.
b. A child under six may invent a story in response to a question.
c. An older child, from six to ten, may tend to distort the story.
d. Young children are given to flights of imagination.

60. Which of the following are recognized exceptions to the Fourth Amendment search warrant requirement?

    I. consent search

   II. vehicle exception

  III. crime scene exception

  a. I only

  b. III only

  c. II and III

  d. I and II

61. Which of the following is not a blood type?

  a. A

  b. AB

  c. O

  d. AO

62. All of the following are presumptive signs that indicate death, with one exception. What is the exception?

  a. a bluish color on the body's outer extremities

  b. cessation of breathing and respiratory movements

  c. absence of heart sound

  d. a loss of flushing of nail beds when pressure on the nails is released

63. Of the following, what is considered to be the best test to determine if a stain is human or animal blood?

  a. the precipitin reaction test

  b. the microspectroscopic test

  c. the Hemming crystal test

  d. the phenolphthalein test

64. You are the sergeant in charge of an investigation unit and you are responding to the scene of a homicide to aid your investigators, who are already at the scene. Upon your arrival, you are met by one of your investigators. She tells you that she has located about eight brownish blond hairs in the right hand of the victim. She asks you what the best means of collecting these hairs for future examination would be. To follow sound forensic science procedures, how would you advise the investigator to proceed?

  a. Tell her to place the hairs in carefully folded paper and seal them inside an envelope.

  b. Direct the investigator to place the hairs in a clean test tube containing a saline solution.

  c. Tell the investigator to leave them in the deceased's hand and transport the body to the lab.

  d. Direct the investigator to place the hairs in a clean test tube containing distilled water.

65. Which of the following will not contain any rifling markings?

  a. a bullet shot through a .9 mm handgun

  b. a bullet shot through a .22 caliber rifle

  c. a slug shot through a shotgun

  d. an expended shell ejected from a .40 caliber handgun

66. How many latent fingerprint points must match the suspect's fingerprint for courts to consider the latent print positive identification?

  a. 10 to 12

  b. 12 to 15

  c. no specific number

  d. 7 to 10

67. Which one of the following is considered by forensic medical doctors to be least accurate regarding suicide committed by hanging?
  a. When the body is found hanging by rope, cord, or wire, it should be cut between the knot and the object to which it is tied.
  b. Postmortem lividity will be most pronounced in the lower portions of the arms and legs, as well as around the face, lips, and jaw.
  c. Most suicidal hangings are a painful and very discomforting process, since death is caused by the victim slowly choking to death.
  d. It is common in suicidal hangings for the victim's feet or even the knees to be touching the ground.

68. When someone is poisoned by sulfuric acid, what is the most evident symptom?
  a. yellow vomit
  b. reddish skin color
  c. blue-green vomit
  d. black vomit

69. A body is found lying face down. Upon investigation, the investigating detective finds that there is significant pooling of blood, known as "lividity," on the back side of the entire body. What is the most plausible conclusion that can be drawn from this observation?
  a. The victim has been deceased for at least 24 hours.
  b. The victim died as a result of arsenic poisoning.
  c. The victim was asphyxiated.
  d. The victim was moved after death.

70. Which one of the following statements concerning a crime scene search is least accurate?
  a. Graph paper is the best paper to use in preparing a crime scene sketch.
  b. A large variety of colors should be used to identify objects or points of interest on the sketch.
  c. The coordinate method is a technique that involves measuring the distance of an object from two fixed points.
  d. The triangulation method is particularly useful in an outdoor situation where there are no easily identifiable boundaries of fields or roads for use as baselines.

71. A fundamental aspect of most investigations is the neighborhood canvass. It is estimated that systematic canvassing of the neighborhood within a short time after the commission of a crime produces positive information of value to the investigation in approximately what percent of all cases?
  a. 15%
  b. 20%
  c. 50%
  d. 60%

72. Blood specimens should be taken only by a physician, medical technologist, or other person with similar qualifications. In taking the specimen, the skin and the instruments must carefully be disinfected. When disinfecting the skin and instruments for the purpose of taking blood specimens, which one of the following should be used?
  a. bichloride of mercury
  b. alcohol
  c. ether
  d. sodium fluoride

73. Making plaster casts of evidence can be important for many reasons. Plaster casts are used for most kinds of footprints, motor vehicle tire tracks, and many other impressions left by the criminal and the tools used by the criminal in committing a crime. The best procedure for making a plaster cast of an imprint in sand (before adding a layer of gauze or wire to reinforce the structure) is to
   a. apply the plaster and then spray shellac.
   b. spray shellac and then apply the plaster.
   c. wet the surface with water and then apply the plaster.
   d. spray iodine, let dry, then apply the plaster.

74. The greatest number of safe crackers employ the following technique: First, gather the required tools (an electric drill or a brace and bit and a sectional jimmy or a crowbar); next, make a hole in the upper or lower left-hand corner of the safe door; and finally, place the jimmy into the hole and pry the door up until it is exposed to a point just beyond the dial. This technique refers to what?
   a. rip job
   b. punch job
   c. chop job
   d. touch job

75. In one form of swindle, two people enter a jewelry store and ask the person tending the counter to show them some loose diamonds. Generally the attendant is smart enough to leave only one or two stones out at a time for the prospective buyer to examine. At this juncture, a third person enters the store and distracts the attendant for only a few seconds, but it is long enough for one of the first two people to switch the genuine stone and a lookalike fake. This type of theft is
   a. the smack game.
   b. the launch.
   c. pennyweighting.
   d. the switch.

76. Invisible laundry marks are usually discovered by
   a. iodine fuming.
   b. an ultraviolet lamp.
   c. an infrared lamp.
   d. oblique lighting.

77. In recent studies by community relations experts, it was found that police officers perceived that the least cooperative citizens were
   a. individual teenagers.
   b. individual grown men.
   c. teenagers in large groups.
   d. sports fans in large groups.

78. What is considered to be the basic goal of community policing?

    a. to decentralize operations to the maximum degree

    b. to get the officer on the beat more involved in the community

    c. to assign patrol officers and first line supervisors in a temporary capacity to a particular neighborhood

    d. to allow the police and the community to interact in a climate of dysfunction

79. Officer Monaco receives a call regarding a burglary. Officer Monaco responds to the call, conducts the investigations, collects all relevant evidence, makes the arrest, writes up all necessary reports, and prepares the case for prosecution. Which type of organizational structure does Officer Monaco work in?

    a. line organization

    b. staff organization

    c. functional organization

    d. line and staff organization

80. When work is delegated to a subordinate, the subordinate should perform the tasks necessary to complete the assignment so that all that is left for the supervisor to do is to review the work and sign off on it. What management concept does this describe?

    a. control

    b. direction

    c. completed staff work

    d. organization

81. Sergeant Wells is teaching a course at the police academy. A recruit officer raises her hand and asks Sergeant Wells a question. Sergeant Wells listens to the question and then calls upon another recruit officer and asks him to answer the first recruit officer's question. Which question technique did Sergeant Wells utilize?

    a. rebound question

    b. overhead question

    c. rhetorical question

    d. relay question

82. What is repeatedly cited as the greatest barrier between police and the community?

    a. heavy caseloads

    b. lack of understanding of the police by citizens

    c. lack of understanding of citizens by the police

    d. the squad car

83. Sergeant Schneiderman is delegating away a work task to an officer in her unit who she knows is capable of completing the task. What should Sergeant Schneiderman be aware of regarding the delegation process?

    a. You must also delegate authority and responsibility.

    b. You can't delegate authority, but you should delegate responsibility.

    c. You must delegate authority, but you can't delegate responsibility.

    d. You can't delegate either authority or responsibility.

84. In which of the following situations would a sergeant be justified in filtering information from his or her supervisors?
   a. when the information is unfavorable news
   b. when the information is positive news
   c. when the information is not noteworthy
   d. never; sergeants should never filter information

85. Who provide the major point of contact between the police and the community?
   a. police dispatchers
   b. patrol officers
   c. traffic officers
   d. police detectives

86. Perhaps the most important approach to improving relations between the police and the media is
   a. the ombudsperson approach.
   b. the press council approach.
   c. the mutual education approach.
   d. the teleconferences approach.

87. Policing is most effective when
   a. officers stay on the same beat.
   b. officers are regularly assigned to new beats.
   c. community members play decision-making roles.
   d. community members participate in ride-along programs.

88. Three important elements of a police officer's job are (i) danger, (ii) authority, and (iii) efficiency. According to experts in psychology, these elements give rise to three personality characteristics in the typical police officer. Those characteristics are
   a. an ability to be discreet, isolation, and brutality.
   b. guardedness, flexibility, and indecisiveness.
   c. an ability to be innovative, flexibility, and independence.
   d. isolation, a sense of police solidarity, and guardedness.

89. What right is implicated when the state treats a class of defendants who happen to be indigent differently from other defendants for purposes of offering them the opportunity to appeal a court decision?
   a. equal protection
   b. due process
   c. double jeopardy
   d. *habeas corpus* concerns

90. With regard to self-representation, which of the following statements is most accurate?
   a. When a defendant wants to act as his or her own attorney, the court must allow him or her to do so without any further obligation on its part.
   b. A state may, even over the strong objection of the accused, appoint a standby counsel during the trial.
   c. When a person represents him- or herself, that person is not compelled to follow rules of procedural and substantive law, as a member of the bar would be.
   d. A person who represents him- or herself and loses at trial may not appeal.

91. Armed with two arrest warrants for Joe Bradford, police were watching a house where they believed Mr. Bradford lived. The police observed cars pull up to the house, whereupon Mr. Bradford would come out and talk to the person in a car, go back to the house, return a moment later, and lean in the window of the car. Police believed they were observing narcotics transactions. Finally, when Mr. Bradford was returning to his house from speaking to a person in a car, the police arrested him on his front steps, before he could get into the house. The police then entered the house and made a cursory inspection to ascertain if anyone else was present; when the defendant's mother and brother entered the house, they were told of the arrest and an impending search. Sometime later, when the search was conducted, a quantity of narcotics was found in a rear bedroom. The Supreme Court held that

a. the search was illegal because there was no exigency to justify a warrantless search of the arrestee's house.

b. the search was legal as a search incident to a lawful arrest.

c. the search was illegal due to the "taint" of an unlawful arrest.

d. the search was legal because the "sweep search" was performed for the officers' safety.

92. A suspect appeared at the stationhouse voluntarily for questioning concerning the strangulation of his wife, at which time the police noticed what appeared to be blood on his finger. Although they had probable cause to arrest him, they did not formally place him under arrest at that time. The warrantless taking of scrapings from his fingernails in this case was held to be

a. constitutionally permissible as incident to arrest under the scope of *Chimel v. California*.

b. constitutionally reasonable as a search to preserve the highly evanescent evidence under his fingernails.

c. unconstitutional, as the suspect was not under arrest even though probable cause for the arrest existed.

d. unconstitutional, because a search warrant was not obtained.

93. Which of the following is NOT considered a seizure in the Fourth Amendment sense?

a. an arrest

b. an investigative stop

c. a subpoena to appear before a grand jury to give testimony

d. taking a suspect to the station for questioning and holding him or her there

94. As a supervisor, you may be called upon to oversee suspect interrogations. An important aspect of any interrogation is to balance the rights of the accused with the need to get pertinent information about the crime. Which of the following incidents recounts a violation of the right to self-incrimination as embodied under Miranda?

a. Officer Kruter arrests a suspect, fails to read her rights to her, and asks her, "Where did you put that loaded gun?"

b. Officer Kruter stops a person he reasonably suspects is committing a crime and asks her, "What are you doing here?"

c. Officer Kruter transports a suspect to a police interview room and says, "Tell me how you committed the crime."

d. Officer Kruter asks a person walking by him to identify herself.

95. Immediately following the adoption of the Fourth Amendment, a certain practice whereby probable cause is reviewed by a higher court furnished the model for criminal procedure in the United States today. There are indications that the framers of the Bill of Rights regarded this practice as a model for a "reasonable seizure." These statements are most likely making reference to what practice?

a. a writ of *habeas corpus*

b. a writ of *corpus delicti*

c. the process of arrest

d. the due process clause

96. The Supreme Court established the exclusionary rule in *Weeks v. United States*. The exclusionary rule states that

a. evidence obtained by unreasonable search and seizure can't be used in court.

b. evidence obtained by private citizens can't be used in court.

c. anything that the defense argues should be kept out of court should be excluded.

d. anything that directly proves the defendant's guilt or innocence may be entered as evidence.

97. The Supreme Court has concluded that an issuing magistrate must meet two tests in order to conform to possessing "warrant authority." He or she must be neutral and detached and

a. must be a judge.

b. must be an attorney.

c. must be capable of determining whether probable cause exists for the requested arrest or search.

d. must be capable of understanding the procedures of the court and the rules of evidence.

98. Of the following, what has traditionally been applied to determine probable cause?

   a. The "two-prong" test has traditionally determined probable cause.

   b. The "totality of the circumstances" test has traditionally determined probable cause.

   c. The traditional test to determine probable cause is the "weight of the veracity and reliability" test.

   d. Specific tests must be satisfied by every informant's tip before probable cause is determined.

99. When does the right to counsel attach?

   a. at the time of formal arrest

   b. when the suspect asks for an attorney subsequent to arrest and following the Miranda warnings

   c. at the suspect's lineup after he has been indicted

   d. when a defendant is formally charged or first appears before a magistrate

100. "It is intended to vindicate society's interest in having its laws obeyed, and it is inevitably accompanied by future interference with the individual's freedom of movement, whether or not trial or conviction ultimately follows." This statement, made by the Supreme Court in *Terry v. Ohio*, most nearly refers to

   a. a frisk.

   b. a full search.

   c. an arrest.

   d. the investigatory detention.

▶ Answers

1. d. The main advantage of the visibility provided by patrol officers is crime prevention. The mere presence of an officer on the streets tends to inhibit criminal activity.

2. b. Although police officers rarely have discretion as to whether or not to charge someone with a crime, they often have a certain amount of discretion in issuing citations in traffic cases; nonetheless, an officer's opinion about the fairness of a traffic law should not be a consideration in issuing a citation.

3. a. It would be unnecessarily dangerous for an officer to attempt to disperse a large, possibly hostile group alone. Instead, an officer should stop at a location from which he or she can observe the crowd, then notify the dispatcher as to the nature of the incident, the number of people gathered, whether they are armed, and any other important information.

4. d. In most jurisdictions, the medical examiner or the coroner is in charge of the body, and all personal property and clothing found with the body, until the cause of death is determined. Medical examiners are usually medical doctors specializing in pathology. A coroner, however, may or may not be a medical doctor; many coroners are morticians.

5. a. The inability to maintain equilibrium is known as the "Romberg sign." "Frankel's test" is the test in which the subject is directed to walk a line by placing the heel of one foot against the toe of the other for approximately ten steps; "Fournier's test" refers to an officer taking notice of the subject's balance in the walking and turning. An intoxolyzer is a machine for measuring blood alcohol level.

6. a. Each skid mark needs to be measured to within the nearest inch. All of the marks from one car should be added together, even if not all of the tires left marks. The total is then divided by the number of wheels on the vehicle to find the average length of the marks. Minimum speed can then be computed by using a device such as the skid-speed chart.

7. b. Foot patrol is the oldest type of police patrol; it is still a highly effective way of combating such crimes as robberies and street muggings. Foot patrol can do little to prevent organized crime, domestic abuse, or white-collar crime.

8. a. With improvements in modern electronics, this disadvantage will gradually disappear. Other disadvantages of bicycles are the restrictions in the amount of equipment that can be carried and the distance they can cover compared to motor vehicles.

9. c. It is generally wiser to explain the basis for your suspicions before taking action. The citizen who is not engaged in unlawful activities is likely to extend cooperation and may well have a satisfactory explanation for his or her presence in the area. If a suspect is uncooperative or unable to explain his or her presence in the area, the officer will need to investigate further and may need to consider frisking the suspect if the person's behavior causes the officer concern for his or her own safety.

10. b. In most cases, the sergeant as a supervisor is responsible for directing field units. Unless there are some particular circumstances in this investigation, one patrol unit can complete the preliminary investigation.

11. c. Although motive—the "why" of a crime—may be important, it is of more concern to courts and prosecutors than to police officers. It is not necessary to uncover motive in order to arrest a perpetrator.

12. d. The Constitution was created to protect citizens against unfair treatment by the government. This includes any derivative governmental organization, such as the police. The Constitution does not protect against the actions of other citizens.

13. c. The U.S. Supreme Court is the highest court in the nation. This is the ultimate court of last resort. All decisions rendered by the Supreme Court become the law of the land for all states.

14. b. The court has ruled that this type of speech is not protected under the Constitution. Other examples of unprotected speech include "fighting words," words likely to elicit a violent response, such as obscenity and defamation.

15. c. When no verdict is reached in a trial because of a hung jury or a mistrial, the defendant may be tried again; also, actions that are illegal under both state and federal statutes may be prosecuted by each (the crimes usually have different names, even though they are based on the same incident). However, once a defendant is acquitted, that defendant cannot be tried again, regardless of any new evidence that arises.

16. b. Secondary complaints are those made by second parties, often attorneys, elected officials, representatives of organized groups, or parents. Primary complaints are those received directly from the victim of a police action.

17. d. Other examples of situational barriers include unpopular rules or policies and inconvenient scheduling. Physical barriers are things in the environment of the individual, such as a malfunctioning flashlight, a sticking door, or bad brakes on a police car. Psychological barriers are conditions inherent in the individual, such as depression or worrying about a loved one. Human barriers are caused by the people in an officer's life and could include problems with a spouse, partner, or supervisor.

18. c. Although it may become necessary to search the house of the lost child and the area around that house, the immediate area from which the child disappeared should be searched first. This is true even when parents or friends indicate that they have already looked there. Most children are found very near to the area where they were last seen.

19. b. When psychological problems go untreated, they become worse. This in turn may begin to affect the employee's performance and the performance of those working around the affected officer. These problems rarely, if ever, subside or lessen in intensity.

20. b. Typically, four steps are involved when dissatisfactions degenerate into formal grievances. In the first step, the supervisor or the employee representative receives the complaint. Usually the issue can be resolved at this level. Should attempts to resolve the matter at this level fail, the matter becomes an official grievance. This is the second step, in which the complaint is referred to a higher level of management for resolution. Should the grievance not be solved at that level, it is transmitted to the top level of management within the organization. If unsuccessful there, it moves to voluntary arbitration, the fourth step.

21. a. Lack of organization can make a class feel that the teacher is wandering in his or her presentation. Experts consider lack of preparation resulting in a sense of aimlessness the single most important cause of ineffectiveness in teaching and student frustration.

22. c. Problem solving and role playing are excellent teaching devices that allow students to practice applying the principles they learned in the introduction and presentation steps.

23. a. According to experts, an employee mourning the loss of a loved one can be helped by undertaking a physical activity or helping someone else. In addition, in these cases, it is always important for a supervisor to display understanding, patience, and tact. A vacation does not generally help someone "get away from it all," but rather focuses a person even more on his or her problems.

24. d. The charm-school approach, or the democratic method, can bring excellent results when applied sincerely, with common sense, and with good intentions. If applied superficially and insincerely, it eventually will produce bad results.

25. b. When members of a conference are from a variety of ranks in a hierarchy, it is said to be a *vertical conference*. A *horizontal conference* is one where members are of equal (or nearly equal) position or rank. (These tend to be more productive than vertical conferences, since everyone tends to speak up more.) Neither the term *structured conference* nor the term *spontaneous conference* refers to the rank of the participants.

26. a. Although the other ingredients may be important to supervision, directing is the essence of supervising others. It involves giving orders with some instruction on how to proceed (training) and monitoring the tasks to see that they are being properly done (follow up).

27. d. Questions framed in positive terms allow for a continuity of thought on the part of the prospective employee and result in responses that are complete and informative. Attempting to lead a prospective employee results in inaccurate information. In addition, questions should be framed so that the train of thought cannot be stopped by a "yes" or "no" answer.

28. d. Of course, punishment should be fair and impartial, but fair and impartial punishment does not deter future misbehavior as much as when a worker is certain that punishment will follow any serious infraction. Failure to deliver promised punishment leads to workers who know they can break the rules with impunity. In addition, punishment does not always have to be swift. At times, a cooling-off period is necessary; sometimes, punishment should be delayed in order to allow an investigation to be completed.

29. b. The question is asking who has the principal responsibility for maintaining discipline in a particular unit. If the unit doesn't have a sergeant, then the person responsible for discipline in the unit might be the lieutenant or a senior patrol officer. That person would be considered the immediate line supervisor of the unit.

30. c. Unity of command dictates that subordinates should answer to only one supervisor. Generally, it is understood that supervisors from other units should avoid giving orders to subordinates of other units. An exception occurs when an employee's or a citizen's safety is endangered or when the organization's reputation is endangered.

31. d. Training is an example of positive discipline. Choices **a**, **b**, and **c** are all examples of negative discipline. Negative discipline should be used only when positive discipline fails.

32. c. Experts recognize three stages of problem drinking: the early stage, the intermediate stage, and the acute, or late, stage. In the early stage, one may display minor symptoms, such as a tendency toward arguments, tardiness, absenteeism, or frequent hangovers. In the intermediate stage, a problem drinker's work habits start to deteriorate and absenteeism increases. In the acute stage, physical deterioration often sets in. The problem drinker becomes physically and psychologically dependent upon alcohol and becomes unsuited for the demands of police service.

33. **d.** Employees who do not improve but also do not deteriorate are rated highly by lenient supervisors because those employees tend to be easy to manage. The error of leniency is by far the most common of all errors in the rating of personnel. It is recognizable when a supervisor marks an inordinately large number of the rating reports as "very good" and "excellent," or perhaps even "excellent" and "outstanding."

34. **c.** Communicating with employees is the most effective way to learn about them on several levels. The skillful supervisor learns about subordinates by hearing others talk about them, by analyzing their work through the inspection process, and by reviewing their reports. But each of these methods provides only discrete bits of information. Talking with employees provides a more complete picture of them.

35. **d.** Supervisors should tread lightly when intervening into an officer's personal problems. Generally, it is understood that a supervisor should avoid "butting in," but a supervisor has a duty to intervene once an employee's performance is negatively affected.

36. **c.** Suggestions or implied orders are often abstract to the point where effective follow up

is nearly impossible, since the orders may be subject to more than one reasonable interpretation. Orders to inexperienced or unreliable employees should be given in a more direct manner than by suggestion or implication, allowing follow up to determine compliance.

37. **d.** In the employee-centered interview, little can be learned if the interviewer talks too much, whereas a lot can be learned through listening. Therefore, the wise interviewer will adopt a "big ears, little mouth" approach to the interview.

38. **c.** When a supervisor wants to achieve strict accountability with the provisions of an order, the supervisor should memorialize the order in written form. Orders should also be in written form when they are meant to convey a message to several different units or are meant to last for a long period of time.

39. **b.** A marginal worker might attempt to intimidate the supervisor into awarding a better-than-deserved rating. One method for doing this is to accuse the supervisor of partiality. The hope is that, in order to avoid being accused of partiality, the supervisor will award a higher rating. An outstanding worker has no need to engage in such tactics, and an average worker will often be content with an average rating. A poor worker, at least one who knows he or she is a poor worker, knows that intimidation will not result in a high enough rating to matter.

40. **c.** While it is rarely appropriate to discipline or chastise an employee publicly, experts agree that it may occasionally be necessary in order to stop a continuing breach of order.

41. **b.** This type of management works well when circumstances permit employees to participate in the decision-making process. But it does not call for complete democratic participation. There are occasions when managers must act as autocrats. Delegation of authority is an effective management technique, but not the definition of *participatory*. Finally, training employees to realize their own goals is not effective management.

42. d. The *introduction step* is where the teacher prepares the student to learn. The *presentation step* is where the teacher presents the subject matter. The *application step* is where the student gets the chance to apply what he or she has been taught. The *test step* is where the teacher finds out what the students have learned. (The fifth step, *follow-up*, was not offered as an answer choice; it occurs after instruction and assessment are over, to see if the lesson stayed with the students.)

43. a. Although it is often necessary for investigations of personnel to remain confidential, that is not a goal of the investigation. Nor is determining punishment usually a goal of an investigation into personnel complaints, although that may happen once the investigation is complete. Finally, while it might be helpful to know why an employee behaved a certain way, it is not the ultimate purpose of the investigation.

44. a. There should always be a record of this type of interview, to prevent inaccurate information from being entered into the final report. Note taking during the interview is the best way to assure accuracy. Waiting until after the interview is over may result in incomplete notes. However, there may be times when notes taken during the interview need to be expanded after the interview. Since this is not a counseling situation, it is not necessary to avoid note taking in order to put the officer at ease.

45. a. Without a well-trained staff on the line, the department's work will grind to a halt. Allowing training to trickle down from the top, even if it could be done, would be inefficient and counterproductive. The other choices are important, but nowhere near as important as effective initial training of personnel.

46. b. If punishment is uncertain, a supervisor may relinquish authority over subordinates. While there are situations that call for delay, none call for indecisiveness.

47. c. While upward, downward, and lateral communications all occur in organizations, lateral communication is the most effective in coordinating the efforts of organizational units. With lateral communication, peers communicate with each other and are able to coordinate efforts.

48. d. Directing, leading, and controlling are all activities a sergeant must undertake at times; taken together, they result in supervision.

49. c. In order to effectively delegate, a supervisor must have well-trained subordinates upon whom he or she can rely.

50. d. When people fail, they often attempt to explain away their failure in order to avoid embarrassment. This action is termed *rationalization*. Supervisors should be aware that frustration may also set in.

51. c. Addressing questions to the whole group allows any one of the trainees to volunteer the answer and opens the possibility of group discussion. It is not necessary to arouse emotions or to suggest answers in order to foster group involvement. Addressing questions to particular trainees may actually discourage group involvement.

52. a. Supervisors should treat all officers fairly. Equally is not an appropriate choice, because people have different personalities and to treat each in the same manner would not recognize these differences.

53. b. This type of behavior is called upward discipline. This refers to an attempt by a subordinate to discipline a supervisor.

54. c. Although different types of leadership vary in effectiveness and may be relied on in certain situations, too much use of the *laissez-faire*, or free-rein, style will provide workers with no leadership. As a result, they will be isolated, without guidance or direction. Then morale, discipline, efficiency, and eventually production will all begin to deteriorate.

55. d. Overhead questions are those directed to the entire class; these are most commonly used in teaching. Relay questions are asked by one student and relayed by the trainer to another student for an answer. Reverse questions are those where the trainer will refer the question back to the person who asked it for an answer. A rhetorical question is one asked for effect, where no answer is expected or the answer is implied within the question.

56. a. While all the choices are management principles, a supervisor does not know which are effective until he or she observes and inspects the unit. Only by knowing exactly what needs to be done can a supervisor exert control.

57. d. The rating error known as "personal bias" occurs when the rater gives exceptionally high or exceptionally low ratings based upon the fact that a subordinate holds the same beliefs as he or she does. This may seem that it is related to subjectivity, but the key is that the rater bases his or her rating on the fact that they both have the same opinions on an issue.

58. c. The term *hot shot* usually refers to heroin that is contaminated with substances that can lead to

death. The term is also used to refer to heroin whose contents are more pure than expected and which, when taken, can lead to death.

59. a. Actually, middle-aged people have reached a point in life where they are more keenly aware of their fellow human beings than at other ages. In addition, the knowledge and perception they have gained through life experience makes them among the best witnesses.

60. d. There is no such thing as a crime scene exception to the warrant requirement. In addition to movable vehicles and consent searches, warrants are not required for searches incident to lawful arrests, plain view searches, and *Terry* type frisks.

61. d. There are four blood types; A, B, O, and AB. AB blood is the rarest blood type, belonging to less than 10% of the population. O is the most prevalent blood type, belonging to just over 40% of the population.

62. a. Cessation of breathing, absence of heart sounds, and a loss of flushing when pressure on the nail is released all indicate death; a bluish color of the extremities is not conclusive.

63. a. The Hemming crystal test, the microspectroscopic test, and the phenolphthalein test all confirm the presence of blood, but it is the precipitin test that can distinguish between the blood of a human being and that of an animal.

64. a. Hairs and fibers should be handled in this manner when found on a homicide victim. (The best way to fold the paper so nothing falls out is commonly referred to as a *druggist's fold*.) However, when hair is found attached to an object, particularly one that may have been used as a weapon, the object itself with the hair still attached should be forwarded to the laboratory for examination.

65. c. The majority of shotguns are smooth bore and do not have any rifling in the barrel. This means that any projectile shot through a shotgun would have no rifling markings. The other answer choices do have rifling patterns and would transfer these patterns to any projectile shot through the barrel, allowing for forensic identification.

66. c. The number needed for a positive match depends on how uniquely the points match. For example, there could be 15 points from a latent print that match the suspect's fingerprint, but if there should exist an unexplained difference, then a positive identification could not be made.

67. c. Doctors believe that when a person commits suicide by hanging, the victim will slowly squat until the noose is tightened, creating pressure that painlessly cuts off blood flow to the brain, at which point the victim slips into unconsciousness. The full weight of the body will then cut off the oxygen to the brain until death ensues. The victim suffers no pain.

68. d. Poisoning by sulfuric acid results in black vomit. Carbon monoxide poisoning causes the victim's skin to turn a bright cherry red color. Nitric acid poisoning produces yellow vomit, and copper sulfate poisoning causes blue-green vomit.

69. d. Lividity is the pooling of blood after death due to gravity. It presents as a red hue of the skin. If a body were lying on its back after death, the blood would pool on the backside, and if it were lying on its stomach, the pooling would be observed on the face and stomach.

70. b. While color may be used to distinguish objects or features, using a large number of colors may be confusing and eliminates the ability to reproduce the sketch quickly.

71. b. The extent of the neighborhood canvass is dependent upon a number of variables, such as the type of offense, the time of day, and the characteristics of the crime scene. To be most effective, the canvass should begin within a short time after the commission of the offense.

72. a. A 1:1,000 bichloride of mercury solution should be used as disinfectant and two blood samples of at least ten cubic centimeters should be taken. The samples should be collected in wide-mouthed tubes and closed tightly with rubber stoppers. Five grains of sodium fluoride should be added as a preservative.

73. b. The spray should be directed against a piece of cardboard and permitted to settle over the impression. In this way, the imprint is protected from any distortion or obliteration by the force of the spray. (Hairspray can be used in place of the shellac.)

74. a. The description is of what is known as a rip job. The punch job is the second most common method of opening safes. In the chop job, the safecracker simply turns the safe upside down, drills a hole in the bottom, and uses a crowbar to gain access. A touch job is one in which a safe is opened by using the sense of touch on the dial.

75. c. This is an extremely successful form of theft, mostly because the attendants believe they are protecting themselves from a would-be thief by putting out only a few loose diamonds, which they feel they can monitor.

76. b. This process can also identify manufacturing marks.

77. c. Experts theorize that large groups of teenagers, especially males, are hardest to handle because of the pressure on the teens not to back down in front of their peers.

78. b. In community policing, patrol officers and first line supervisors are assigned in a semipermanent capacity to a particular neighborhood and are encouraged to develop a positive rapport with the residents of the community. The officer develops a higher sense of responsibility for the crime rate and other problems in his or her district. The community policing approach was designed to bring the police and the community closer together.

79. a. A line organization is the simplest type of organization. It is found only in very small police departments. A downfall of line organization might be that there are no specialists to do the many tasks necessary to complete a criminal investigation successfully. Therefore, officers working in these organizations are often called upon to do the work of specialists.

80. c. Subordinates should complete all tasks delegated to them in such a way that all that is left for a supervisor to do is review the work and approve it. Any less would be considered incomplete, as it would require further work on the supervisor's part.

81. d. A relay question is a question taken from one student and given to a different student to answer. A reverse question involves fielding a question and giving it back to the person asking it to have them explore the answer. An overhead question is a general question given to the entire class.

82. d. The squad car is a strong barrier if the officer stays in it listening to the police radio and waiting for the dispatcher to call. On that kind of patrol, the officer rarely gets out of the car to mingle with the public unless he or she is responding to a call, and this isolates him or her from the public. Community policing is designed to get away from this style of policing.

83. c. When delegating a task to an officer, you give that officer the authority to complete the task, but you can never delegate away responsibility. The responsibility for the task will always rest with the delegating supervisor.

84. d. Sergeants should avoid filtering information at all times. This is true during both upward communications and downward communications.

85. b. Members of the public are more likely to interact with patrol officers than with those in other positions. Choice **a** is not a good one since calls to 911 are taken by 911 operators and then passed on to police dispatchers, who rarely talk to members of the public directly. Most police detectives are tied to their chairs and telephones (despite what we all see on television) and don't mingle with the public much, making **d** a poor choice. Finally, traffic officers are usually either working collisions or writing tickets and have contact with a much smaller segment of the public than patrol officers do.

86. c. This involves giving both sides new insights into the rights and responsibilities of those on the other side. Police officers learn about the press and the press learn about police officers.

87. a. When officers stay on the same beat for long periods of time, they get to know the people and patterns of the community, which results in more effective policing. While ride-along programs and (to some extent) consultation with community members are helpful, they are not as effective as the regular presence of the same officers in the same community over time.

88. d. These personality characteristics are also supported by the paramilitary structure of the police organization, which discourages innovation and flexibility and encourages dependency. As the rigidity of the structure increases, the degree to which these characteristics are emphasized also increases.

89. a. The equal protection clause prevents governments from creating improper classifications. Laws that are applied to classes of people risk violating the equal protection clause.

90. b. Courts are obligated to determine if a defendant is knowingly and intelligently waiving the right to an attorney. The court also warns the defendant of the dangers of self-representation and may appoint a "second-chair" attorney to assist the defendant. Although courts will be somewhat lenient, a defendant who represents him- or herself must follow rules of procedure and law.

91. a. A search is incident to an arrest only if it is substantially contemporaneous with the arrest and is confined to the immediate vicinity of the arrest. If a search of a house is to be upheld as incident to an arrest, the arrest must take place inside the house, not somewhere outside. *Vale v. Louisiana*, 399 U.S. 30, 90 Sup. Ct. 1969, 26 L. Ed. 2d 409 (1970).

92. b. The Supreme Court in *Cupp v. Murphy*, 412 U.S. 291 (1973), approved the warrantless search in this instance when probable cause existed to arrest the defendant but no arrest had yet been made. However, the court specifically limited its holding to the prevention of destruction of highly evanescent evidence—in this case, debris under the defendant's fingernails—and even then only permitted a search limited to that purpose, not a full search of the person.

93. c. According to the Supreme Court, "it is clear that a subpoena to appear before a grand jury is not a seizure in the Fourth Amendment sense, even though that summons may be inconvenient or burdensome. The personal sacrifice involved is a part of the necessary contribution of the individual to the welfare of the public."

94. c. The right against self-incrimination as embodied by Miranda attaches to an incident when the person is in police custody and is asked questions about a crime. Choice **b** does indeed rise to a custody situation, but the question asks for a situation that the court has allowed under this type of stop. Choice **a** recounts a public safety exception to Miranda.

95. a. *Habeas corpus* is a Latin term meaning "have the body." If a defendant receives a writ of *habeas corpus* from an appeals court, he or she will be released from unlawful imprisonment. *Corpus delicti* is a Latin term meaning "the body of a crime." The "body" of the crime consists of the elements needed to consummate the criminal act, for example, the burned building in arson. Courts are not involved in the process of arrest, and the due process clause is contained in the Fourteenth Amendment.

96. a. The exclusionary rule was created by the Supreme Court and is not contained in the Constitution. The purpose is to protect citizens' Fourth Amendment right to be secure in their persons, homes, papers, and effects against unreasonable searches and seizures.

97. c. The court rejected the notion that all warrant authority resides exclusively with a lawyer or judge; sometimes magistrates are not attorneys. The court further stated that a clerk of the court possesses the requisite detachment, as he or she is removed from the prosecutor and police and works within the judicial branch subject to the supervision of the municipal court judge.

98. b. The Supreme Court has determined that the Fourth Amendment's probable cause requirement is best served by "the flexible common sense standard," which is determined by analysis of the "totality of the circumstances" test.

99. d. The right to counsel first arises at the time the Miranda warnings are read. However, the right does not attach until the "critical stage"

commences. The court has recognized a "critical stage" as a formal charge, an indictment, an arraignment, or a preliminary hearing, presumably as early as the first appearance before a judicial officer.

100. c. This case is where the phrase *Terry* stop was coined. In this case, the court determined that an arrest is a different kind of intrusion upon individual freedom than is a limited search for weapons or a stop of an individual to briefly investigate a crime. An arrest is the initial stage of a criminal prosecution and is the commencement of the adversarial judicial process.

Preparing for Assessment Center Exercises

When you first hear the term *Assessment Center*, you might think it is a place like a youth center or a senior center. This is not the right picture. *Assessment Center* is a term used to describe a process by which a series of evaluative exercises are administered. If your department uses one or two such exercises to reach a decision about promotions, it uses assessment exercises. If the department uses multiple exercises (three or more), it uses an Assessment Center.

The Assessment Center is a process in which candidates participate in a series of systematic, job-related, real-life situations while being observed and evaluated by experts in policing, supervision, and management. Trained evaluators, called *assessors*, observe the candidates, individually and in groups, performing exercises in scenarios that simulate conditions and situations a sergeant would encounter in real life. It is this attempt to simulate actual working conditions that separates Assessment Center testing from the academics of written exams and the subjectivity of oral tests. Assessment Center testing was originally developed during World War II. The agents of the Office of Strategic Services (OSS) knew that pure academic training and education were not adequately preparing their operatives for real-life situations in wartime. Their candidates scored well on academic tests but did not always perform well under pressure and were unable to apply academic principles to real people, places, and scenarios. The same situation exists in police recruiting and promotion. A recruit may score 100% on a written test about how to subdue a violent person yet be unable to do it when the occasion arises.

Developing the simulated exercises usually begins with a job-task analysis. The specific skills, behaviors, and characteristics important to being a sergeant in your police department must be determined. These are the criteria on which you will be evaluated. Although they may vary from one police department to another, there are certain constants that the examiners will always look for. In any case, you must become familiar with the particular exercises in which you will be participating, since there are many varieties of assessment exercises.

With regard to police officers taking the sergeant examination, the Assessment Center is a process in which police officers who hope to be promoted to sergeant participate in a series of exercises simulating actions that would be required of them as sergeants. This gives the examiners an opportunity to judge how well the officers would perform as sergeants. It is important to understand that these exercises have been developed from an analysis that breaks the job down into the different actions required of sergeants in a particular department.

The first thing to do before attending an Assessment Center is to find out as much as you can as soon as you can about the exercises you will be doing. This does not mean trying to get information about the specific content of the tests. It does mean getting a good general understanding of the nature of the examination, because different types of examinations require different strategies. Experienced police professionals have demonstrated that advance training and preparation can absolutely improve a candidate's performance on an Assessment Center examination. Next, the candidate should find out as much as possible about the police department in his or her own jurisdiction. It's also a good idea to explore the environment of the community in which the police department is located. If you are already an officer in that department, you are familiar with most of this information. Finally, the candidate should examine his or her own strengths and

weaknesses as they relate to the job for which he or she is being tested, and attempt to maximize the one and minimize the other.

The first thing the candidate must investigate is whether the center will be testing "technical" or "generic" skills. To answer this question, the candidate must understand the difference between technical skills and generic skills. Technical skills refer to specific knowledge that is applicable in your own police department but would not necessarily apply to other departments. Generic skills, conversely, are those skills that are necessary in every police department.

The best example of a technical skill is a thorough knowledge of the rules and regulations of your police department. Obviously, a police supervisor—or any supervisor—must be familiar with the rules and regulations in order to enforce them. While there are many similarities in such rules and regulations from one police department to another, no two police departments operate under exactly the same policies and procedures.

Another example of a technical skill is knowledge of a particular body of law. The penal code of your own state is something with which you should be familiar before you take the test for promotion. Such bodies of knowledge can be made available to you within your own department and should be studied before you even consider taking the test for promotion.

There are a number of categories on which you will be judged at your Assessment Center. Although they may seem intimidating at first, when you study them you will see that you are probably familiar with them already. They include, but are not limited to, the following: oral communication, written communication, planning and organizing, training/coaching, problem analysis, judgment/decision making, responsiveness/sensitivity, conflict resolution, delegation, leadership, meeting/management, and technical knowledge. (You have already answered written questions in many of these areas on the practice exams and in the minicourse.) Oral communication and written communication are discussed in other chapters of this book, but let's take a look at the others.

▶ Planning and Organizing

Planning and organizing require the ability to formulate a plan of action for the candidate him- or herself and for others. The candidate must realize that the resources available to him or her are not limitless and that adequate documentation may not always exist. It is important for a sergeant to realize that planning, like training, is a continuing process.

The first step in planning is recognizing the need for a plan. It is always a good idea to include those other members of the department who will have the responsibility of carrying out the plan at the earliest stage possible. When formulating a plan, it is important to gather as much information as possible and to keep the plan flexible. As stated above, planning is a continuing process. This means that plans should be evaluated as time goes by, and if the plan is not achieving its results, it should be altered.

In organizing the division of work, a supervisor should apportion it as fairly and equally as possible among all workers. It's never a good idea to pile too much work on one individual, who will become discouraged. Also, anytime a subordinate is given responsibility for a task, that individual should also be given the necessary authority to perform it. It is the supervisor's responsibility to make sure that the subordinate understands his or her assignment and the time frame in which it is expected to be accomplished.

By the way you answer questions about planning and organizing, you will demonstrate that you will be able to handle similar situations in real life once you achieve the role of sergeant. These questions will probably be multiple choice but may also be in essay form;

see the "Report Writing" section on page 199 for information on how to handle a writing exercise.

▶ Training/Supervision

The first line supervisor, that is, the sergeant, is undoubtedly the key person in the training process in a police department. In a formal training program, the instructor must accept the major responsibility for the success of the program. When you train an employee, you should prepare the employee, present the information, have the employee apply the information, and then test the employee to determine what he or she has learned. Any formal program must include an evaluation phase to determine the effectiveness of the training. Remember that you may be training personnel other than police officers. For example, you will probably be in a department where civilian clerks do a fair amount of the paperwork. Since they will not have had the advantage of police training, they will need more supervision before they begin their work.

It is important that a supervisor be aware that it is necessary to publicize among subordinates the details of new procedures—and of old ones if they are being ignored. If, during an assessment exercise, you note that a procedure is being violated, suggest training as one of the solutions. The most common "point losers" in the training/supervision exercise are indicating that you would tell a subordinate to correct a problem without indicating how to correct it, making absolute rules that can't be carried out, and telling a subordinate in general terms to "take care of" a problem.

▶ Problem Analysis

The first step in intelligent problem analysis is the correct identification of the problem. The second step is the gathering of information about the problem. Only then should you attempt to solve the problem. A key component of successful problem solving is the capacity for gathering information from different sources. For example, if you were being tested on solving a problem about a particular officer under your jurisdiction, the examiner would award points if you indicated that you would first find out all you could about the officer, his or her background, job history, and so on. The person who scores high on problem analysis is the person who keeps asking for more information before making a decision. You would also gain points for indicating that you were aware that certain solutions that seem obvious could create further problems.

Another, often overlooked dimension in problem solving is the ability to forestall problems before they arise. Suggest to subordinates ways to avoid problems. For example, teach them how to keep a "tickler file," a chronological listing of due dates, meetings, and appointments. Basically, this is just keeping a calendar with notations on it.

It is also important for a supervisor to recognize that a problem may be only the tip of the iceberg. It is possible that there is a more profound problem underlying the obvious one. Once again, don't indicate to the examiner that you believe you have solved the problem presented without further investigation. When appropriate, show concern and offer counseling to a subordinate who appears to have a personal or job-related problem. Note that the offer of counseling has to be consistent with departmental policy. Most departments offer counseling to alcoholics. Some, but not all, offer counseling to employees with drug problems.

There are priorities in problem solving: life over property, constitutional rights over departmental regulations, needs of the department over the needs of the individual. All of these priorities should be identified by the candidate and observed in responding to questions.

▶ Judgment/Decision Making

Although it's been said before, gathering all available information before answering a question is essential. At no time is it more important than when the candidate is answering questions relating to judgment and decision making. The most common point loser, according to experienced examiners, is the answer that indicates that the candidate would take extreme action based on surface information. The second most frequent point loser is the failure to take action when action is required.

Students in face-to-face training often express concern over being able to distinguish between the two, that is, knowing when to delay action pending the gathering of more information and when to take immediate action. An example of the first error would be taking disciplinary action against a subordinate without first gathering facts from a number of sources; an example of the second would be failure to prevent an intoxicated officer from getting behind the wheel of a car. Here, action must be taken immediately.

▶ Responsiveness/Sensitivity

First and foremost in this area is the candidate's awareness of the chain of command in his or her department and an indication that he or she intends to follow it. Next is the ability to give necessary criticism in a civil, adult manner and not to embarrass or humiliate a subordinate. There is an old adage that is appropriate here: "Praise in public and criticize in private." Another indication of sensitivity to others is the response by a candidate that he or she would deal with two antagonists separately. Threats are nonproductive. Remember the seriousness of complaints made by others. If something bothers a person enough to cause him or her to complain, it must be serious to that person; be sure to indicate that you would treat it seriously too. Examiners look with favor on the candidate who displays concern for people who have problems, whether they are crime victims, homeless people, or emotionally disturbed subordinates or colleagues. Someone noted for his or her competence and concern is the image of the police officer that the department wishes to present.

▶ Conflict Resolution

What the examiners are looking for in the exercise called "conflict resolution" is an indication that the candidate knows what action to take to resolve a conflict. A candidate can earn points by indicating that he or she intends to suggest alternatives or compromises to resolve conflicts but also never intends to compromise on a violation of the law or of departmental policies, rules, or procedures. Where possible, the candidate should plan to use compromise, but if compromise fails, the candidate should indicate that he or she will use established departmental policy and that he or she knows what that policy is. It is also wise for the candidate to indicate that he or she is aware that conflicts similar to the one presented might arise in the future and that steps can be taken to prevent this from happening. Examiners will be impressed by a candidate who can offer positive recommendations in such a situation. Once again, the candidate should be specific in answering questions. Examiners do not give much credit to candidates who give vague answers or issue unclear instructions.

▶ Delegation

Delegation is the art of managing subordinates effectively. It is the ability to assign work to the subordinate you judge will do it best. It also requires the supervisor to be able to indicate clearly what result is expected from the subordinate to whom the task is given. In the assessment exercise, the candidate is usually given information about the subordinates with whom he or she will be working. It is important to study this information in order to determine which subordinate is best suited to the task at hand. For instance, before making an investigative delegation, a supervisor must make sure that the person to whom an investigation is being assigned is not him- or herself involved in the investigation. It is also important to follow up on jobs that have been delegated to make sure that they are being done in a timely manner. Your own "tickler file," like the one you suggest subordinates keep to forestall problems, will come in handy here.

▶ Leadership

Leadership is defined as the ability to influence others so that the job at hand is accomplished effectively and efficiently. Leadership can be demonstrated through the proper training, disciplining, monitoring, counseling, directing, and developing of subordinates. A candidate can earn leadership points if he or she indicates in writing how he or she would behave in a variety of situations. For example, in some circumstances a good leader would take charge of the situation him- or herself immediately. In others, a good leader would take charge by issuing specific instructions to subordinates. In another case, a good leader would recognize that a subordinate needed counseling and recommend how that counseling could be obtained through the department. Again, the successful candidate will demonstrate that he or she would obtain all possible relevant information before acting. Examiners deduct points for responses that ignore the department's policies when the candidate is placed in a situation that calls for leadership, as well as for responses that fail to call for the training, disciplining, and counseling of subordinates where those resources are indicated.

► Meeting/Management

Of all the abilities tested by the assessment exercises, management is the easiest to display. It is basically the establishment of procedures to monitor and control your own activities and those of your subordinates. The fundamental principle of management is that the manager cannot escape final accountability for responsibilities properly assigned to him or her. It is closely related to delegation. In a written exercise, management can be demonstrated by indicating how one would follow up on tasks that have been delegated. If a calendar is provided at the Assessment Center, the candidate might indicate on it the dates and times when a follow-up call would be made to a subordinate assigned a particular task. Another management tool is the requirement that a subordinate report back to you, preferably on a specific date and at a specific time, with an update on how the job is proceeding.

It is also important for the candidate to indicate that he or she would meet with subordinates to make sure that they understand the tasks delegated to them. Demonstration of communication skills is likewise important in management exercises.

The effective supervisor demonstrates the ability to improve the functioning of the group by being aware of the skills of subordinates and taking advantage of them. This also reflects the candidate's ability to encourage a cooperative spirit among individuals.

► Community Relations

An area not mentioned yet, but one that is of vital importance to a police department, is that of community relations. The police need the cooperation of members of the community both in solving crime and in keeping the peace. Community relations are, of course, a two-way street, involving communication from the police to the public and from the public to the police department. In recent days, much media attention has been given to the relations between police departments and the public in major cities. Although there has been a lot of negative publicity, there is also a lot of good news on the topic, and the candidate should be aware of this. In many suburban departments, police have set up special units to deal with the public in an effort to prevent problems. Many of these units are specifically focused on the kinds of problems caused by teenagers, such as graffiti, vandalism, and public intoxication.

The most important aspect of any community relations program is the attitude of the individual police officer who comes in contact with the public. For a police officer to be truly effective in a given area, he or she must be familiar with and understand the culture of the people in that area. A police department should be "a part of" the community, not "apart from" the community. The assessors will look for candidates who demonstrate a knowledge of and an allegiance to a community-friendly attitude.

► Video Simulation

Assessment Centers frequently use video simulation exercises to judge both specific and generic skills. A video simulation exercise is a written exercise in which a candidate first views a police-related scenario on a television monitor and then is asked questions about the appropriateness of the actions taken by the police officers portrayed in the scene. It is often called a "job sample" exercise, since the scenario presented must always be a representative sample of the police job as it is actually performed in the jurisdiction where the exercise is being held. As with other assessment exercises, there is a "structured" video simulation exercise, in which the candidate is asked multiple-choice questions about the actions taken by the police in the scenario, and an "unstructured" version of the exercise, in which the candidate is shown the scene and asked to make his or her own comments on the actions taken by the police.

For example, suppose a candidate for promotion to sergeant is shown a scenario unfolding, in part, as follows:

> Two uniformed police officers on patrol are given an assignment by the radio dispatcher to respond to the scene of a family dispute. Upon arrival at the scene, the officers are admitted into the house by a woman who says that one of her sons attacked the other with a knife. She wants the alleged attacker, the older son, arrested. The older boy says that he was only fooling around with his brother, but his brother confirms his mother's version of the "attack." The older boy then approaches his brother with what the police consider a menacing attitude, and the police have to physically restrain him.

In a structured version of this exercise, the candidate might be asked the following multiple-choice question:

> Which of the following would have been the most appropriate action for the police to have taken?
> **a.** The officers acted properly in attempting to get the entire story.
> **b.** The officers should have separated the brothers before attempting to get the rest of the story.
> **c.** The officers acted properly, since hearing both sides of the story is the best method of getting at the truth.

The correct answer is **b**, since it is a well-established principle in domestic disputes that parties in such a dispute should be separated in the fact-gathering stage.

In the unstructured version of the same scenario, the candidate might be asked to write a commentary on the way the officers handled the situation. In this case, the correct response would be something like the following:

> The officers should have separated the brothers and their mother and questioned them separately. In this case, one officer would do the questioning and the other would remain with the other two participants.

The way the video simulation exercise usually works is as follows: The candidate, usually without any advance preparation at the site, is brought into a room where there is a television set. He or she is then shown a video simulation of a police incident. After seeing the video, the candidate is asked questions about it. There are two common variations on this exercise. In one, a number of two- or three-minute scenes are shown and the candidate is asked questions about each of them. In the second variation, the candidate watches a longer scene, but the video is stopped every three or four minutes and the candidate is questioned about what has happened up to that point.

A candidate who is going to take a video simulation exercise should speak to members of the police department who have achieved the rank of sergeant and ask them for information about the form and content of their own tests. Find out if previous exercises given in the same jurisdiction were released, and if they were, obtain them and study them. Video simulations involve the most common or the most critical of street situations. Particular favorites of past examiners include investigations of vehicle accidents, making arrests and issuing summonses, dealing with sick or injured people, crisis intervention in a situation such as an attempted suicide, dealing with street disorders, evidence gathering, and dealing with domestic violence situations.

In order to prepare for a video simulation, you should be sure you understand the procedures you have been taught to follow in a given situation. For example, if the video is of a vehicle accident, you need to know what to do, and when, in investigating an accident. The correct procedure includes first obtaining medical care for anyone injured in the accident. If you are familiar with the correct procedures before you see the video, you will be prepared to identify the behavior you see on the screen as correct or incorrect.

The video simulation exercise is sometimes given in conjunction with an "in-basket" exercise. In this case, the universe established for the in-basket exercise also applies to the video.

▶ In-Basket Exercises

So-called in-basket exercises constitute an important segment of the Assessment Center. In these exercises, the candidate assumes the role of the position for which he or she is being tested. In-basket exercises are generally classified as administrative tests. The work amounts to reviewing various pieces of information and answering questions based on that information. The examiner presents each candidate with a set of paperwork that a sergeant might find on his or her desk at the beginning of the day. The paperwork might include memorandums, written reports of oral complaints, investigative reports, internal documents, letters, and telephone messages. Along with the enclosures, the candidate receives written questions designed to test how he or she would complete the exercise, that is, how the candidate would deal with each document. Candidates are given a specific amount of time to complete the assignment.

At the beginning of every in-basket exercise, the candidate is given a set of instructions setting the stage for the exercise. As one retired police captain put it, these instructions create a simulated universe within which the candidate must function. At the very least, the candidate must be told what role he or she is to play in the exercise and the current date and time. Other facts with which the candidate may be presented include the command to which the candidate is assigned, the organizational chart of that command, the number of officers under his or her supervision, a map of the assignment area, and the tour of duty the candidate is working. Pay attention to such facts! They will be important when answering the questions. When a police situation develops, given the set of facts that has been supplied, the candidate must be aware of such details as time and place, because the correct response may differ as these factors change. In other words, a response at 3:00 A.M. might differ from a response at 10:00 A.M., and a response in one area of the police precinct might not be appropriate in another area.

Here are some examples of possible in-basket items:

- a note from your lieutenant relative to a citizen complaint against an officer in your jurisdiction. The lieutenant has attached the complaint and instructs you to report back on a specific date and at a specific time as to actions you have taken.
- a telephone message from a reporter at your local newspaper requesting information about a crime of which the reporter has heard rumors
- an interdepartment memorandum from your commanding officer concerning high-speed pursuits that he or she wants read to your subordinates
- an arrest report completed by one of your officers and submitted to the court. Attached is a note from the lieutenant saying that the report is

incomplete and requesting that you take appropriate action and report back.

As in the other exercises cited, there are two types of tests given for the in-basket exercises, the structured and the nonstructured. If the exercise calls for a structured response, you will be given a set of options as to how to deal with the situation. In other words, the exercise becomes a multiple-choice test. For the first item in the box, the complaint from a member of the public concerning one of your officers, you might be given the following options:

a. Call the officer in question in to see you and get his side of the story.
b. Institute immediate disciplinary action against the officer.
c. Respond to the commanding officer that it is unfair to accuse the officer of anything based on unsubstantiated information.
d. Begin an investigation of your own to uncover the facts of the situation.

The correct response is **d**, and all you would have to do would be to mark **d** down on the paper.

If the exercise is a nonstructured one, the appropriate actions to take might be the following: You would first write a memo to your lieutenant saying that you have received his or her note and will investigate the complaint against your officer. In order to begin your investigation, you might request the records of the officer's assignments, particularly as they relate to the kind of activity about which the lieutenant has received the complaint. After obtaining the facts, you might send for the officer to come in and discuss the affair with you. You would then make a determination as to the facts of the case based on your investigation and, if necessary, outline remedial action. In this case, you would be graded on the quality of your actions.

You would receive points for keeping your commanding officer informed, for outlining a specific plan of action, for sensitivity in dealing with your subordinate, and for good judgment in not taking action in advance of having all the facts.

The importance of reading questions carefully before you begin to answer them cannot be overstated. In exercises of this type, you should first be sure you know how much time you will have to complete the exercise. You must also know precisely the title of the role you are supposed to be playing (for example, desk sergeant). A good idea at this point is to schedule your time. Give yourself sufficient time to read the instructions carefully. Make an estimate of how long it will take you to answer the question(s), and give yourself time to review your answer(s).

In-basket exercises take time. If you are told that you will have three hours to complete such an exercise, first count the number of items in your in basket. If there are 12 of them, plan to allot 10 minutes to each. Obviously, some will take longer than others, but 12 at 10 minutes apiece will take two of your three hours. That gives you 30 minutes at the beginning to plan your strategy and 30 minutes at the end to review your work. The time allotted is purposely short, because the object is to place you under pressure to complete all of the tasks contained in your in-basket within the time allotted.

▶ Report Writing

The typical format for a report-writing exercise is one in which the candidate, acting the part of the position for which he or she is being tested, is given written instructions from a commanding officer to write a report on a certain topic. The instructions contain general guidelines as to the content of the report. The candidate is also given information relating to the report.

Such information is usually given in the form of letters, memos, or department orders. The candidate's task is to review the information and select the specific information that should be included in the report. After identifying the information, the candidate writes the report, making sure to use the standard format of his or her department.

This exercise is intended to test the candidate's ability to write clear, concise summaries of data, statistics, and other information and/or to write a memo that interprets or adapts broad general principles. This is one exercise in which the candidate may be required to express a personal point of view. The candidate's report is reviewed by the assessor and judged on grammar, spelling, punctuation, form, and, finally, content. A candidate is normally given approximately one hour to complete an exercise of this type. Take the first part of the hour to sort out the information, use the major part of the time to write the report, and leave sufficient time to review your work.

▶ **Summary**

According to a police research study, candidates have been consistent in their comments regarding Assessment Centers. They report that the centers are difficult and challenging but also fair and relevant. Assessment Centers present a candidate with an opportunity to demonstrate his or her skills and to learn something about what is required to become a successful officer. Various problems in the Assessment Centers will not have simple solutions, just as real-life situations do not have simple solutions. The candidate should remember that the answer to a question must be the best answer possible, not necessarily the perfect answer.

Preparing for Your Oral Board

No matter what kind of oral board you face, one thing is clear: the oral component of the police sergeant exam can make or break your chance to succeed. The typical oral component of the police sergeant exam accounts for 40% of the total score, so it stands to reason that substantial time should be allotted to preparing for the oral. Yet the oral boards are frequently overlooked when it comes to preparation. Some candidates seem to feel that they need only show up and do the best they can, that scoring in the orals is "politically" influenced. Comments like "They already know in advance who is going to score high in the orals" or "It's who you know, not what you know, that counts" are common refrains. Maybe at times these statements contain a grain of truth, but even when they do, thinking like that is self-defeating.

Not taking the oral boards seriously, and therefore not preparing adequately, is one of the biggest mistakes you can make. As one chief said, "Some officers are better test takers than others. A patrolofficer who wouldn't necessarily be a good supervisor can get a high written-test score, but at the oral exam we have a better chance to find out what kind of person we're dealing with. I've seen more officers blow a chance for promotion in the orals than I have in the standard part of the test." One reason for this may be that the oral component normally is not scheduled until after the written component. In fact, in most departments, only those who pass the written component with an adequate score are offered a chance to stand before the oral board. Some may feel that to prepare for the oral before they even know if they are eligible is silly. Well, that kind of thinking is unproductive, and it does not display the attitude of a potential supervisor. No learning is a waste of time. If it doesn't pay now, it will pay off later.

The oral boards are not just a place where you can "blow it." The orals are also a chance to shine. Everyone takes the same multiple-choice objective test. They earn a certain point score. The odds are that many of the test scores at this stage are close. The one way a candidate can stand out is to impress the board at the oral. This is your chance to show why you are the best one for the job. Try to look at the oral board as an opportunity to show who you are and why you deserve a promotion. The benefits of a positive attitude should not be minimized. The board will like to see you display, as a potential supervisor, a contagious "can do" spirit.

To do well in the orals, you need to prepare. To prepare, you need to know what you are preparing for. This means research. You need to find out what kind of oral board or oral interview you will face. Start with the police sergeant exam announcement. It should give you the pertinent information: the who, what, when, and where. Most likely it will also describe the type of testing and the weighing of the components. Don't stop there, however. There is much more to be learned. Talk to colleagues, your sergeant, and other superiors who have successfully stood before your board. What was it like? Do they have any advice? Would they do anything differently now? Is there a way that they might recommend to prepare for the oral? Logic may tell you that the best information will be gleaned from those who succeeded and are now supervisors, but don't fail to ask others who have taken the police sergeant exam before without getting a promotion. They, too, may offer valuable advice. In fact, they may be taking the test again with you. These officers are potential partners in practicing for the oral board, putting you through the paces of an interview. Practice would help them, too, so don't be afraid to ask.

In order to prepare effectively, you will need to know the type of oral board/oral interview that you face. You will need to know who staffs the board. Is it all civilians? A mix of civilian and law enforcement personnel? What kind of law enforcement personnel? Human resources? Police psychologists? Training personnel? Supervisory personnel? Are supervisory personnel from other police departments called in to sit on the oral board? What are the numbers? Might the board have a liberal or a conservative bent? Any clues as to the "flavor" of the board may be invaluable to you. Remember, you will be playing to an audience. Knowing as much about that audience as possible will be to your advantage.

▶ Kinds of Oral Boards/Oral Interviews

The kind of oral board you face well may depend on the type and size of your police department and the level of civilian input. Three panel members staff a traditional oral board. The origin of these three panel members can vary tremendously from one police department to another. Increasingly, spurred on by the growing importance of community policing, civilians are named to sit on the oral boards. These may include city or township council members, members of civilian review boards, or others. Keep these panelists in mind when preparing for your oral boards: They may be looking for different types of responses than other panel members coming from a more traditional law enforcement environment. You will need to address both factions in your responses.

It would even help to think of your responses in terms of two parts. First, respond to a question, situation, or role-playing exercise as a police sergeant addressing a superior officer. Then expand your response to include issues that might be of interest and importance to a civilian panelist. This will not be as hard as it might seem if you begin to think in these terms now and keep civilians in mind as you prepare and, especially, practice for the oral component of the police sergeant exam. For example, if a question or a situational role-playing exercise involves a public setting, you will want to know the proper departmental procedure and the codes involved. Answer or address these points confidently, but then go further, explaining how and why the procedure you have just suggested will affect the community. What issues might be raised? How might you follow up on the situation to keep the community, or the civilian board member, informed?

This may take seeing things through the civilian panel member's eyes, something that will take practice. When preparing for the oral exam component with colleagues, take some turns as the civilian on the panel. Try to see the response that your fellow study companion gives through the eyes of that civilian. Considering the civilian perspective will prepare you for your own responses. Some police departments, such as Haverford township in suburban Philadelphia, Pennsylvania, use all civilians on the three-member panel. In such a situation, if you do not incorporate appropriate responses, ones where a civilian point of view is considered, you will be at a serious disadvantage compared to a candidate who does. Remember, even if only one civilian sits on your panel, that person controls 33% of your score. Don't ignore the civilian perspective.

Most traditional oral boards will have some, if not all, law enforcement professionals as panelists. In the quest for objectivity and the avoidance of litigation, the law enforcement professionals on the panel will not, in most cases, be from your own department. Other police departments will be contacted to volunteer appropriate supervisory personnel, usually lieutenants, captains, and chiefs, to sit on the oral exam panel. These assignments are not taken lightly. The visiting law enforcement personnel are not only representing themselves, their own departments, and their own cities; they also know that this task will most likely be reciprocated. They are aware that supervisory personnel from outside departments will be major factors in deciding who gets promoted in their own departments. You can be assured that these panelists will not be fooled by vague, incomplete, indecisive, or unrealistic answers. If you are not ready to be in a supervisory

position and have not done your homework and prepared for the oral exam, that will be readily apparent to the professionals on the panel.

Traditionally, the panel in an oral board will agree to ask certain questions or propose certain situations to each and every candidate in order to have a level field of play. The candidates will then be rated on their responses. Follow-up questions to the candidate's response are not necessarily planned in advance, but do count in the overall rating. Panelists will typically have a rating sheet with a list of factors to which they will assign a value, up to 100. The factors will most likely include some or all of the following:

- attitude
- reasoning ability
- knowledge of responsibilities
- ability to handle stress
- confidence
- communication skills
- appearance
- maturity
- judgment

Depending on the department, some factors may be weighted more than others. Again, try to find out ahead of time which, if any, factor is deemed most important to your board. The scores from the panelists will be averaged to determine the applicant's final score.

Some oral examinations are fairly technical in scope. Though less common, these are designed to evaluate the candidate's competency in certain skills and may be given by different panels, each designed to evaluate a specific skill, such as supervisory practices, state law, municipal law, and so on. The larger departments sometimes administer the more technical oral boards. Preparation for the content in these would be the same as for the multiple-choice objective exam content. This chapter's general advice on poise, appearance, and attitude will be of considerable value in facing a panel. It is not enough to have the knowledge and skill; you must also be able to communicate the mastery of that competency with "grace under fire."

A new trend uses various video and computer-generated interactive programs to simulate the "fire" under which you are to display your "grace." These more modern interactive oral exams call for more specialized preparation, not necessarily in content, but in presentation. For this kind of test, you will want to practice in a simulated test environment whenever possible. Have a spouse or your study partners use a video camera, and practice performing in front of the camera. Nothing could be worse than to know what you are doing and why, only to fall victim to a case of stage fright. In fact, even if you don't face this particular kind of exam, practicing in front of a camera is a wonderful way to get a realistic picture of the way you come across. No one is thrilled at the prospect of facing a camera. We cannot dismiss the quirks of posture, the tics of speech, the number of times we say "um" or "you know." It can be a rude awakening, but better to face it in yourself now than to let the panel of the oral board discover these flaws for you. A video camera is a worthy tool to use to help prepare for the oral exam. By the time you get accustomed to answering questions in front of the camera, you should be able to respond to the members of your panel with confidence.

Using a video camera is a particularly fine way to practice if the oral exam you face involves role playing. Take turns portraying different roles, that of supervisor and that of subordinate, for all of the situations that might be presented to you. Critique your performance and that of your study mates as if you were the panelist scoring the test. Help each other figure out what you could do better and, just as important, why. Once you've figured out why one response is more appropriate than others, the odds are better that you can transfer that knowledge to different but similar situations. Again, the more closely you can mimic actual test conditions, the better.

▶ A New Study Plan

Just as you prepared a study plan in preparation for the multiple-choice component of your police sergeant exam, you will want to have a new plan for the period after the multiple-choice test right up until the moment you sit before the your oral board. Use a day planner or calendar and designate specific times to study. As before, pick realistic times and stick to your schedule as much as possible. Preparing a little at a time and building momentum as the date of the oral exam approaches will make the task manageable. It will also build confidence—and you want to be confident! An air of confidence, though not to the point of cockiness, is what the examiners want to see. Confidence is what a supervisor should have and be able to instill in others. At this point you will also want to coordinate times when you can meet with study partners to quiz each other and practice responding. If you did not utilize practice with other candidates for the multiple-choice part of the exam, you should reconsider this tactic for the oral component. The oral exam is, by nature, interactive. The way to prepare is with interaction. This rehearsal can make a world of difference. If you have practiced responding to others in a lifelike situation, when the real test comes you will be able to concentrate on what you say without worrying so much about how you sound or look.

As you develop your study plan, try to schedule more work with others as the test time gets closer. Early on, you can plan to develop a set of possible questions and your possible responses. In the later stages of your plan, you can set up and practice oral examinations. Enlist your study partners, family, and friends, if need be, to staff the panel. Reproduce as much of the actual exam situation as possible. Arrange the seating as it will be for the real test. Have a start time and enter the exam room as if it is exam day. Film the whole process, if possible, and then critique your performance along with those of the other performers. By this point, if you have been studying together, a certain rapport should have developed. Try not to consider yourselves competitors at this point, even if in reality you may be. Instead, you want to be each other's coach, someone who will critique honestly, without being brutal. Honest feedback is what you each need. The goal of every member of the study group should be to improve the performance of all the members. It may sound contrary in a cutthroat world, but cooperation and the ability to work well with others are also the attributes of an officer who has supervisory potential. Helping others to see what they can do better is likely to make a better candidate of you. As any teacher will attest, one of the best ways to learn something is to teach it to others.

▶ Things That Should Go without Saying

Be on time. It sounds simple, but you would be surprised at the number of candidates who for some reason or another arrive late for their oral board. No matter how good an excuse you have, lateness will hurt your score. Candidates have been late because they assumed they knew where the testing site was but didn't, or they didn't allow for traffic or parking. So know exactly where the test is being held and when. If need be, make a practice run to be sure you know. Allow time for parking if that might be a problem. You don't want to put a major effort into a study plan and then blow your chances on the oral exam with a simple mistake.

Look right. Unless you have been told otherwise, show up in uniform. Allow enough time to look the best you possibly can. Groom meticulously. Creases should be sharp and hardware polished. Imagine that you are on display, because you are. Many experienced panelists have stated just how important the candidate's visual impact was in their scoring. A potential supervisor will represent the department, and board members want the candidate to represent the department well. From the moment you drive into the parking lot, conduct yourself as if you were in front of the panel. Don't slouch, even on the hallway bench. You don't know when a panelist might appear. You will be judged any time you are seen by a panelist, so act as if you are on stage from the moment you hit the grounds. Considering you are on stage at all times is a good way to approach the process. In many ways, this is a play and you are the star. Your practice (rehearsals) will help your performance and keep you from blowing your lines or getting stage fright. Sit straight. Look the panelists in the eye. Be polite. When they say to sit, say, "Thank you." When in front of the panel, take your hat off. One candidate, when told he could take his hat off, replied that he'd keep it on. He might have been thinking it was a trick question, but the effect on the panel was negative. For the next twenty minutes, that hat sat large and dominated the thoughts of everybody in the room. A candidate who otherwise might have scored well didn't.

▶ Kinds of Questions

You will need to prepare for the kinds of questions you are likely to face. Odds are these questions will not be technical in nature, but will be designed to test other qualities such as character, communication skills, and judgment. In fact, the first question you are likely to be asked may not seem to have a lot to do with the job of sergeant. It's common practice to break the ice with a general question, both to get to know you and to set a friendly tone. These types of questions are about you, not necessarily what you know. Possible warm-up questions you are likely to hear include:

- Tell us a little about yourself.
- What first got you interested in law enforcement?
- What kinds of interests do you have outside of your job?

Be prepared for these questions. It's surprising just how many officers are ready to answer technical or situational questions, yet open their oral exam stuttering and stammering while they try to figure out what to say about themselves. Practice responding to these questions, preferably on camera in front of others, just as you practice for the questions that more closely pertain to the job.

Some departments require you to submit a resume when applying for a promotion. If this is the case in your department, make sure you know just what is in your resume. If the board members have your resume in front of them, the last thing you want to do is to contradict what you have submitted.

The sample questions that follow have all been used to test potential police sergeants. Keep in mind that your response must be appropriate for your particular police department and the population you serve. You also need to be mindful that each response you make is as a supervisor, the sergeant you aspire to be, not according to your rank at present. Responding as a subordinate is a common mistake, especially when the questions pertain to possible discipline. In the "them versus us" mentality, you must think as "them."

You will want to be prepared for these questions, but you should not memorize a particular response and give rote answers. You want to sound prepared, not mechanical. To accomplish this, it is important to have a strategy. Any question you are asked or situation you need to address can be broken down into steps. If you know these steps and their priority, you can use them to solve any problem thrown at you.

- **Identify** the problem. This sounds simple, but a quick response is not the right choice if no real problem exists or you address the wrong problem. Verify the facts.
- **Analyze** the facts. What is really going on? Do you have reliable information? What does the information mean?
- **Act** appropriately.

- **Review** the results of your action and react accordingly.
- **Learn** from the experience.

If you approach any problem, question, or situation the board presents by thinking in terms of identifying, analyzing, acting, reviewing, and learning, you will respond in a way that will earn you the most points possible. Let's look at this strategy in dealing with a question commonly asked by oral boards.

Panelist: What would you do if it were reported to you that an officer on your watch was sleeping on the job?

1. Identify

Candidate: Well, first I would try to verify the facts. Is this officer, or has this officer really been, sleeping on the job? Is there a possible grudge involved? By this, I mean is the person who reported the incident likely to be telling the truth or have ulterior motives?

Panelist: Let's assume for this instance that the facts are true. Your officer has been found asleep in his patrol car.

2. Analyze

Candidate: If that were the case, I'd want even more information. I'd want to learn whether this is the first time this has occurred, an isolated incident, or whether it's been going on for a while. I'd also like to know if there were any extenuating circumstances.

Panelist: Like what, for instance?

Candidate: Well, for one, is this officer a new father? Maybe he's sleep deprived.

Panelist: He's still sleeping on the job.

Candidate: Yes, and that is a serious situation.

3. Act

Candidate: Some sort of action is definitely called for, but the proper action might be to arrange a scheduling change if this officer is in all other respects valuable to the department. If there are no extenuating circumstances, and this is still an isolated incident, a direct confrontation with the officer is in order, including a stern warning.

4. Review

Candidate: In either case, I would keep an eye on the situation to see if the rescheduling and/or warning has the desired effect, which is to make sure I have a fully staffed, alert watch on duty at all times.

5. Learn

Candidate: I'd also like to think I would learn something from this incident. Maybe I should try to be more aware of any personal situation that might affect the performance of my officers. I should know who just had a baby or is caring for an elderly parent, circumstances that might affect the amount of rest my officers are getting and therefore their effectiveness. Or maybe officers on watch should report or call in more often than was the case at the time of this incident. Then if I didn't hear from an officer on time, I could investigate.

One thing this example demonstrates, besides the value of using the **identify**, **analyze**, **act**, **review**, and **learn** model, is the need to be flexible. If the candidate in this case had memorized a specific answer to the question originally asked, it might not have withstood the interjection of the panelist. By "reasoning" his or her way through a response, the candidate is prepared for different twists on the topic, ones he or she may not be specifically prepared for. By using the strategy we've outlined—**identify**, **analyze**, **act**, **review**, and **learn**—a candidate can tackle any problem.

Let's look at another example and see how this strategy might work there.

Panelist: Let's assume that a major event has occurred on your watch. What do you do?

1. Identify

Candidate: Well, a lot would depend on the nature of the event itself.

Panelist: Let's just say it's a major event, one you and your department probably have not faced before.

Candidate: OK. First and foremost, I'd want to verify that this event is for real. If it's a major occurrence, one that might cause the public to panic or cause the department or the city embarrassment, I'd want to be pretty sure there really is a problem. If there is a problem, I'd want to know exactly, as far as possible, what the facts are.

2. Analyze

Candidate: Depending on the facts of this event, I would try to determine what my next move should be. I'd determine who should be notified first and if there's a need for more officers.

3. Act

Candidate: Next, I'd assign the dispatcher to begin notifying extra personnel to either report or be on call, with an imminent possibility of coming on duty. While this is happening, I'd call my superior and notify him or her of the event.

4. Review

Candidate: Once the event was addressed, I'd review my own and my personnel's performance. Were we able to react to this event effectively, with the staff it called for?

5. Learn

Candidate: What might have been done better, and how would I react if this event, or one like it, occurred again? What policy might be put in place in order to be better prepared for events of this kind? Since this was a major event, I assume it must have had some effect on the community. With that in mind, I'd want to analyze the public reaction and consider how the community might be better informed or served.

Notice that the candidate in this response addressed community concerns. While this would be important to any law enforcement personnel on the panel, addressing these concerns would speak directly to any civilians sitting on your oral board. The civilian panelists don't have your law enforcement background, so you must make sure your answers are ones that make sense to them, too. Remember that they control a large portion of your score on the oral examination.

You will have addressed a number of issues before your oral exam is over. Toward the end of your allotted time, be on the lookout for a wrap-up question. Just as your panel will likely begin with warm-up questions, it will also likely have an exit question. This is your chance to leave a lasting impression. Make sure it is a good one. Prizefighters are coached to come on strong toward the end of a round, to leave the judges with a good impression as they begin to score. And you, too, should end the exam scoring points and leaving a lasting impression. The following is a typical exit question.

> *Panelist:* If you get this promotion, how will you deal with officers who may be jealous that they didn't get the sergeant's job?
>
> *Candidate:* Well, I think I'd deal with it by being the best sergeant I could be and by assuming that since I'd gotten the promotion I'd deserved it. If problems arose with an officer because of it, I would try to have a private talk with that officer and make it clear that I was, in fact, the sergeant and I expected that officer to act professionally at all times.
>
> *Panelist:* And if that officer didn't?
>
> *Candidate:* Then I'd implement whatever discipline was appropriate under the circumstances.

I'd like to think it wouldn't get to that point, though. I'd hope that a heart-to-heart talk would prevent such measures, maybe by asking for the officer's input to solve department problems, acknowledging the officer's strengths.

> *Panelist:* And what if you don't get the promotion? How will you feel then?
>
> *Candidate:* I'd be disappointed, that's for sure. With all due respect, I'd think that the board had made a mistake. I think I'm ready for the sergeant's position, but I'd live with the decision. I'd do my job to the best of my abilities and I'd give the new sergeant the respect due his or her position. That's what would be best for the department. I'd show by my performance that I'd be ready the next time.

However you respond specifically to this type of wrap-up question, remember that the board members will be looking for a response that shows that you definitely want this job and feel confident that you are ready for it, but that you put the department first. If you cannot respond honestly in this way, then maybe you're not ready for the job. But you are, so respond in a way that shows it.

▶ Summary

- Have a study plan and stick to it.
- Do your research. Find out what you can about the test.
- Give yourself enough practice time. Make preparation a priority.
- Work in teams.
- Videotape yourself answering sample questions in a realistic setting.
- Practice, practice, practice.
- Practice some more.

CHAPTER

9 ▶ Preparing for Your Writing Test

What do sergeants do and how do they do it? How do they spend most of their time? One analyst says that sergeants spend 40% of their time supervising those under them, 20% in administration, 10% on departmental procedures, and 10% on criminal law. Of course, these percentages differ in specific police departments, since a major urban department may require different skills from those needed in a suburban or a rural one. However, wherever they are and whatever they are doing, police sergeants must be effective communicators. According to state civil service departments, every promotion examination contains questions on the subject of communication. Communication is the transmission of an item (a report, an order, a suggestion, a problem, and so on) from one person to another by various means—verbally or in writing.

People planning to take the police sergeant exam must understand the basic responsibilities of the job. Candidates must demonstrate that they know what a sergeant does (and how a sergeant does it), what characteristics are most important in a sergeant, and what tasks require most of a sergeant's time. The nature of a police sergeant's work is largely supervisory, directing an assigned squad of patrol officers. His or her work involves responsibility for the efficient and prompt performance of patrol officers performing booking, transmitting, and/or receiving duties at the police desk; supervising prisoners within booking facilities; and writing reports about their cases. All police work, of course, is performed in accordance with departmental rules and regulations. For this reason, it is important that sergeants demonstrate the ability to communicate clearly both to subordinates and to the superiors for whom they write reports. Sergeants are the key officers who pass information down to subordinates and up to superior officers and managers.

Most police communication goes from the top down. It can include orders, memoranda, bulletins, and training instructions. These communications are intended to provide officers with the information they need to do the job on the street. Upward information advises management about the performance, morale, needs, and grievances of those under a sergeant's supervision. In some departments, police personnel also get the chance (and the responsibility) to communicate with the public on department affairs. While this responsibility may in real life be assigned to just one sergeant in the whole department, be ready to be tested on it if your department offers a written exam; it is a general enough skill that it is sometimes tested on written examinations.

The sergeant test you take may or may not include a specific essay-writing section. Most sergeant exams today don't include an essay component; departments are relying instead on multiple-choice exams (which are easier to administer and score). However, as you probably know from your own department, and as you saw in Chapter 7 of this book, Assessment Centers are on the rise as a means of evaluating potential sergeants, and Assessment Center exercises often do involve some writing. Look back again at the portions of Chapter 7 on in-basket exercises and report writing for a reminder of what to expect in this regard.

There are two distinct areas in which candidates for any job are judged—aptitude and achievement. (The tests used to measure those skills are a lot like the ones you took in high school, the aptitude tests and the achievement tests.) Aptitude tests gauge a person's natural qualities, such as how well he or she reasons logically and how easily and quickly he or she grasps written matter. These things are hard to study for, because such tests are really designed to tap into inborn abilities.

In contrast, as you are well aware by now, you can and should study for achievement tests. The multiple-choice portion of the sergeant exam is an achievement test, and so are writing tests. The remarks in the rest of this chapter are designed to help you prepare in case your department tests your writing skills. Furthermore, as noted, Assessment Centers often include in-basket exercises and exercises in report writing, both of which can involve a good-sized chunk of writing. You'll do best to sharpen your writing ability before exam day to prepare for these exercises as well as explicit essay questions. (If you know for sure that all you will face on test day is a multiple-choice test or a multiple-choice test and an oral board, you do not need to spend time on writing skills and should direct your efforts elsewhere.)

▶ Writing Skills: Clarity, Finding What's Important, Keeping It Simple

Written tests are usually achievement tests, whereas oral tests tend to be aptitude tests. Because a written test gives the examiner an opportunity to test the candidate's ability to communicate, it is most important for the candidate to remember one word: **clarity**. A sergeant's instructions to his or her subordinates must be clear. There can be no ambiguity or confusion about an order or a requirement. It is important to clarify ideas in your own mind before communicating them to others. Therefore you should know precisely what you are trying to communicate before you set it down on paper.

In the rare case when essay questions appear on a civil service exam, it is important for candidates to understand them and then devise outlines to answer them. On the game show "Jeopardy," it is frequently stressed that contestants may know the answer to a question, but when they don't listen carefully to the question being asked, they sometimes give a wrong answer. Make sure you read the question on the exam carefully and answer the question before you, rather than demonstrating how much other material you may know. One police commander says that more police officers fail promotional exams because they don't understand or answer the questions than for any other reason. He recommends that candidates take a number of practice exams before taking the actual exam.

What's Important?

When taking a writing test, think the situation through. What do you want people receiving your message to do? What instructions will they need in order to perform the task in a satisfactory manner? Candidates should always be on guard not to use words that can be misunderstood. If something is to be done at once, the instruction should tell the subordinate to proceed *immediately*, not soon. It is also important that the most vital information be given first. In fact, on some multiple-choice exams, there are exercises in which candidates are given five or six sentences and told to put them in order of importance. A writing exam is similar; you should place the most significant information up front. Include only relevant information, whether in instructions to subordinates or in reports to superiors.

The report writing exercise involves the preparation of a written report designed to test a candidate's writing ability, ability to write a report in accordance with the format used by his or her department, and ability to identify the pertinent information that should be included in the report from a larger body of information. The big job here is sifting through all the material to **find the important information** and then dealing with that in a prominent way. Don't forget the details, but don't get lost in them, either. Your report should give a reader a clear, quick idea of the overall situation at the very beginning. You can then go on to fill in all the details that someone actually working on the case will need. Make sure you understand the big picture before you begin to write; then write a report that gets this big picture across to the reader.

A candidate's report will also be judged on grammar, spelling, punctuation, and form, so it wouldn't hurt to get a friend who is skilled in writing to read over some samples of your work and give you pointers. A second pair of eyes always helps, and practice in writing is vital.

Keep It Short and Simple

One of the most common errors new writers make is using too many words and not the right ones. Think before you write. What point are you trying to make? What is the simplest possible way to get that point across? If your officer saw a man standing on a corner talking to a woman in a car, and the man resembles the suspect in a mugging, you may need to report that. What you will need to get across are the facts: who, where, when, and why it is important. You don't need to dress this up by making fancy references to the goals of the department or the criminal code that would be of no use whatsoever to the person getting the report.

Remember that it is easier to write correctly if the writer keeps it **simple**. It is often better to use a **shorter** word than a longer one if the meaning is the same. Write *use* rather than *utilize*. The meaning is the same, and the shorter word keeps the message clear. The same goes for phrases. Write *since* instead of *owing to the fact that*; and *I didn't know* instead of *I was unaware of the the fact that*. If you are writing a sentence and find yourself unable to complete it properly, scrap it and begin again. Shorter sentences are almost always preferable to longer ones, just as shorter words are preferable to longer ones. Long sentences can create confusion.

Having said all this, we will qualify it: You should not use shortcuts at the expense of clarity. For example, do not use nicknames unless everyone will understand who or what you mean. If you expect to use abbreviations, a good rule is to write the words in full plus their abbreviations the first time you use them and then, later, just use the abbreviation for convenience.

The expert grammarian William Strunk once wrote: "Vigorous writing is concise. A sentence should contain no unnecessary words, a paragraph, no unnecessary sentences, for the same reason that a drawing should have no unnecessary lines and a machine no unnecessary parts. This requires not that the writer make all his sentences short, or that he avoid all detail and treat his subjects only in outline, but that every word tell." These words could have been directed at a candidate for police sergeant as well as to beginning authors. The sergeant must make every word tell or, as we would say today, **make every word count**.

As with any other skill, whether it's shooting baskets or learning to play the piano, the key to success is practice. Take a few minutes each day to write something simple. And before you start writing on your test, make sure that you understand the instructions. When you finish taking the test, you'll be on your way to being the person giving the instructions in the future!

Special FREE Offer from LearningExpress!

LearningExpress will help you be better prepared for, and get higher scores on, the police sergeant exam

Go to the LearningExpress Practice Center at www.LearningExpressFreeOffer.com, an interactive online resource exclusively for LearningExpress customers.

Now that you've purchased LearningExpress's *Police Sergeant Exam, 2nd Edition*, you have **FREE** access to:

- **A full-length law enforcement practice test** that mirrors the official police sergeant exam
- **Immediate scoring** and **detailed answer explanations**
- Benchmark your skills and focus your study with our **customized diagnostic report**

Follow the simple instructions on the scratch card in your copy of *Police Sergeant Exam, 2nd Edition*. Use your individualized access code found on the scratch card and go to www.LearningExpressFree-Offer.com to sign in. Start practicing online for the police sergeant exam right away!

Once you've logged on, use the spaces below to write in your access code and newly created password for easy reference:

Access Code: _____   Password: _____